A Penny a Kiss

A penny a kiss, a penny a hug
We're going to put our pennies in a big brown jug.
A penny a kiss, a penny a hug, oh how rich we're going to be.

I'm going to save a penny every time I hold you tight,
And we're going to watch the pennies grow.
I'm going to save a penny every time we kiss goodnight,
And darling when we're married we can build a bungalow.

A penny a kiss, a penny a hug
We're going to put our pennies in a big brown jug.
A penny a kiss, a penny a hug, oh how rich we're going to be.

"A Penny A Kiss"
Words and lyrics by Buddy Kaye & Ralph Care, 1951

A Penny a Kiss

Memoir of a Minnesota Girl in the Forties and Fifties

Judy McConnell

NORTH STAR PRESS OF ST. CLOUD, INC.

St. Cloud, Minnesota

Dedication

To my children,
Libby and David

Copyright © 2014 Judy McConnell

ISBN 978-0-87839-728-0

First Edition: June 2014

Printed in the United States of America

Published by
North Star Press of St. Cloud, Inc.
P.O. 451
St. Cloud, Minnesota 56302

northstarpress.com

Acknowledgements

I am indebted to the following people for providing candid feedback on the manuscript:

Instructors Simone Di Piero and Mary Carol Moore; friends Sally Bosanko, Merl Edelman, Nelly Hewett, Ruth Horner, Ingrid Lund, Judy Proudfit, Ted Seeley, Carol Souter, and Mary Swanson, with added thanks to special friend Marvin Walowitz for tromping the old Los Angeles haunts with me; editors Nancy Raeburn, Lane Rosenthal, and Toni Hull; and members of my writing group and classes too numerous to name.

Also, I am grateful to the friends who have tolerated my holing up for those first two years and my family for noticing my absence.

The experiences related in this book are products of my own perception, based on diaries, journals, letters, and memory. The names of some characters have been changed to protect the guilty and expose the innocent.

Part I

Early Imprints

Me at Virginia Beach—1939

Chapter One

❧ Eastern Beginnings ❦

EING BORN WAS EASY. All I had to do was open my mouth and scream, and I was initiated into the world. After that nothing worked. I never paid any attention to growing up or any of that. Life just drifted, carrying me along like an insect floating downstream on the current, upside down, legs in the air or belly flopped and watching the watery scene below move by. It was an easy way to go through life, buoyed and cushioned from the responsibility of walking on hard surfaces.

Even now, memory dim, I look back through a fog and see only feeble outlines. I see the house where we lived in Washington, D.C., and I recognize the upstairs bedroom where my mother sat in a maple rocking chair silently sewing at the window under a print of Gainsborough's *Blue Boy* hanging on the wall above her. Her white fringed blouse and rose colored necklace shone soft in the yellow light.

I walked into the room and across the blue carpet flowing like a vast pool of velvet in front of me. There I stood staring at her through the stillness, watching her creamy white hand draw the needle into the air, curve around and pierce the needle into the garment, lengthening a neat row of stitches. I wanted to sit on her lap to soak in the warmth of her bosom and look out the window, but her lap was a flurry of business. Her hand waved back and forth, consuming the space above the lap I coveted. Even at age four, I understood in some visceral way that when she hid away in her room like that, it was a stay-away signal.

No, I couldn't go to Petey Haines's house, my mother told me. I was too young to cross the street by myself. Without my playmate there was nothing to do. I was tired of wandering through the house and around its orderly tables and tall-backed living room chairs, and I was tired of sitting on the window sill staring out at one small cherry tree and a sidewalk that wound around two sides of the yard. There was no sign of life. If only *something* would move.

So the days droned on. One afternoon, when Petey was allowed over, we raced through the house until Mother, who was upstairs in her rocking chair listening to the radio, sent us and our noise outside to play in the yard. We yelled for Thumper, the neighbor's cocker spaniel, who came running and licked our faces before heading straight for the garage. The dog had a habit of weaseling through the Barberry bushes when no one was around and pooping in our detached one-car garage.

Petey and I followed him inside. We were entranced by the steamy odor he left that clung to the damp walls and the shadows lurking under the opaque window. This time we decided to try it ourselves.

"You go first."

"No, you go first."

We stood looking at each other, then out into the shadows of the garage. An uneasy thrill of daring stormed my limbs, and finally I slipped into a dark corner, pulled my pants down and squatted. Petey immediately did the same. We were giggling. The thrill was immediate, like we'd pulled off a bank robbery. We returned to the house savoring the power of a dark secret.

After a few weeks the lumps piled up and my parents started asking questions. "How did all those dogs get in the garage?" Petey and I said nothing. We switched to pulling worms from the garden and watching them wiggle in buckets of ammonia water lifted from the laundry room. But the punch wasn't the same.

☙ ◆ ❧

IN 1939, WE MOVED TO Minnesota and settled in a small two-story house on Wooddale Avenue in Edina, complete with an attached one-car garage. I was sent to school a half-mile down Wooddale on the corner of France Avenue. There wasn't a bus for the half-day kindergarten kids, so every morning a taxi arrived at the front door. My mother stuffed me into my long red coat, and I walked to the taxi all by myself. It felt like a real adventure, like I was going to England or someplace, and I pretended that at any time I could turn to the driver and say, "Airport please."

Afternoons I waited on the school steps and watched as the other kids climbed into cars that pulled up with a parent behind the wheel and drove off. I kept a lookout for the taxi to take me home. One warm spring afternoon the taxi never arrived. I waited, twisting my fingers uneasily as one by one the kids left me sitting stranded on the steps. Cars were motoring back and forth, going about their business. When the school yard was deserted I stood up uneasily, not sure what to do. Clearly, the window of pickup time had passed, and I realized the taxi was not coming. Surrounded by the still, flat emptiness of the dirt school yard, I felt nervous being entirely cut off and on my own.

Finally—doing nothing was out of the question—I crossed France Avenue and trudged down Wooddale Avenue along the curb, as there were no sidewalks. On the other side of the road the Edina Golf Course stretched into the distance, and I caught a glimpse of six miniature figures inching across the turf between the pine trees like a far off caravan in the desert. I knew exactly where I was. Easy!

An automobile swept by giving off a slight puff of gas. As I walked I nudged stones along the curb with my toes and sent them spraying off into the grass. As the stones flew to my touch, a new sense of power flooded through me and my uneasiness evaporated into the warm air. All at once everything around me seemed sharper and more vibrant than usual, as if I were seeing the row of white clapboard houses and block yards for the first time. This was the first time I'd been away from home, by myself in the world, and every action was of my own making. A vision of our house hidden further down the road was clear in my mind, and, feeling happy and secure, I sent a single stone flying into a nearby tree where I watched it fall with a meek thud. I couldn't help laughing.

Mother was upset when I sauntered into the house. It was far too dangerous for me to walk home alone. What was I thinking? Where was my common sense?

"But it was easy, there weren't any cars." Well, only one or two.

To no avail. I received a serious scolding. With only one car, Mother couldn't drive me. If the taxi didn't show up I was to wait. I had clearly done the wrong thing, but in a faraway place in my mind I had doubts. A furtive sense of pride persisted. Hadn't I gotten myself home on my own? Hadn't everything turned out fine? Wasn't that what counted?

The rage at school was trading cards. Kids would gather outside on the steps to haggle, everyone clutching their collection box trying to exchange single playing cards for superior ones. Those who knew how to pull an advantageous deal accumulated beautiful cards of fairies, animals, vivid flowers, portraits—all scenes of interest to an artist. Especially coveted were playing cards of puppies and kittens. Trading became a passion. I had one of Dad's cigar boxes packed with cards begged from my parents and their friends. Next, I solicited the houses in the neighborhood, knocking on doors and collecting old decks people didn't want.

It was exciting to get brand new decks, which I stored in a special shoe box. The cigar box held a card from each of the decks, plus the singles acquired from trading and extra jokers. (The cigar box, hinges dangling, still sits on my basement shelf.) These trading cards were divided by index sorters into flowers, people, statues, horses, dogs, twins, scenery. Pairs were either similar in subject or identical but in different colors, and were especially valued.

The best cards were rich in colors and detail. My favorite was a head shot of a proud chestnut horse with a long white star down his nose, gazing intently through his mane with soft brown eyes. I collected elegantly posed roans, sleek collies, colts, and spaniel puppies. These I didn't give up readily, and insisted on two or three traded cards for each one.

I kept the boxes hidden in a bottom drawer in my bedroom underneath the pajamas—there wasn't anyone to hide them from, but I wasn't taking any chances. These cards were a lifeline. I was pretty sure I was accumulating the best collection in school: bright ruby and emerald birds, handsome black stallions, sweeping green landscapes, rare matching pairs and artistic street scenes. Prizes of beauty and variety. Each afternoon in my room I reviewed the takes with a sense of accomplishment and importance, relishing a sense of purpose.

Gloria's scheming sharpened my trading finesse. I had been at Joanne's house next door, cutting out pirate paper doll clothes and folding gold swords and swashbuckling hats on sinister black-haired men with crater-pocked faces. When I returned, Mother met me at the door and announced in a low conspiratorial tone that someone was there to see me. I wondered who it could be. No one except Joanne ever came to see me. This was strange.

"Upstairs," Mother said. "She's waiting in your bedroom."

I recognized my visitor right away. She sat on my bed looking like the queen of a ship with her head cocked and her corkscrew blonde curls surrounding her bright, smiling face. Something about the way her hands rested calmly in her lap irritated me. So did the proprietary way she gazed around the room as she sat square in the middle of the bed in a compelling upright posture.

"Gloria!"

"Hi!" she squawked.

It was the same tone of voice that cried out to be first in the Kool-Aid line, pleaded to be allowed to pass out cookies, and pushed kids into line with an air of privilege, as if she were Shirley Temple on the set commanding the crew. I didn't like her then and I didn't like her sitting on my bed now as I waited for her sweet voice to assail the room and me.

"I talked your mom into letting me wait here," she said. "She gave in after I told her we were best friends and that my mother was late for something and would be back to pick me up in an hour. I said you wouldn't mind."

Now that she had jumped down from the bed and stood facing me, a whole two inches shorter with thin legs covered by a flouncy red skirt, Gloria seemed to promise something exciting, something to break the monotony stretching ahead until dinner. I softened, overcome by curiosity. Best friends? Here was someone to play with.

"Look, I knew you wouldn't mind, but I saw your card box on the table and look what I found." She held out a pack of cards, a new deck I had just gotten from Mrs. Helm down the street.

The cards she held in her hot little hands showed a beautiful golden, chocolate-dotted cheetah sitting regally on a tree stump with a broken branch curved to one side like the horns of a fallen beast. His ears were back and his mouth slightly open, as if ready to fly into action. This was better than any of my other animal cards, a prize I knew would bring me many trading trophies.

Running to the dressing table, I looked in the card box. My blood raced, my toes tingled, my body stiffened. I swung around and glared at Gloria.

"What? You've been in my cards?"

Gloria's smile slackened.

"Oh, I didn't take anything. Just looking. You know I have the best card collection in school. My mother buys decks just for me at the Hallmark shop. I want these cards." She held up the deck. "I'll give you better ones."

"No way. Give that to me."

"But Mrs. Helm promised this deck to me just last week. She knows my mother. They're mine! Why did she give them to you?"

"Maybe she likes my face."

Unable to contain myself, I snatched the deck from her pasty little hands. Gloria screwed up her nose, shook her shoulders, and walked defiantly out of the room. I listened as the front door clanged shut. Mother was puzzled.

"She got in my cards," I said.

"But she was so nice and polite," Mother sighed.

"Mom, she's a fake."

After that I'd see Gloria by the swings or pressed against the brick wall of the school. She would be surrounded by admiring kids and flashing her cards, negotiating exchanges with other girls carrying large boxes.

I traded every day. Trading involved hard bargaining, and sometimes I had to give up treasured cards to get a collie or stallion I wanted. At first I offered single cards backed by hidden decks of the same card. The idea was to not let anyone know which cards I had entire decks of (less valued, of course), and to trade these and guard the good singles that I had no more of. Sometimes I had to trade one of my favorite beauties to get a card I really wanted. A few were too prized to trade, so I used them for enticing other traders, allowing the trader to believe they were available, then steering them to lesser temptations.

My collection of prize cards was rapidly filling the cigar box. Even Gloria eyed the most artistic ones with envy. She came running up to me one day.

"Look what I've got," she smirked, flashing a shiny pair of matching peacocks in front of me. "They're brand new; my mother gave me the jokers."

The cards she held were beautiful—rich blue, violet, and orange feathers gleaming against a soft yellow background. I instantly wanted them.

"Will you trade?" I asked.

"Maybe. I don't really want to give them up. What'cha got?"

I pulled out the stack of my choice duplicates cards, I had plenty more of stashed in my bedroom, and watched Gloria thumb through them.

"None of these, they're creased," she observed. "No, you don't have anything that can match mine."

I pulled out a pack of cards from the end of the box, a pack I rarely showed. These were the irreplaceable ones I absolutely would not give up. I used them as come-ons. Gloria studied them closely.

"Well . . ." She fingered a pair of palomino stallions that I had given six of my best cards for. "I like these."

"Not those."

I didn't think she was serious about trading her peacocks, but could see she was aroused. After twenty minutes Gloria lost patience.

"You won't trade any of these! Why do you even show them to me?"

"I never know when I'll get just the right offer," I shrugged.

Three days later, when she'd tired of the peacocks, I got them for twelve of my most prized cards—all from the duplicate pile. I was ecstatic. I'd worn her down.

The peacocks were added to my never-to-be-traded pile, which was getting larger and more splendid every week. I carried the feeling of self-sufficiency with me all during the school day. I even got up the nerve to ask Gloria to pull her rug next to mine during snack-time.

෨◆෨

MY PARENTS, JUANITA FOUGHT and Harold Bradford, were born in 1903 and 1904 and grew up in a small town of three thousand huddled in the hills of West Virginia.

The town of Pennsboro was a pinprick on a map. It was a typical southern town, I suppose, with a one-screen movie house above a five and dime, one hardware store, and a corner drugstore with a malt machine and stools. A railroad passed through the little town and young people in fur coats walked along the tracks on sunny Saturday afternoons. Its steep hills gave off the smell of warm oil and dust. In the early days, before paved roads, the streets of Pennsboro were covered with carefully laid out stones so the wheels of the horse-drawn buggies could roll through more easily. On Sundays, bells in the Methodist Church tower pealed brassy Winchester notes that echoed across the three downtown blocks and over the hills to the cemetery where scores of Bradfords, Yateses, Wileys, and Kennedys were buried beneath cement markers.

Although Mother and Dad grew up together and certainly attended the same school, all we know about the early years is that Dad attended Mother's tenth birthday party. After that the record is mute. When her mother died of breast cancer when Mother was twenty-two, she and her father moved to an apartment on the street below the Bradford house where Dad's large family resided. The two families became fast friends.

❧ ◆ ❧

As the oldest of seven, Dad was expected to help keep order in his family's household under the silent, no-excuses command of his strict father. A photo of Granddad Bradford in his Shriner uniform shows him looking preacher-stern, with a grim pencil-straight mouth, a chalk-white Anglo-Saxon face and pin-point eyes, his expression grim and unyielding. Watching the way his brown and white pointer crept around his feet, lowering to its stomach, tail pulled between its legs, I became terrified of him myself. It didn't help that Granddad Bradford rarely spoke, often turned his hearing aide off and walked around ramrod stiff without turning his head.

From his high school days, Dad was driven with searing ambition. Being a summer clerk at the corner grocery was not for him. He was a go-getter, an instigator with a magic touch. Early on, Dad decided that Pennsboro was too small to hold his dreams and upon completing high school in three years, he made up his mind there were lands out there to conquer and he was just the guy to do it. Maybe he was influenced by his future father-in-law's worldliness, or his own glimpses of higher distant things. Maybe swimming at the top of a small pond Dad caught whiffs of remote seas, propelled by his I-can-do-anything attitude.

Although no one in the family had ever attended college, and Granddad Bradford, an insurance salesmen who traveled constantly, had neither the interest nor the finances to help, Dad set off in 1919 for the University of West Virginia. After completing his degree, he was determined to enhance his career by obtaining further credentials and the place to go was Harvard. He applied for a post-graduate program. An automatic letter of rejection shot back in the mail. Ignoring this response, he showed up at Cambridge and was denied admittance by the watchdogs at the registrar's office. Undeterred, my father applied to higher authorities, showed up hat-in-hand and somehow talked his way in.

With no money and no connections, Harold Bradford was admitted to Harvard Business School.

Dad thought it may have been his ambition and humble, small town background that sold him to Harvard's officials. Unknown candidates from remote West Virginia towns did not often show up at Harvard's doorstep. Years later, as he related this story to me, I had to wonder if it was not his manner of earnest honesty that sold him.

Dad explained that although as a student he was wooed by fraternities and invited to parties in Cambridge by the local society—the Bradford name was held in some esteem in that part of the country due to the reputation of Massachusetts Governor Bradford and others—he turned them down. With his meager funds he could not afford the wardrobe necessary to appear at the old-name homes and felt he did not fit in with the Ivy League standards upheld by the other students.

One by one his siblings followed in his footsteps, going on to college and settling in Charleston, Clarksburg, and Huntington, West Virginia. There is not a Bradford remaining in Pennsboro today.

After Harvard, Harold married his love, Juanita Fought, the daughter of a Pennsboro landowner and publisher of the *Pennsboro News*. Mother was twenty-two, beautiful and flirtatious. When Dad left for the University of West Virginia in 1919, the letters between the two glowed with passion and yearning. They dated in Baltimore, where Mother was attending Goucher College. As Dad built his career, they started a family and moved to a remote northern state. Their love endured, tightened by common roots, and they stayed together for fifty-seven years.

Early in his career, Dad received unexpected publicity. The securities industry in West Virginia had for years evaded the National Association of Security Commissioners regulations, undercutting industry standards for their own advantage. In his position as security commissioner for West Virginia, Dad, president of the NASC in 1935, challenged the crooked bankers. Local newspaper articles Scotch-taped into our frayed family scrap book give various accounts of the determined efforts of a Harold K. Bradford to clean up the underhanded practices that had been tolerated in West Virginia for far too long. Reports of his efforts spread through the investment world, written up in papers like *The Chicago American Financial* and the *Charleston Gazette*. Al Quinn's column, dated May 1935, described Dad's promotion to the Federal Securities Commission in Washington, D.C.:

> *There goes Bradford.*
>
> *Today the soft-spoken young man who put a wallop in the erstwhile little-known securities department of the state auditor's office will leave for Washington to take an important post with the Federal Securities Commission.*
>
> *That might be good news to crooked stock dealers who used to find a fertile field in West Virginia were it not for two facts. And one of them is Bradford, who will be in a position to keep an eye on the goings-on in the home state.*
>
> *When Simms took office in 1933, he looked over the field of candidates for a post with the federal Securities Exchange Commission. He reached into Clarksburg and got Bradford, the W.Va. cleanup man.*
>
> *Bradford went right to work. New legislation stiffening regulatory laws was passed. Some of the companies showed signs of rebellion. Bradford informed his boss that some of them were big names. Sims replied that none of them were bigger than the state of W.Va. If they had something to hide, let them hide it elsewhere.*
>
> *That was all Bradford needed to know.*

My father's reputation paved the way to a post with the Security and Exchange Commission in Washington, D.C. Two years later an offer came all the way from Minneapolis, Minnesota, offering him an outstanding position in the growing company of Investors Syndicate (later Investors Diversified Services, then Ameriprise Financial). Mother claims they had to consult a map to find out where Minnesota was. Before long the two West Virginians from the sleepy south were transplanted to the cold north, and their children became bona fide Minnesotans.

Dad's arrival at Investors Syndicate was written up in the *Minneapolis Star-Tribune*. In those days, with the population of Minneapolis at three million, there was a small town interest in every tidbit of news. A photo of Mother and me appeared in the society section of the paper announcing our move from Washington, D.C. Mother was dressed up in blue velvet, and I in a print seersucker dress and yellow hair ribbon.

The picture showed only one of my two sides; the one Mother dolled up in cute print dresses, curls, lamé ribbons and Mary Jane's for church, visiting, and other special occasions. The other side, the real one, a girl in jeans scrambling for frogs in a vacant lot, hair stringing, skinny arms smeared with dirt and smelling of hard-boiled eggs, was nowhere to be seen.

The following year Mother's picture was published under the headline: RETRIEVE RETRIEVER OR I'LL BE IN THE DOGHOUSE. The text explained that our Labrador retriever had run off, and Mom was in grave trouble as it was her husband's hunting dog. The serene young woman in the picture didn't look like she was in trouble at all, seated upright in the carved chair with her shoulders back, her hands poised gently on her lap, and her face smiling unselfconsciously into the camera. I guess the paper wanted a story, not just a picture of a wife.

Over the years my parents kept in close touch with their southern birthplace. The *Pennsboro News* that came to our house regularly from West Virginia detailed card parties, engagements, out-of-town visitors, and described how Jake Myers' three-legged pig adopted a blind chicken that had wandered off the Macgregor farm. Also in the *News* was a photo of Mr. and Mrs. Simpson's Hoover wagon, a stripped Ford newly rigged and pulled by two horses, a form of transportation popular during the Depression when no one could afford gas.

Every summer at 5:00 a.m., Dad corralled the family, grouchy and sleepy-eyed, into the car, and we set out over the 1,500 miles across country to West Virginia. My brother and I squirmed the entire two days, counting cows (pure blacks were two points), watching for the lineup of Burma Shave road signs, reading comic books, and arguing and punching each other to fill the long hours caged in the back seat. Such imprisonment was the most grueling thing I'd ever endured and I fidgeted, whined, and stared

Newcomers to the City

THE MINNEA

NEWCOMERS to the city are Mrs. Harold Bradford and her daughter, Judith, who with Mr. Bradford and young Harold, Jr., have recently moved here from Washington, N. C. The Bradfords are living at 5329 Wooddale avenue.

Mother and me newly arrived in town, from the *Minneapolis Star Tribune*—1939.

peevishly out the window at the dry, monotonous mounds of trees, streaks of wild grass, and barren fields. This, I imagined, was where life ended, the final destination, a wasteland, where somewhere we were to destined to land, desolate and alone.

Our arrival in Pennsboro brought a flurry of festivities. Everyone knew each other. Grandma and Grandpa Bradford's house was crowded with aunts, cousins and neighbors; there were dinners and cocktails on the front porch and spontaneous visits. Sometimes Mother and I climbed the steep hill across the street to drink lemonade on Lucy Wiley's porch, or pass by the homes of Icky and Lena King, Mabel Kennedy, or Creed and Katie Cling. People sat exposed on front porches in those days, and if you walked by chances were you would be invited in for a visit.

While the grownups made merry, I spent hours nosing through the dusty attic above the garage where Granddad Bradford kept his black, 1920s Ford. It was in this attic that Granddad Bradford plied his taxidermist skills, which he had picked up on his own. Besides the stuffed heads of fox, deer, and a muskrat with green glassy eyes, the attic was loaded with hunting and fishing gear: khaki pants, plaid hunting shirts, and shotguns. There were trunks full of old photo albums and stacks of Victrola records. On one wall hung a photo of the four Bradford boys and their father: Granddad Bradford, Dad, Bert, Bob, and Tom, standing side by side dressed in hunting shirts and ankle boots, shotguns perched vertically in front of them like an infantry lineup.

My favorite place was the swimming hole. I watched the older kids leap on a swing-rope, arc far out over the water, and drop flailing and shouting into the brown depths. When later in my teens I spent a summer in Pennsboro, this became my favorite pastime (along with playing casino with Grandma Bradford until midnight in the upstairs bedroom). I loved the breathtaking fling into the air and plunging into the dark mystery of the warm water below.

అ◆ఇ

WEST VIRGINIANS DON'T KNOW the meaning of winter. When snow arrives, they act as if they've never seen it before. The schools are closed and cars tucked into garages. Even up north, no one was prepared for

Mother, Dad, Harold, and me in Pennsboro, West Virginia—circa 1939.

the Armistice Day Blizzard of 1940 that hit Minnesota and North Dakota. The mild weather had extended the hunting season and, in the early afternoon of November 11th, duck hunters out in their boats were removing their hunting jackets. The first threatening sign was swarms of ducks the hunters saw blackening the sky overhead. The winds were rising and gaining strength, and within hours reached eighty-five miles per hour. Thousands of birds scattered over the sky and funneled into the Mississippi River Valley, seeking protection from the swirling snow.

Without warning, hundreds of duck hunters were trapped. The storm cut a 1,000-mile path through the middle of the country, killing forty-nine people in Minnesota and 150 nationwide. The storm didn't let up until the next day, burying cars, rendering passenger trains snowbound, and leaving Minnesotans stranded throughout the state.

When the blizzard hit, my mother was downtown shopping. As the snow drifts accumulated, she was barricaded, along with hordes of others, inside a department store. No one could get in or out. The snow fell all night in large crisp flakes that fluttered down from vast reservoirs hidden in the dark sky, dropping silently, relentlessly, insidiously. Hour after hour they came, accumulating in banks of up to twelve feet tall, up to the second stories of buildings, burying buses, creating white towers of shrubbery, and stretching across landscapes in glittering ocean waves. The next day bulky machines charged out into the stark brightness and plowed into snow banks, piling mounds that stretched across roads and walled driveways until there was no place left for the snow to go.

Dad hung on the phone trying to locate Mother at her favorite stores and bombarded authorities to obtain information on the state of the downtown streets. We sat glued to the radio as the announcers revealed the extent of the unexpected storm and the total immobilization of transportation. Was Mother stranded in her car? Was she buried inside some store or filling station? Why hadn't she called?

My brother Harold and I sat motionless on the couch, not feuding for once. I held my chin while nursing mixed feelings of worry, curiosity, and expectation. We could see nothing out the snow-blasted windows, and the radio announced that throughout the Twin Cities driveways were blocked. Dad paced up and down, then called a number for the fifth time and still failed to get through.

A tinge of fear edged along my spine. Something terrible must be going on. Dad walked over and spoke soothing words. He said if Mother didn't contact us, it must be for a good reason. But he continued to stand by the phone table, twirling a pencil around one finger, balancing on one foot, then another. We waited, cut off, powerless, stranded like castaways on an isolated island. Finally, he sent Harold and me to bed and stretched out fully clothed on the couch next to the telephone.

The following day about noon, Mother showed up at the front door. She looked frazzled and worn. Her wool coat drooped on one side with moisture, there were shadows under her eyes, and strands of hair hung over her forehead. In place of her hat she had a long neck scarf wrapped around her head with the ends tucked into the collar of her red coat. I wondered what happened to the hat.

Behind my mother a strange man towered in the doorway. I stared at him. He looked like he might have materialized from a snow bank himself. His wool overcoat was moist and wrinkled as if slept in. The cold had burned his cheeks red, and under the brim of a fedora hat wide brown eyes looked out at Dad, Harold, and me, full of anxiety, gratitude, and evasion. I didn't trust him.

We got the story in a rush of words alternating between the two of them: they had been stranded at Young Quinlan's along with a mass of other shoppers, and crowded into a back lounge where Mother had spent the night in a stiff wooden chair. She hadn't slept a wink and didn't know if she were coming or going. She calmed down as she spoke, even laughing as she described the stench of sleeping bodies and the piercing sound of clogged nostrils from those lucky enough to drift off. She glanced coquettishly at the stranger as if to corroborate her words.

"Mr. Mathews was kind enough to drive me home, bless his heart," she said. "He was standing next to me when the store manager announced that we would have to spend the night until the plows got though." She turned to Dad who was standing immobile, taking all this in. "Thank heavens for this nice gentleman."

She laughed again, with a soft lilt, and unwrapped the scarf while her goulashes dripped clusters of snow on the hall rug.

"We were worried sick," Dad said. To him this was no laughing matter. "The phones were out."

"Yes, indeed. No one was able to call in or out. We figured our families would hear it on the news," Mr. Mathews replied.

Dad reached out his hand to the stranger and thanked him for his assistance. The stranger's hand was cocked and smooth, as if made from clay. In fact, it hardly looked human. It was then I noticed wet fabric in Mr. Mathew's hand, which he now handed over to Dad.

"Say, thanks for the protection. Nita let me use this to cover my head. Would have ruined my hat." Now Mr. Mathews was all amiability, looking at Mother.

"Nita is full of kindness," said Dad dryly.

"Oh, those are the pajamas I bought for Judy," chimed Mother. "It was the least I could do. Judy won't mind." She gave another jingling laugh, accompanied by a wave of eyelids.

Judy *did* mind. Who was this guy anyway? What right had he to be here? I eyed my pajamas, patterned with little daffodils and pink ferns, now stained and ruined. Mr. Mathews, who had brightened, continued telling his version of the previous night. Dad shifted from foot to foot, and I willed Mr. Mathews to go. He had no place here. He had no right to corral Mother when we needed her at home.

I blamed Mr. Mathews for keeping Mother out all night, for her outlaw condition, and for the storm. The truth was I didn't want to share her, even for her benefit. I was also angry at her for giving my new pajamas to this overbearing, over-smiling man. The next thing you knew he'd want to stay for supper. Well, there was just enough for us, so there!

It wasn't the storm that upset me, it was Mother. Flurries were raging in my stomach, ice tingling through my blood. Part of me wanted to protect her, to save her from the rages of the storm that had stolen her in the shape of this snow-coated demon with the scheming eyes. Part of me was furious at the amiability, the gratitude she lavished on him. I wanted to be lavished on. I knew like a biblical fact that she had only so much caring to dispense, and it was being used up on this stranger.

I felt my world shrinking. Dad, I could see, wasn't happy with the situation, either. I willed the door to open and suck the strange man out so our family of four could sit by the fire around Mother and be one. I wanted Dad to take us for a drive in the new Studebaker, down France Avenue and over to the seven lakes, stopping at Bridgeman's for banana splits.

Finally the stranger left, disappearing into the mountains of snow. I stared forlornly at the remnants of my pajamas hanging on the hall table, a little pool of water shimmering on the floor below.

Mother at the piano at Wooddale Avenue house in Edina—circa 1940.

Chapter Two

❧ A Special Case ❧

My BROTHER HAROLD, five years my senior, was a thin boy, freckled, with a swatch of straight reddish hair that fell over one side of his forehead. He had Mother's good looks and gentle manner. He didn't like me. He saw that I continually received the benefit of the doubt, as the youngest and a girl and all. He stood by cautiously, watching the dramas I created and the wealth of attention they produced. Unlike me, he was strictly disciplined by Dad.

Bursting with high-strung antics and impulsiveness, at the age of five I began showing signs of nervous susceptibility. I never stopped. Climbing over the house furniture like a gymnast, I'd swing over the back of the couch and cartwheel across the room, legs crashing against the walls. Mother would clutch her hands together in desperation. "Stop that! Settle down." When I ran to her with a fresh bruise, seeking her lap, she twisted away, drawn into the other room by some urgent task. "For God's sake, don't be such a cry baby."

I developed tics. When I lifted my chin and picked at my neck bone at the dinner table, my parents looked on in astounded silence. Mother lowered her fork slowly. "Judy, stop picking at your neck. Must you do that? You'll damage yourself. Brad?" she called out helplessly. At the far end of the table Dad, a hazy figure in a brown business suit, sliced his knife back and forth over a crisp pork chop.

"She should get outside, get more exercise. She's got more energy than a newborn heifer." Dad was fond of using country language, a humorous reference to his backwoods background that we later suspected was deliberate. When they could afford to attend cultural events, Mother lured him to an opera, and he left shaking his head and declaring never again; he'd heard enough hog calling back home in West Virginia.

I looked down at the chunks of food swirling into each other on my plate as I jerked my finger around. My picky eating habits caused a continual dinner-time struggle. All attention focused on my difficult behavior. I sank down in the chair. If I could just bury myself under the fold of the table! As my parents conversed, my eyes shot up to a silver-framed print on the wall behind Mother's head. It was the picture of a young girl standing in a garden under a flowering arbor, slender and impeccable in an icy blue frock. She exuded confidence, serenely at home in her starched dress and white ribbons. My explosive emotions could never be tamed like that, never molded into quiet shapes and smooth limbs. I could never be that girl!

I knew that something about me was not right. I jerked; my shoulder, leg, mouth would tighten in quick little lifts from voltage shooting from some inner control center. The doctor prescribed rest and exercise and my brother was sternly warned not to aggravate me. My protection at his expense probably intensified his lifelong animosity. The days of enforced rest, a word I abhorred, had begun.

At age seven, I was still taking afternoon naps. I dreaded them. Every day after lunch I had to lie down in my room, with blinds lowered and the door closed. No games, no distractions—just lie there. The idea was to learn to *relax*. This was a word I did not acknowledge. Nothing was worse than lying in a silent room with nothing to do. I rolled and squirmed on the bed, unwilling or unable to settle into the disarming quiet. I would peer under the shade at my friend Joanne's house a few yards away and think of her loose and carefree while I was forced to endure this torture. Joanne, who had quit napping three years earlier, must have thought I was something of a baby. This idea was insufferable.

I complained—Mother called it whining—but in this one thing she was adamant. As soon as the doctor prescribed rest for me, Mother threw herself into the plan. This was something she could do, when so much of the time she at a loss with us. She guarded my rest periods and sleep time like the crown jewels. Occasionally she would come in and rub my back for a few minutes while sitting calmly on the bed, her gentle touch rounding on my shoulders. Sweet vibrations and the scent of White Shoulders perfume lingered in the room after she'd left. After this I lay more quietly, missing her, watching the minutes pass one by one, stretching and slowing down until they seemed to span the entire afternoon.

When not under afternoon bondage, I was parrying with Harold. His main occupation, his ghoulish pleasure, was teasing me. Maybe he was bored. Or maybe, with my intense reactions, I was a tempting target. His antics drove me to boiling, and my defensive outbursts goaded more teasing. Mother's fragile nerves were stretched to the breaking point. He was relentless and I was unstoppable. She was beside herself.

I fell into Harold's snares with naive regularity.

"Judy, come down here, I want to show you something." He would lead me downstairs, then dash up, slam the top door and lock it, leaving me crouching in the dark on the other side, the dank basement at my back.

"You cannot get out," he hissed through the crack. "You're all alone. Watch out for monsters below. They're coming up the stairs—look out!"

One of his favorite tortures was to wrestle me to the living room floor, sit astride my stomach and tickle me by plowing his head back and forth on my chest, demanding that I say, "I'm a monkey." For the first seconds I squealed with glee as his arms pinned my wrists to the floor. I loved the close contact and the playful thrusting, but as his weight dug into mine I felt my muscles crunch into tight fist-like nodules. The pounding on my chest sent jack hammer currents firing through my body. Whipped into submission, I lay defeated, tamed, primed for the kill. I clenched my mouth into a knot as long as I could bear it. Finally I spit out, "I'm a monkey," and ran like a broken gazelle, crying and protesting to Mother.

The only defense was to threaten to tell. The minute she heard my squeals, Mother's forehead creased and she shook her head, a look of resigned endurance creeping over her face.

"Stop this continuous squabbling! Your Dad will hear about this tonight."

"But Harold was tickling me!"

"Oh, for heaven's sake, he's just playing." And to Harold, "Stop it. She doesn't like it. You'll answer to your Dad." Then, with a sharp sigh and look of desperation, she fluttered out of the room.

Mother was at a loss. She had grown up among adults, listening to their conversations and sitting quietly at the corner of the card table while they played bridge. She was rarely with someone her own age. Her biggest treat was a summer visit with her cousin Florence Musgrave in Spring Park, where the two girls thumbed through picture books of the Adirondacks while the adults conversed in the parlor. Discipline in Mother's household was twofold: her dad's not-to-be-countered orders, administered in sharp phrases, and her mother's non-interfering compliance, which amounted to no discipline at all. The powerful voice of Granddad Fought reverberated through the house even when he wasn't there. Obedience was automatic.

When Dad returned home, Mother briefed him on our antics and he either blew it off, saying we were bound to have spats, or stormed into the living room to confront us. Harold and I offered up our conflicting versions, and most often he grabbed Harold by the shoulder and sent him to his room. "You're older. You're the boy," he'd say. "You're supposed to look after your little sister." And with a scuff on the neck from his powerful hand, Harold was sent upstairs. "And you, sister, you have to learn not to pay him mind," was all I got.

Those days Dad was in no mood for foolishness, especially since he was working days at Investors Syndicate and attending William Mitchell Law School at night. Dad hadn't the time or patience to hold an examining court. He used his temper to keep us in line. Its heat would create a larger and larger circle of tense space around him as we all backed away from it and merged into the depths of the house. Back then it was Harold who took the brunt, who was the target of the fast one-shot discipline method, while the rest of us trembled in the background.

Mother suffered silently, and reliving, no doubt, the explosive bouts of her father, she dissolved into the shadows. With maturity my father learned to manage his rage, but the terror I felt at the sound of his voice crashing against the walls stayed with me long after.

Revisiting those years today, I see that power was used as a molding device in our family, a fierce, barricading male power that ruled by fear. As a dependent small thing I was overcome with fear—an accusing, crushing fear that threatened obliteration. I felt myself shrink, shrivel into timidity like a night creature trembling in the blindness of the forest. As I grew older, as if by some alchemy churned in my intestines, another feeling emerged and made its way to the surface, accompanying my teenage years and far beyond, eventually dominating all others: anger. As I got to know both my grandfathers, I saw the same temper that dominated our house. The men needed to get things done. The women took refuge.

As we grew older, Harold endured consequences that, as a girl, I was spared. The harder Dad came down on him the more distant he became.

Harold spent hours hidden away in his room, or I'd hear him slam out the back door. I saw enough to understand that he was popular with his friends, with whom he joked and laughed in a devil-may-care manner. If he and a friend locked themselves in his room, I lingered outside the door and listened to their mumblings. At meals he didn't say much, just answered questions or responded with a slight smile. It was Mother who lightened the mood with rounds of small talk. Sometimes I saw across the table a glint of confusion in Harold's eyes that sent a hot wave through me, streaks of wonder and gloom that I couldn't bear. I was ready to do whatever he asked if it would only take away that look.

His disdain only increased my longing to be included in his life. I worshipped him but the attachment was one-sided. As we grew up we never discussed things or did anything together, like throw a baseball or go on picnics. Often I watched him stride through the house with an elusive air, going off to do something that didn't include me. I was banned from his room. With equal determination I wanted to be wherever he was and doing whatever he was doing. Often I heard him up in his room listening to the radio or buried in eerie silence. What was he doing in there? Evenings I watched him lying on the rug in front of the fire hugging Zip, our red Irish Setter who never left his side.

Hearing blasts from the trumpet as he practiced in his room upstairs, I waited to catch a glimpse of him on his way out. "Where are you going?" "Nowhere," was all Harold would say, and he'd vanish around the corner without a word, Zip at his heels.

I delved into his drawers to inspect his treasured coin collection and the Red Sox or Dodgers baseball signed by a well-known pitcher. I didn't care about his privacy—I'd do anything to get into his world.

When I was ten Harold was sent to Shattuck Military Academy—presumably to dislodge the chip from his shoulder—and nearly got booted out for bringing girls to his room. After high school he joined the Eighty-First Airborne Division in Fort Benning, Georgia, where he took on parachute training "because the pay was good." Eighteen months later he entered Duke University, where I assumed he launched into his usual round of bar-hopping and girl-chasing.

Looking back on those years, I wonder how my life-long yearning for his affection in the face of his indifference influenced my relationships with men. I seem to have absorbed his rejection with uncritical admiration—maybe I even grew to desire it. Was I weaned on a negative emotional relationship pattern with my brother that I was doomed to seek for all time because it was familiar? Did I harbor a need to confront and tame the unaccessible to resolve some need? Why didn't I reach out for what contributed to me, instead of habitually attaching to people who were in reality absent?

Harold.

❧✦❧

WHEN I WAS SEVEN, Mother decided it was high time I was baptized. Not that religion played a prominent part in our lives, but with a minister grandfather, Mother guarded a serious religious strain. She selected Easter Sunday for my big day at the Presbyterian Church at the corner of Wooddale and France, the denomination of her youth in West Virginia.

We spent the morning getting spiffed up for the occasion. Mother loved to doll me in Shirley Temple curls. This penchant of hers conflicted with my horror of having my hair combed and styled, which took a large part of the morning. After a shampoo in the bath tub, my wet hair was toweled down and I was seated on Mom's dressing table stool in front of a gilt-edged mirror. Mother tugged a pearl-handled comb through the snarly strands of my hair. I endured every yank on my skull with loud complaints. "Stop, you're hurting me! I don't want curls. Get your own curls!"

But Mother would not give in on this one. Her face was determined, if tormented. Her hands waved above my head while she wove the hair brush in and out, separating strands of my damp, permed hair, combing out flat sections and wrapping them tightly around the brush handle. She then dried each curl with an Eskimo hair dryer until set, and carefully withdrew the brush handle, allowing the curl to air dry for a minute. She admonished me to sit rigid, but no matter how hard I tried I couldn't.

"Hold still!" Mother implored.

The curls were little works of art, perfect corkscrew swirls, cascading from a part running across the top of my head and encircling my crown like floppy lusters. When she had finished, Mother secured two blue ribbons with Bobby pins on each side above my ears.

"That's enough." I said. "It looks fine."

"I guess so," Mother responded, not stopping. "Just a bit here . . ."

I looked at the mirror and caught her image raised above mine, like a sculptress bent over her carving. She was decked out in a rayon crepe lavender dress with scooped neck. As usual she looked impeccable, hair soft and freshly styled, with a tiny amethyst and pearl pendant set in gold hanging daintily from her neck. She wore matching pearl and amethyst earrings and bracelet.

She looked worn under her makeup, her face tight. Our tug of war had exhausted her and left me pouty. We surveyed the result in the mirror. I faced a little girl in a blue-and-white print dress with a white lace collar, a single strand of pearls, and a head of fresh bouncy curls, looking big-eyed and sour. I raised my eyes to Mother's satisfied smile above me. Her hand rested on my shoulder: she had done a good job.

"Judy, where's your other shoe," she asked as I climbed off the stool.

"Don't know, can't find it. I already looked."

"Well, for heaven's sake, go look some more. And don't forget your handkerchief and white gloves. We have to leave in a few minutes. Hurry."

She tapped downstairs to clear the lunch dishes off the kitchen table. I poked about my room. Nothing. I picked up a stuffed yellow Pooh bear and idly twisted its black eye in circles. A whiff of lemon hit my nostrils, the odor of an autumn flower. I let it flow in. . . .

"Judy," Mother yelled up the stairs. "Come and finish your lunch."

"I'm not hungry," I yelled back.

"You have to eat. For heaven's sake, she hasn't eaten her lunch yet!" I dragged down the stairs and stood in the kitchen doorway.

"I don't want it. I can't eat." I looked at the egg-salad sandwich and untouched glass of milk on the Formica table. My stomach tightened at the sight.

"You have to eat or you'll get cranky."

"I'm cranky now. I can't find my shoe."

"What is the matter with you, child?" Mother groaned as she began to put away a row of gold-striped Tiffany glasses washed the night before. As soon as her back was turned I darted my hand out, grabbed one of the tall glasses, and in a frenzied attempt to grasp the milk bottle, felt myself falling. To my horror the glass splat against the white china sink and cluttered in sharp pieces to the floor, while a spray of while liquid flew out and soaked the skirt of Mother's new lavender dress.

She looked down at her dripping skirt.

"Oh, my Lord!" she exclaimed, her forehead scrunched into a circle of deep ridges. "Can't you ever do anything right?"

"I'll just get my white gloves." I dashed upstairs and pulled out the top drawer of my bureau, where I found a mismatched pair of brown and blue suede gloves. The white gloves were missing and so was the handkerchief with the blue-and-white delphiniums stitched around the edges.

My mother's voice reached me from the living room as I descended. "I don't know what I'm going to do with her!"

When I came down Dad and Harold were seated on the couch, coats in their laps.

"We'll be late. We'd better go," urged Dad with irritation.

"Brad, Judy has lost her shoe. And her handkerchief." She came in the living room and I saw a wet circle on her dress where she'd sponged the stain. "I certainly haven't had time to look." She jerked on her coat. "And what have you done with your gloves? I laid them here on the table an hour ago." She threw a severe look at me.

Everyone stood waiting by the door, staring at me. Dad's stood by impatiently, a sour look on his face, and Harold scanned the wall with an eye-rolling expression. Mother frowned and her eyes swept around the room nervously.

There was nowhere to turn. My head drooped and my eyes locked dully on the floor. I wished myself sucked into a galactic hole or buried in a crater in the desert. Or anywhere else! I squeezed my eyes, and they locked into a frozen pose of humiliation. Today I was the star, but the stars weren't shining. I couldn't do anything right. I hated it. I hated everything.

Harold swung his arm in the air. "Here's the shoe. It was under the couch," he said with a slight grin on his face.

I stared at him, incredulous. I'd already looked there. Was this another trick? But there was no time for suspicion. We had to leave, without my white gloves or handkerchief. Dad hastily snapped our picture, showing me morosely holding a corsage of yellow and white flower buds, backed by a heavy white doily, my mother wearing gardenias, and Harold placid in his new tweed suit.

Once inside the gray stone church we hurried to a forward pew. The scent of sour candle oil drifted over from the altar. When my turn came, I stood at the chancel and the minister sprinkled water on my head from a marble font, with Mom, Dad, and Harold looking on. Far from enjoying the attention focused on me, I felt lost in the enormity of it all and gripped with the sting of an acid stomach.

From some mountainous distance the notes of an organ bellowed into the chapel like a cornered animal and for a split second the gold crucifix and the black silhouette of the minister's arms looming just above my head mesmerized me, ground me into a tiny star in the dark pool of the marble floor.

My parents gazed anxiously at my drooping face, willing my mood to change. When I glanced at Harold standing in the background, he jerked his head away as if touched by a hot wire. I expected him to fly off at any minute out the door and into the sanity of another life. I wanted to fly with him.

Mother, Dad, Harold, and I on my baptism day—1941.

☙ ◆ ❧

THERE WERE ADVANTAGES to being a girl. I was pampered and primped in velveteen dresses, and brushed and combed and groomed like Mother. I wanted to be like Mother. At first I was a cute little thing (until I grew gangly and tomboyish). I had a little girl voice and innocent little girl eyes. I was valued. I had a unique place in the family. I was the only girl they had.

This was not to last.

Most of the time, Mother was out shopping, playing bridge, stirring pans in the kitchen, or resting upstairs. While she dressed for a social event, I hung in her bedroom, mesmerized by the faint scent of White Shoulders as she glided by in her swishy dress and tiny suede heels with bows, carefully selecting clip-on earrings and matching bracelet. Sitting at the dressing table smiling serenely into the mirror as she brushed her soft brown hair, she looked so contained, so mature, womanly and lustrous. It was clear that even grown up I wouldn't look remotely like her, never claim her soft gentleness. I would never match her grace and confidence or draw a continual beam of admiring glances. But I didn't give up wishing.

One afternoon, I spied a pair of identical mother/daughter dresses in a catalog. The cotton dress had a red, blue and yellow patterned skirt, which was connected to the bodice by a wide elastic waistband in the same colored plaid pattern, running in the opposite direction. Mother was unenthusiastic, but I thought it had a smart, perky look. When she finally gave in and ordered the dresses I was ecstatic. I could hardly wait for our twin outfits and the splash we would make as look-alikes.

When the dresses finally arrived, it was too late. I was told, in hushed tones, that with a new development in our household Mother was no longer able to concern herself with elastic dresses. She and Dad were expecting a newcomer to the family—a baby. Wow. There was to be another person in the house to play with or even better, to hold and protect. Someone for me to love, they said. Now this sounded tricky. I heard a tone of expectation and wondered exactly what role I was supposed to play. It would be an exciting, happy event—but that was all I was allowed to know. It was a delicate topic, and I would have to wait and see.

When I learned that Mother's stomach would be getting bigger and she would not be wearing the dress after all, I thrashed out of the house and hid behind an oak tree. The dream of Mother and me parading hand in hand in our matching red dresses had crumbled to pieces. The safe arms where in lucky moments I drew warmth, the center of life, the source of nourishment was being withdrawn. Once I wore the red dress on my own, but it had lost its appeal. It hung in the closet with the red, blue and yellow colors lost in the shadows like a flag after the celebration was over. The sight of it reminded me how the shape of my little world had changed. There were challenges afoot as I was faced with consequences that displaced my visions of baby allure. The new addition had already, from inside my mother, started to change her and to vary the complexion of our family life.

When the big day arrived, I sat on the piano bench by the window, peering up the road for a sign of the car. Finally our brown coupe appeared between the stone gates and scooped down into our driveway, and I rushed to the garage door, cries of excitement bubbling in my throat. Mom, Dad, and baby Susan burst out of the car. I stared at the bundle of pink fleece and lace and into a little face so innocent and helpless it made my heart stop. The baby was to stay in the spare room over the garage, which was not a true bedroom since it connected to the hall through Harold's room. We'd only lived in the Tyrol Hills house a year and it was already too small. It would be six years before we moved closer to town. I wasn't allowed in the nursery, so I stood in the doorway and peered at the bundle of pink wiggling in the wicker basinet. Mother, wearing a gold bracelet set with four red stones Dad had given her and a blowy peach-and-cream dress with pearl buttons, glowed as she bent over the crib.

I wasn't allowed to go near Susan. Week after week visitors passed the growing baby from hand to hand, while I looked on from the dining room, doomed to be forever standing the shadows. The baby needed protection, I supposed, from accidents or foolishness, which Mother seemed to think I would amply supply. In later years I learned that the obstetrician had given strict orders to keep me away from the baby. The fear of germs was rampant—diseases could maim, kill. Visitors had to wear masks and siblings had to keep their mass of contagion at bay. The doctor's expertise was not to be challenged. The live-in nurse proved to be a strict sentry.

Mother faded into the nursery. Sometimes, when the house was still and the only sound was the rhythmic slurping of the baby on its bottle, I kneeled outside the door and peeped in, watching Mother's form in the maple rocking chair, her head curved over the bundle on her arm. The look on her face was tender, her shoulder under the rose-colored robe soft and inviting, and a hypnotizing scent of gardenia drifted from her presence. I imagined myself curled in her lap, enveloped in a halo of brightness, pure contentment. As I pressed against the jamb, a pounding in my throat threatened to explode into my head. When the nurse padded across the room and shut the door the vision flooded my mind for some time.

After that I kept my distance. The plaid dress hung in my closet untouched, reminding me every time I opened the door how empty and cheated I felt and that it was all this baby's fault. I spent more and more time in my room reading in bed, where I fell contently into a make-believe existence, and the blaze of jealousy raging through my limbs became absorbed in the pages of far-off reality.

Everyone said the baby looked like Dad. Mother was pleased. Here was a little girl who wasn't bothered by things, who was perky and positive and laughed happily. Who remained quiet and content. And who to my annoyance retained the aura of cuteness that accompanies infancy far beyond her infant years.

Despite my disappointment about the dress, I wrote a two-page story, something about the wonder of babies, especially a baby sister. I vowed I would teach her how to say her prayers and let her know right off that she would never be lonely. Mrs. Moore, who lived next door, praised my enthusiasm and said to guard the piece carefully for my sister to cherish one day. Three months later I ripped it up.

For being so tiny, the new baby consumed a great deal of household energy. She filled the room with gushing visitors and the scent of talcum powder, and seemed to require the attention of every adult in the house at all times. As the months passed I stopped minding the "look-not-touch" ban. I had other things to think about—like how to fill an entire afternoon.

When Susan started wandering into my room, the first thing she did was waddle up on shaky legs and grab whatever I was holding. At first I ignored her, but it became clear that whatever I wanted Susan would get, and whatever focus Mother was able to give to child-raising was beamed on her. Gradually I developed ploys to keep her away. If I heard little footsteps approaching my door and stopping outside, I refused to respond, and when she invaded the living room where I was playing paper dolls with a friend, I herded my friend upstairs to my bedroom. She constantly trailed me about, but I kept my bedroom door shut.

One day, Susan was in the back yard, carrying our new Labrador puppy draped over her arm by its stomach, with its legs dangling and its head pumping as it uttered little cries of protest. I ran outside to put a stop to this torture, but Mother intervened, insisting Susan have her rightful turn. Banished to my room, I peered out the window and watched the puppy struggle as Susan twisted it around like one of her stuffed toys. I was determined to wait until the puppy was released from its misery, no matter how long it took, my stomach clutched into a ball between my ribs.

Finally, after Susan became bored, I sat on the bed with the puppy in my arms, and stroked the golden head that smelled of warm milk and acorns. Across the room the plaid dress drooped in my closet. Suddenly I was overcome with anger. This little sister was anything but the bundle of joy I had been led to expect. I felt the well source of my feelings shrivel and a sense of loss threatened to extinguish my very breath. The days of curling against Mother's warm breast were over—she was busy elsewhere. I would never wear the dress alongside her, and worse I would never *be* her. Eventually I balled the dress up and stuffed it in a corner of the closet behind some shoe boxes.

Susan and me in Tyrol Hills, 1946.

Chapter Three

❧ Into the Woods ❦

*T*HE FAMILY MOVED IN 1941 to Tyrol Hills in Golden Valley, and we now resided in a self-contained neighborhood surrounded by thick woods and an air of secluded liberty. I had reached the ripe age of seven.

I launched with enthusiasm into a new freedom where I could roam at will, safe within the confines of the large yards with brick and clapboard houses scattered among the hills. Since the single entrance to Tyrol Hills was through a stone gate bordering the service road along Highway 12 (later 394), cars passing in and out were local. Safety was guarded by the presence of bustling mothers in each house, keeping watch with eagle eyes at the windows. It was not long before I knew every hill, every door stoop, every shortcut between garages, and how to navigate the trails around the low-lying swamp in the early moonlight.

Our French provincial house had a large bay window overlooking the back yard, second-story dormer windows, and connecting fireplaces in the living room, master bedroom, and basement. Above the back stoop, a small hatch opened to a metal slot where the milkman inserted glass milk bottles two or three times a week. For the master bedroom Mother purchased an antique poster bed of dark mahogany with a white ruffle running along the top of the four posts and a queen mattress, considered oversized in those days. A matching hourglass dressing table with a stool and mirror and a tall mahogany chest of drawers stood against one wall.

I loved the house, with its carved woodwork, the surprise angle of the walls, the split Dutch front door, and especially my parents' unorthodox closet that consisted of cupboards, rods, shelves and drawers built into the walls of a narrow corridor that ran all the way from the master bedroom to the other end of the house. Beyond this corridor was a spare room that was first a den and later converted to a nursery when Susan was born. This room led into my brother's room, which in turn opened to the upstairs hall, completing the circle.

We lived on the outskirts of Minneapolis, a short commute to the Roanoke building in Minneapolis. Dad could drive down Highway 12 between stretches of wooded hills where the Prudential Insurance building now stands, past Dunwoody Institute and down Hennepin Avenue and be sitting in his office at Investors Syndicate in fifteen minutes.

Dad set about improving the house. In the basement he built divider walls for an amusement room, poured concrete, installed paneling, and cut a door to the back yard. Nothing was too big to tackle; if he hadn't done it before, he'd find a way. The next year he built a

House in Tyrol Hills, Golden Valley.

screened porch on the back of the house and beyond it a brick barbeque grill. He thrived on the work, the sweat, the accomplishment, and the thought of all the money he was saving.

A coal furnace at one end of the laundry room resembled an old iron frigate. To fill the firebox a truck pulled up to the side of the house and poured coal down the steep chute into a dusty basement bin. Several times a week Dad cranked open the heavy iron door and shoveled crumbled black coal into the blazing red depths. The flames crackled and roared, creating a throbbing ball of fire that scorched your face if you peered too close. When the air was humid the cankerous smell of coal ash seeped up the stairs and through the laundry chute to the above floors.

After burning, Dad had to cart the ashes outside to be trucked away. Carbon dust settled everywhere, and yellowish particles produced a haze in the air and coated our gray Pontiac with thin ash. Little Bobby Ludwig ran around the neighborhood with a black mask covering his asthmatic nose. Not long after we moved in Dad replaced the coal furnace with a streamlined gas system. Mother acquired a new wringer washing machine, a round chrome tub on legs topped with two abutting rollers. Wet clothing was fed between these rollers, powered by a side handle rotated by hand. Each dripping piece was tucked in the crack between the rollers and drawn through, emerging as a flat mass of folds that resembled a floppy fish. To scrub stubborn stains, Mother used a wavy metal washboard. In summer our sheets, bright off the outdoor line, stretched smooth across the beds, newly ironed and smelling of fresh daisies and ivory soap.

Mother was welcomed into a close-knit South Tyrol community of like-minded stay-at-home moms who loved to socialize as much as she did. There were continual Saturday night parties, bridge games and barbeques. She and the neighborhood ladies commiserated about overworked husbands, the best dentists for children, and the latest styles at Young Quinlan's. Mother kept some of these friends for years after she'd moved her social focus to the Lafayette Club and the popular downtown restaurants. With Mother busy much of the time, I was left to my own devices. I didn't have, in second grade, homework or any tasks around the house. There was really nothing I had to do except obey and not make trouble. I would have much rather operated the washing machine or performed a task that would let me into the adult realm so I could feel a part of something. Instead, I had plenty of time to fret and wander around feeling isolated, to contemplate my lacks and failures, which my parents often found the most compelling thing about me.

EVERY MORNING I WAITED for the school bus at the stone entrance pillars along Highway 12. On frigid days, as the wind whipped through, piercing everything in sight, I huddled behind a pillar, inching round the sides to escape the frigid onslaught. With my coat clutched around my throat, I shivered until I spied the nose of the yellow school bus down the road. I leaped on and stared out the window as the bus wound through North Tyrol, down Glenwood Avenue and across the Highway 100 overpass to a square two-story red brick building just beyond.

Meadowbrook School held four classrooms: grades one/two and three/four were set across from each other on the first floor, with identical rooms for grades five/six and seven/eight directly above them on the second. Along the front of each room ran a separate cloakroom with an open archway on either end for winter gear and lunch pails. While the teacher stood at the front desk teaching one grade, the students in the other grade were bending over their assignment in their half of the room. You could go through a grade twice if you listened carefully to both lectures. Not that anyone ever did, of course.

They didn't work us too hard. During my eight years we were not given take-home assignments and there were no organized sports. The boys tossed basket balls into the hoop standing in the school yard, and baseball teams, which included girls, were thrown together casually during recess. The younger students played on the swing set.

During second grade, I got into real trouble. Every morning Mrs. Bolton had us sing *Faith of our Fathers*, a hymn that went on and on, verse after verse, until we spaced out—we thought *Battle Hymn of the Republic* had much more zing. Timmy Olson and I shared one of those beige two-seater desks with lifting lids and a cut-in ink well. Timmy sang out, he loved music. Not only did he play Chopin—his mother was a piano teacher—but he could draw lifelike pictures of animals and created birds of all types with ease. His slender fingers could make a blue-bird come to life on the page, standing on a twig or guarding a nest. I tried to copy his sketches, but my birds didn't even enter the ranks of the living.

One afternoon while Mrs. Bolton was instructing the first graders, Timmy's elbow pressed against mine. He opened a lettering book and between the pages I saw he had drawn a naked woman. I pressed my lips together into a half smile and glanced at him, trying not to blush. He withdrew the book and in a minute slithered it back to me. This time he had drawn a naked man and I had to swallow a giggle. We took turns adding parts to the figures, inventing and exaggerating and stifling our titters as best we could. This went on for several days and no one seemed to notice. We were in stitches, burying our heads in our books to look busy, then slipping out the drawings when Mrs. Bolton was preoccupied elsewhere.

This frivolity did not last. Our close heads must have given us away, for we heard a *snap snap* along the floor coming closer and stopping at our desk.

"All right, you two!" Mrs. Bolton swept up the two pieces of paper from the book, started to raise them as an example of our naughtiness, but changed her mind and simply barked, "This is unacceptable!"

Out to the hall we went, feeling chastised until we decided that the punishment was almost as much fun as the crime. We liked to sit on the floor in the empty hallway talking and laughing. After a half an hour Mrs. Bolton called us back into the classroom, complaining we were making too much noise. After class we were given a stiff talking to and placed in separated seats for the rest of the year and that ended my artistic endeavors.

Timmy became my best friend as we moved up the grades, despite the pressures for little girls play with other girls, which never made any sense—Timmy was much more fun. I would spot his tan sweater in the hallway, with his straight ginger-brown hair framing his narrow face and his long feet lending a slight lilt to his step, and we would sneak off to peek at the naked pictures in the *National Geographic*. Mostly we stayed out of trouble. Like most kids in the forties, we were geared to obedience. To talk back to an elder was unheard of. Timmy was acquiescent, in contrast to my willfulness. He let me boss him and was forgiving when I chewed him out. Our close friendship lasted until seventh grade when a new girl named Jean entered our ranks and a burgeoning awareness of being of the opposite sex and all that might entail drove a wedge in our friendship.

≈◆≪

MOSTLY I WAS ON MY OWN. As spring buds on the bushes fluttered open and rains brought tree roots to life, I broke out of the house into the surrounding woodlands, wandering endlessly, sometimes tramping across Highway 12 and through the forest of pine, maple, aspen and oak to Theodore Parkway, breathing in the odors of wet bark and oats. Without destination or timeline, I listened to the whoosh of wet leaves underfoot and felt the fresh air on my arms, stopping from time to time to smell spongy pine cones. Reaching Birch Pond, I sat on a rock and inhaled the rubbery-sage smell of still water and mud. Curious ducks ventured up and then shot off sleek across the water like marbles on glass, motionless and mysteriously silent.

My special hideout was high on a wooded hill overlooking the curved roads of Tyrol Hills, where I sat on a carpet of long silky grass flowing between two tall oaks. Leaning against a tree, with a jacket stuffed behind my back, I occupied my own little room, walled by clumps of poplars and underbrush. From this vantage point I could observe Keith Icky's house, where Debby, our Labrador, once ripped through the back screen porch and devoured a birthday cake cooling on a metal chair. We received a phone call.

Occasionally I'd see the lone figure of Mrs. Gibbons or Mrs. Bloomers along the side of the road below headed for a neighbor's house, unaware of the eagle eyes in the woods.

Many days I settled into my wooded den and became lost in a book. I read about the feats of *Lad, a Dog* or Laura cozy in her underground sod house in *On the Banks of Silver Creek*. In Josephine Lawrence's *Stories for Girls*, the golden-haired Rosemary put up with snotty siblings and troubles over which, in her conscientious, good-girl way, she always prevailed. I loved Rosemary, wanted a friend like Rosemary, wanted to be like Rosemary. In her life problems were conquered and kids took on challenges and emerged triumphant and praised.

I would lie in my grassy lair underneath the tree, look up at the sky, and watch white cloud clusters drift in splayed animal shapes across the blue sky. If I closed my eyes, the woods began to stir and come alive with little cracking noises of hidden creatures. Sometimes the wind took up a soft moan, stirring leaves that turned and fanned in the air, and I heard the branch of a honeysuckle bush, like the one in Rosemary's yard, whispering from its hiding place.

There on the hill everything accommodated everything else, powered by an unknown law of nature. There was no fuss, no confusion, no complicated choices about how to act, no rough voices pressing me to be different. I could just be, no questions asked.

The trees didn't say much, but as the minutes ticked by their presence came to life. Just be natural, they hinted, be like us. Animated sounds bubbling at the edge of the wide marsh below drifted up the hill. Here I felt comfortable, alone with the world at my feet, looking down on the neighborhood where I knew every stone and nook, with my house just out of view around the hill. Here I was safe, undisturbed, connected, and detached but still felt I belonged.

Mike and Smitty, my constant companions, were game for anything. Mike, a golden retriever with a rich burnt-gold coat and a noble face, lived two houses away and was more than happy to go anywhere on earth. Smitty was more of a baby and ran to my side at sudden loud noises, but as an imposing German shepherd he had a reputation to maintain, which he enforced by barking wildly at strangers. He bounded up from his house next door when I whistled and couldn't wait to take off. The dogs were indefatigable. We roamed for hours and they never stopped flying through the trees to investigate this or that, tails beating back and forth.

Dogs in those days ran free with no restrictions, could visit whomever they liked, poop where they wanted, and sleep under any old bush. Most dogs really didn't have many places to go by themselves and wandered around the yard sniffing or lay on the back stoop waiting for indoors and company. A readiness something like my own.

≈◆≈

DEATH WAS AN UNKNOWN. I was faced with its overpowering mystery one late fall afternoon, when I rounded the crest of a hill overlooking Brownie Lake and stood looking down at a brown pool of water far below, hushed and immobile in the approaching dusk. There was some curious movement going on at the far shore, half-hidden by the heavy brush, and I made out miniature figures running down the slope. They were focused on something I couldn't clearly see. Some bulge, a mottled form, was lying at the edge of the water. Side-stepping down the hill, I broke through branches and made my way down to the bank.

As a reached the bottom and peered across the lake I made out a group of men in wool caps carrying bundles of what looked like blankets, bobbing down the slope in an eerie rhythm. A couple of the men clutched the ends of two long poles between which stretched a limp cloth or canvas. People following in their wake were gathering at the waterfront, and three boys in faded jackets stood carelessly in the wet muck and stared at the form in the water, looking pale as if the disintegration at their feet had metastasized through their own cells.

As I drew near, I made out a body stretched out among the limp reeds, the lower half buried under the water, its skin splotched purple and black and the features of the face washed into neutrality. The body looked like it belonged more to the mucky swamp than to the dry banks above—the water seemed already to be claiming its own, penetrating and absorbing the loose flesh, drawing the corpse into its black depths.

I was aware of an inscrutable powerlessness enclosing the rescuers and me. What had once been a person was no longer within our ranks and was now more swamp than mortal, more vegetable than animal. The semi-human form seemed remote, and there was an inference emanating from its monotone stillness that we were all contained in the watery grave—a call of the inevitable.

Watching the medics carry the corpse away through the dense brush, I became aware that I was only a minuscule spec in the design of the universe and that some cosmic mastery could at will draw me into an unknowable vastness. A wordless, insistent fear penetrated my body, driving out all other emotions. I pictured my family sitting together around the radio in the blue time of evening that closes the day, drawn by the drone of voices from the console and the crackle of Dad's newspaper. The image was dim and the figures remote as if projected from the long end of a telescope. I was overcome with a terrifying sense of separation. Sweat covered my temples, maybe from having stumbled and clawed my way down the slope or maybe it was the apparition of raw fear that lay there at the edge of the lake.

Where did this fear of the unknown come from? Anger was a known thing, it propelled you to get things done, and it provided a valve to release all those pent up charges. But fear, as I learned in later years while trying to untangle the source of my neurosis, lurked behind most other emotions and appeared to stem from two main threats: pain and annihilation. As the saying goes, pain is inevitable, while suffering is optional. And that leaves extinction, preceded by separation and emptiness. There are times when a child believes there is nowhere to turn and slips into a muggy pool of loneliness.

Such theorizing didn't take place until years later—at the time I only sensed I'd been exposed to some Truth the mystery of which was hidden in the depths of Brownie Lake.

When I arrived back at the house, I pulled out a new *Tarzan* book while Mother stirred fried potatoes in an iron skillet and reached up in the cupboard for a tin of paprika. The warmth of the stove and the smell of toasted garlic swarmed around me and all thoughts of death melted into the circle of steam hovering over the stove top.

❧◆❧

DURING THIRD GRADE, a new girl showed up at school. Patsy was a grade ahead of me. A big hefty girl with wide puffy shoulders, it was clear she was not to be messed with. My being the tallest girl in the third grade didn't impress her, and behind my tallness and urge to be in the forefront she sensed a timidity that drew her predatory instincts. After a few weeks observing the lay of the land, Patsy set about establishing her position. When the bell for recess rang, she followed me to the playground and ran up to the swings where I stood waiting my turn.

"I'm next," she shouted, running ahead of me as the swing came to a stop and a student stepped off, "You had extra turns yesterday. Move away."

"No, I didn't!" I cried trying to grab the swaying swing seat, but Patsy lashed out and grabbed one of the ropes, squeezing her body onto the seat. With a wild push she arched up into the air and dropped back down, sweeping me out of the way.

From then on it was war. If I were sledding down the hill alongside the school, Patsy would grab the piece of cardboard I was using as a sled and disappear around the school building, cackling. One time she discovered the rooms of the little house Jean McIntyre, Snookie Styles, and I had marked out in the earth at the edge of the woods and furnished with abandoned logs, stones, and old towels. Patsy tore through, kicked out the wall marks with her heels, then with broad sweeps of a branch obliterated all signs of our work.

"I'll get my brother after her," exclaimed Snookie. Furious, the three of us concocted a plan to line her coat pockets with wads of used chewing gum. The plan fizzled when Mrs. Graves confiscated the ten packets of Spearmint I had squirreled in my desk. Jean vowed revenge.

But it was me she was after.

During the afternoon recess, Patsy would gather the kids lounging against the walls and offer to start a game of tag. "You know the rules," she cried. "The one who's it counts to fifty and you can't peek." She looked around and saw me hanging by one arm from a swing post. "Judy's it!" and with a yell she flew around the side of the school house, followed by eight or ten girls. When it was her turn she chased after me furiously. At one point I turned my head to see her red-headed, square-jawed face speeding towards me yelling, "There goes Judy *Brat*-ford! Get her!"

Several times she lunged at me, threw me to the ground and pummeled me on the back until the ruckus drew a teacher who put a stop to it—for the time being.

"Now girls, you must try to get along." After seeing our passive faces, all signs of wildness erased, the teacher added, "Run along and behave yourselves."

Stifling my shame, I mustered up a defiance. But before I could conjure up a foolproof scheme for getting back at her, loud peals rang out from the schoolhouse door where the principal, Mr. Williams, stood flicking a wooden-handled bell back and forth, calling us inside. My revenge would have to wait.

Patsy continued her rampages after school. She and her family had moved in four houses down the street from me so we shared the same bus stop. At the afternoon drop off she would scream "BRAT-ford" as I walked ahead of her down the road and disappeared around the corner of my house. Sometimes she chased me through the yards as I dodged around trees, but she could never catch me. Propelled by panic, I was faster. My mother told me to ignore her. Yeah, sure. How do you ignore a bee with a mission?

One day her loud yowling pierced my brain like a firecracker, releasing a mounting cache of anger. The bolt stormed through me, releasing mounds of rage, raw after weeks of defensiveness. As she hurled towards me, yelling that I was a "scaredy-cat," I dashed from behind an oak tree, leapt on her back with a fierce yell and toppled her to the ground. One of her arms had twisted behind her when she fell and I pressed the weight of my body against it, keeping my heel pressed down on her neck.

When she lifted her head, I pressed her face into the dirt with my foot and she uttered a moan. With a thrust of her large shoulders she managed to pull herself up, but before she could get to her feet I flew home, carrying my victory with me. Patsy returned to her house with a torn face and sore arm, while I was untouched. The win was small, but it counted. At school I received no more cat calls from Patsy.

A week later as we walked from the bus, Patsy's mother came out on the front stoop, called us into the house and offered us lemonade. We entered slowly, uncertain, but her mother was so friendly and oblivious that we followed her meekly into the den. She had set out some records for us to play and a painting set with drawing tablets on the table, along with the lemonade and crescent-shaped rolled cookies. Patsy and I sat on the floor and munched the cookies.

"You want to paint?" Patsy asked.

I twisted my mouth down. "Uh, I don't know," I said unenthusiastically. I wasn't sure I wanted to be there and I didn't like painting. Yet here was an intriguing invitation. I felt myself warming up. We sat silent for some time, as if waiting for the referee to come in and tell us when the game would start.

"I can stand on my head," Patsy said finally.

"So can I! That's easy!"

Before long we were doing acrobatics on the thick wool carpet. I could stand on my head longer than Patsy and evidently a headstand was all Patsy could manage. I showed her how to stretch her legs over her head while lying on her back and touch the floor with her toes.

"It's easy for you, you're so skinny," she said.

"No, you can do it too." We did backward summersaults, handstands, and performed some fairly decent cartwheels. Patsy was a natural—chunky but strong. She worked on a backbend and could touch the floor behind her with her hands if I held on to her middle.

After that we spent whole afternoons at gymnastics, our feuding ended. The next year she moved away with her family. I wasn't even glad she was gone.

There were other trials in store. An annual skin-splitting, blood-raging, mind-battering, inevitable event filled me with dread. Every fall Mother marched me like clockwork downtown to the Medical Arts building where Dr. Werness wielded his instruments of torture. He ignored my protests. My teeth were naturally soft, and with no fluoride in the public water and my constant munching on hard candy—the pacifier of the day—I was a dentist's dream: a mouth full of gaping cavities. As we drove along in the car, I stared stiffly out the window like I was heading for an execution. The cheeriness of the receptionist only exaggerated the abyss between her mood and mine. "How are we today?" she would chirp. I was the target and they were ready for me.

Mother and I waited in stiff brown chairs. On the wall loomed a gigantic drawing of a three-dimensional set of teeth with roots in vivid reds and whites, looking like a steel trap, and I imagined the teeth springing from the wall and pinning me in the chair. I fidgeted and stared at the wall. Mother was looking nervous too, as an ordeal for me was an ordeal for her.

A nurse approached and bid me follow her down a long hallway that seemed to get smaller as we reached the end. Finally I stood at a gaping doorway where the shadow of the dentist loomed like the statue of Rhodes, backlit by the one window in the room. I had no choice but to go in. Dr. Werness was all smiles and motioned me into a huge pit of a chair. I lay sunk into the leather folds and stared up at Dr. Werness with his receding hairline and wide nostrils. On the top shelf of the white equipment chest, where the tools he used to scrape, pick, probe, and stab at the insides of mouths were kept, stood ceramic replicas of the seven dwarfs, lined up in a row.

Dr. Werness picked Sneezy from the group and set him on the tray below. This was to be mine at the end of the day's session. I already had Dopey and Doc at home, stuck in the back of my bureau drawer, as far out of memory's sight as possible. Sneezy was not tempting. There was nothing he could offer that would have induced me to stay willingly in that cavernous chair.

Dr. Werness swung the circular tray forward where his silver picks were lined up evenly on a white cloth. I listened to the water swishing around in the white porcelain spit bowl next to my elbow, hissing a sour soda spray. A drill hung above me, a silver tool of torture, its neck swung around and looped into the retaining arm. It hovered in the air near the dentist's arm, ready to plunge into my mouth and find a raw nerve. By now my facial muscles were contorted and my hands were twisted in knots. Clouds of sweat had accumulated in my palms.

"Now this won't hurt much," said the dentist.

I'd heard that before. Dr. Werness lied. I dug my back into the leather chair and pushed my toes against the foot rest.

Dr. Werness paid no attention to my body contortions. "How was school today?" he asked, but I hardly heard him. He could have said "Little girls deserve to be murdered," and I wouldn't have known the difference.

If a cavity was small, Dr. Werness drilled it with no pain-killer because it took only a few seconds. A trillionth of a second was too long. That day five cavities were going to be filled, so Dr. Werness wheeled over the gas machine and the nurse placed a foul smelling rubber mask over my nose and strapped it tightly around my head in a suffocating grip.

"Just relax. This will be over in no time. Sneezy is waiting for you."

The nauseating smell of nitrous oxide crept into my nose. Sometimes this was the last thing I remembered as my eyes clutched desperately at the crust of cloud passing outside the twelfth-story window as I went under. But today, as sometimes happened, the gas did not render me completely unconscious. I could still see the blurred form of the dentist looming over me and hear the screech from the throat of his drill as if in a dream, could feel the needles of pain pressing into my raw tooth and through a network of nerves deep into the far reaches of my body. The cool hand of the nurse rested on my arm like a wet flipper.

At long last the mask was peeled from my face. The smell of sour gas lingered and my throat felt as if it had been sandpapered with brillo.

"All done!" Dr. Werness exclaimed and smiled crookedly. He was as relieved as I was. I shuffled out listlessly, silent, and numb. Dr. Werness told me he would see me in a few weeks and to set up another appointment with the receptionist. *He must be mad!* I told Mother the work had been completed until next year, but the receptionist stepped in and set up another appointment in two weeks.

As we went down the elevator and out the revolving doors to Ninth Street I could hear the screeching sound of a jack-hammer down the corridor. A shudder went through me as I felt the sound echoing in my mouth.

Once outside I experienced a surge of relief. It was over . . . for now.

Chapter Four

❧ Family Dynamics ❧

TRYING TO RECONSTRUCT family dynamics back in those early years is like trying to build a sod house out of crumbled dirt. The memory is selective, releasing only bits and pieces, and I fear the dark parts leap out and block the rest. But I will attempt to describe how it was for me, as best I can, within the limits of my perception.

I was needy. Whatever it was I wanted I didn't have. I was accident prone and I was what Mother termed surly.

Dad kept repeating, "THINK. STOP AND THINK."

Meals were combat zones. I refused to eat. Dinners pivoted around the food on my plate and the dour little face hanging over it as I pushed the peas around with my finger. The family doctor insisted I eat spinach; Dr. Spock said I was begging for attention. As much as Mother tried in her own way to give me whatever I wanted, it was never the right thing or enough.

Anything that could go wrong made a beeline for my door. I didn't remember what I was told. I was late for piano lessons. I broke my glasses. I put a long scratch in the new mahogany dining room table. I lost track of time while meandering in the woods. I always seemed to be coming haphazardly in the back door, leaves stuck to my feet, while the others were going out the front, dressed up and purposeful.

The truth was I didn't like anything. I hated surprises; they threw me into a shocked uncertainty. I drooped around like a basset hound. When people asked me why I looked so glum I reacted with fury. What was everyone so nosey about? I was not feeling bad. I just hated everything.

Since the problem was either with my parents or with me, I decided somewhere along the line to choose them. That way I could imagine that I deserved to live.

Faced with so many failures, I lost my voice. The exuberance produced by my high-strung energy caused too much grief. I learned to clam up, close down, and internalize. I began to feel deprived and helpless. Then came the anger. Anger directed above all towards the one who I was sure was the cause of it all—my mother.

Ours was a love-hate relationship. After enduring the violence of her own childhood, in the form of Granddad Fought's tyrannical battering, all she wanted was peace and quiet. Dealing with me taxed her abilities. She hadn't a clue. She indulged me at every turn, and to Harold's annoyance I rarely heard the word no. In his eyes I got everything my own way, and I don't know if he ever forgave me. If things went too far and I seriously misbehaved, Dad would rush in, beating the room with his voice.

I knew Mother hated me by her glee when I mispronounced a word or when I explained to her friends that a barracuda referred to a bear that had given birth to a cub. Once I came downstairs with a letter I had composed to a magazine editor and meticulously copied onto a sheet of linen paper. She read it aloud and burst out laughing, amused at the pompous last sentence that she repeated, her voice carrying into the next room: "If you will take care of this business as soon as possible, we will consider the matter closed." Mother found this hilarious. When she told her friends about my letter they joined the laughter. As I stood in the shadows of the stairwell, listening while she repeated my words, hot streams of embarrassment surged through my veins. I realized there was nothing I could do to make up for my failure as a human being.

I learned to keep my mouth shut.

My emotional swings and moods grated on Mother's nerves. For the sake of harmony we weren't to argue, weren't to stir up trouble, and weren't to mind anything. Mother hated confrontation, and disturbances disappeared into the pool of good taste that surrounded her. Everyone was expected to keep their internal struggles to themselves and their differences private—nothing was to darken the glow of happiness shining within our home.

It drove me crazy that I never knew what was going on, whether the answer to something was yes or no, or how anyone felt about anything. Looking back, I think a price was paid for this drive for harmony. Without feedback there was no way to test the reality of my perceptions or judge what worked. Without wrangling in the open, there was no way to learn how to resolve conflict in a constructive way.

To boost my self-esteem my parents gave me compliments and exaggerated ideas of my importance. But to identify the vibes in play around me I needed the *truth*. I needed to be told straight on what was up and what was down and not be left hanging in no-man's land. I would have to find out who I was later, through painful encounters in the real world.

In later years I was able to see Mother's perspective. Her determination to maintain a cheerful, upbeat atmosphere in the household was on one front a gift, bestowed with strength of purpose and self-sacrifice on her part. She wanted us to be happy.

Luckily I was not Mother's entire life. She was the epitome of southern charm. People warmed to her assured manner, expansive good looks, graciousness, and intriguing southern drawl. She adored having fun. At parties her usual reserve fell away and she became outgoing and playful. She had a way of tilting her face to the person she was talking to and laughing in unison as their eyes met. She moved through a room with confidence. If a chatterbox threatened to

Mother and Dad ready for another party in Tyrol Hills

imprison her, she would gently deliver the perfect cut-off remark and slip away gracefully.

As I look back, Mother led a dream existence. She watched her diet, exercised, and napped afternoons. She dressed impeccably, visited the beauty parlor every week, and drove her yellow late-model Camaro to an array of bridge games, luncheons, parties, dances at the club, and charity performances. She traveled throughout the world with Dad, antique shopped in New York City, and of course golfed. After they retired to North Palm Beach for the winters, she played eighteen holes of golf, swam in the Turtle Beach Club pool, dined at the club house, and took daily walks around the compound. Throughout all this she was adored by a husband who adhered to the straight and narrow and gave her whatever she wanted. Juanita Bradford led a good life.

Except for me.

~◆~

DAD DIDN'T SEEM TO MIND my outbursts as much as Mother, but he took his job as disciplinarian seriously. One fall Saturday when I was about nine, he sat in the living room reading the afternoon *Star*. Mother was rattling dishes in the kitchen and watching swarms of leaves swirling to the ground like dead butterflies. All at once there was a rumpus from upstairs. Dad rattled his paper and resumed reading, but before he'd read two lines there came a cry, sustained this time. When the cries grew louder he jumped up and dashed up the stairs. He found me standing in the hall peering through a small box-sized opening, and from the other side of the wall he heard the sound of sobbing, mushrooming off and on into screams.

"What's going on here?" he demanded.

The sobs subsided, the door flew open, and Susan stood there, under pants around her ankles, chest heaving.

"She's peeking at me through the window," she wailed. "She won't let me go to the bathroom. She's teasing me. She says I look ugly." Susan stood on one foot whimpering, and peeped at Dad through wide-spread fingers.

A pass-through door from the hall into the bathroom had been too neat to resist, especially after I discovered the extent of Susan's modesty. The eye-level opening, the size of a medicine cabinet, held two rows of supplies and could be opened from either side of the wall. One day I discovered that the view angled directly on the toilet.

Dad glared at me sternly. "We value privacy around here, missy. I've told you before to stop badgering your sister. This has to stop."

I can't honestly say I felt remorse. Didn't she take everything I ever got? She broke the beaded necklace on my American Indian doll and stained its leather dress. She snuck in my room and walked off with things I treasured—if I didn't like it neither did she—and then flew into the arms of our parents, where she was welcomed with accolades and smiles.

Dad bade me fetch a stick from the yard. I knew what was coming and returned to the living room flushed and reluctant. Mother had the water running in the next room. I walked over to where he was sitting and watched him lean over and flail his arm back and forth, snapping the rough bark against my bare legs. *Whap! Whap! Whap!* The humiliation hurt more than the actual stings.

I slunk up to my room, shrunken, determined not to bawl. Flinging myself on the bed, I stared at the bookcase across the room containing titles like *Rebecca of Sunnybrook Farm, Lad, a Dog, The Five Little Peppers and How They Grew*, all of the *Little House in the Prairie* books, *Sunstar and Pepper, Scouting with Jeb Stuart, Little Women, Rosemary* by Josephine Lawrence, *Nancy Drew*, and *King Arthur and His Knights*. I felt calmer as the familiar titles drew me into their comforting worlds. In these stories, I was transported into living homes and became caught up in the characters and their excitement and grief. I identified with their dreams, experienced the glories that illustrated the triumph of decency and justice. These accounts filled me with high ideals—unfortunately, they didn't help me deal with the vagaries of everyday relationships.

Not that I had any relationships to work on. My purview was obedience and compliance. Dad ruled; he took charge and made the big decisions. He commanded a business world that expanded far beyond our single house, a world we knew little about. He was smart, not scatter-brained like Mother and me. I was convinced that there was nothing he couldn't accomplish, and that no Olympian god could overtake him.

I feared and worshiped my father from a distance.

Among his friends "Brad" was well-liked. Handsome, in a non-assuming Spencer Tracey sort of way, he won people over with his affability, a regular guy with a modest, down-home manner, embodying the values of honesty, conscientiousness, and devotion to family. But his never-quit drive overpowered everyone else in the family.

He was only happy when plunged into a project. Weekends he worked in the yard, and I hung around just to be in his company. Under his direction, I raked leaves, stuffed them in wicker baskets and piled them on the burning leaf pile along the gutter. We were not allowed to tackle more complicated jobs. Dad preferred to do things himself; then it would be done now and done right. Harold and I were failures at handy work. When we talked him into letting us paint the porch siding he brooked no slack. Perfection was pursued with a driving impatience. In those early years, there could be no slip-ups. Bricks had to be laid in exact linear order. Expensive tools had to be returned without a mark. Paint splotches were not tolerated, and the inevitable mishaps had to be obliterated up to the last drop. There was no time to tolerate a learning curve—there were only so many hours in the day and each one required its share of accomplishment.

We learned to stay out of his way.

Saturday mornings Dad and I drove to the Minneapolis Farmer's Market and returned with a bushel of tomatoes, a crate of fat succulent peaches, and five dozen sweet rolls he'd found on sale. "Gracious, how will we eat all those?" Mother protested. He liked to be economical and think big.

Occasionally, I accompanied him to the twentieth floor of the Roanoke building. His office walls were hung with photographs of men standing or sitting around a shiny oblong conference table, dressed in dark suits and ties. Except for variations in height, they all looked alike—unsmiling businessmen with a purpose. I poured myself a drink of water from a mahogany serving table. Dad showed me how he dictated letters for his secretary on a newly acquired Dictaphone, a dictation machine that cut a mechanical groove into a wax cylinder while the speaker spoke into the cupped end of a long tube.

The entire floor was lined with rows of desks surrounded by enclosed offices that ran along the sides of the walls and provided window views of the city. While Dad worked in his office, I scooted up and down the aisles on a wheeled desk chair, pushing the floor with my feet to gain as much speed as possible. I snooped through desks, fingering the pencils, yellow legal pads, and fountain pens in the drawers, and I wondered what it would be like to sit at one of the wooden desks and take care of consequential business matters.

Once Dad's secretary—who besides dictation ordered theater tickets, went out for aspirin, and bought anniversary gifts—took me to Snyder Drugs on the first floor for a coke. She treated me like a queen, smiling at me and seeing to my needs. I was transfixed by the atmosphere and the continual bustle radiated by the office. I felt important just being in a place where professional people performed crucial activities that made the world run. I couldn't imagine being bored here.

❧ ♦ ❧

MY PARENTS DIDN'T ARGUE. That is, not around their children. They were members of a mutual admiration society. My dad adored Mother and she, in her roundabout way, catered to his every wish and applauded his every stride up the ladder. At least that's how I saw it. Until one time a midnight scene occurred that shook me to the toes and allowed me glimpse, for a few harrowing hours, the realities of the adult world.

It happened late one night when a sharp voice cut through the wall between my parents' bedroom and mine and punctured my sleep. Behind it I heard the sound of sobbing. My eyes flicked open wide and

I raised my head from the pillow, unable to believe what I was hearing. A male voice continued from the other side of the wall, muffled but the tone was clear. It was stark rage.

There was no way I was going to go near the source of this inferno, but I couldn't lie there and do nothing. A sense of impending danger propelled me up, and I went out into the hall. Standing before the door next to mine, I leaned in close. The sounds grew more distinct. Pressing my ear against the wood frame, I struggled to make out the crush of words.

"How could you!" my father's voice blared. "It wasn't as if you didn't know! And don't tell me . . ."

A burst of sobs cut off the rest, and I recognized the high tones of my mother. My arm floated to the door like it had a life of its own and gingerly pushed it open. The air held a sense of menace, and I stood frozen to the floor.

The minute Mother saw me she let out a cry. "Oh, he'll kill me!" It was the voice of a caged animal.

I stared at the scene before me. Dad stood in his pajama bottoms on one side of the four-poster bed and Mother, wearing her familiar pink lace nightgown, cringed against the bedpost on the other, with her feet planted wide apart, weeping. I had stumbled onto a drama that was being unleashed that had nothing to do with me. The room had transformed from its usual refuge of quiet tranquility, where Mother spent her afternoons, filled now with turbulence. I felt my limbs my shaking.

Gripped by a sense of unreality I moved into the center of the room. All at once I felt needed and experienced a strange sense of certainty. Mother ran to me, clutching me in her arms, and together we crept out of the room, past Dad who watched us, his chest heaving and a worried look on his face. Clinging together, the two of us headed straight to my room and crept into my bed. A few minutes later I could feel Dad climbing in on the other side of me, gingerly so as not to jar the mattress. No one uttered a sound. The three of us lay stiffly side by side, rod-still. Once Mother shifted, burrowing her head in the pillow next to mine.

I lay on my back staring into the darkness. The shock vibes that hung over the bed were so sharp I was afraid they would slice my little world into pieces, like chips off a whirling chain saw.

This conflict contradicted the usual loving behavior between my parents. I was used to the embraces and smiles when Dad returned from work or the coziness as they snuggled over itineraries for a trip to New Orleans, or one of their West Virginia jaunts to the Greenbrier Hotel. At the sight of Mother, Dad would drop his serious expression, and his face took on a light, playful look. He loved to tease her. One afternoon the three of us had been signtseeing in Manhattan and were riding back to the hotel in a black taxi.

"Brad, this oriental sculpture was such a bargain. You see the details on the lion's face. This is not a cheap piece," she told him peering into the oversized box and stroking the lion's nose with her finger.

"I'll bet it wasn't," he replied.

"I got two hundred dollars off. Imagine! Such a bargain."

"That means you must have spent five times that much to get it."

"But look what I've saved!"

"And look what you've spent! A *thousand-dollar lion*. I could get a real one for that."

But he was pleased.

When Mother was happy a soft grin played around Dad's mouth. She smiled, kissed him on the cheek, and he gave a deep, rumbling chuckle. I loved to hear him laugh. I can see them now, the two stretched on the couch watching the ten o'clock news. Whenever Dad yawned Mother quickly popped her finger in his mouth and giggled, at which Dad grinned and tightened his arm around her.

As I lay in the dark staring at the ceiling a thought entered my mind: here I was, lying in bed between the two most powerful and important people in the world, a coveted position, never mind the cause. I could almost be grateful for my good luck. But mostly I lay like a corpse, too terrified to stir, afraid of setting off a fuse that lay just under the covers, ready to explode at the slightest spark.

I woke up the next morning alone in bed. When I shuffled into the kitchen, Mother mentioned in a hushed voice that she'd had a nightmare, and to pay it no mind. Dad drove me downtown to a special lunch at his office, where his secretary commented that my dad was crazy about me. I knew he only said that because he felt badly about what happened. He had a strong conscientious side.

The episode was never spoken of again. It was something big, something adult—something I wasn't to know about. Family life resumed and the midnight scene faded into a shadowy past. Evenings we continued to sit cozily together in the living room listening to the console radio, Dad with his paper, Mother in her chair kitting. It was home and I was content.

∾◆∾

A WAVE FROM ABROAD crashed in and united us by its scope: The War.

Since Decmber 7, 1941, when the Japanese attacked Pearl Harbor, bringing America into World War II, the family had drawn together. Mother taught me how to knit squares that I turned in at school, to be sewn into blankets for the troops. Dad took me with him everywhere, along with his rationing card, and I kept track of the amount of rationed supplies we were allotted—gasoline, sugar, butter, coffee, fuel oil, cheese, preserves, rice, canned fruit, condensed milk—the list kept growing. Even tire sales were restricted, as well as shoes and women's nylons, the latter needed to produce parachutes. The patriotic need to contribute to the war effort drove us all, and we embraced a feeling that we were all in this together.

Riding the wave of enthusiasm, Dad decided to create a victory garden along a strip of our yard bordering South Tyrol Trail. He dug up the turf and hauled in rich black dirt, where we would plant carrots, cucumbers, and turnips. I worked next to him, breaking up dirt with my spade. Other times he helped me tie newspapers into bundles for the Meadowbrook School paper drive. I loved it when we bundled newspapers together, wrapping the string around each pile two ways and throwing them in the trunk of the car, almost in sync. I was proud of the way I kept up, never missing a beat, tossing my pile right behind his. "You're doing a good job there," he'd say. I could have gathered bundles all night.

Every evening we listened to news of the war. We heard of Hitler's invasions of Poland, Czechoslovakia, France, and the U.S.S.R., of the London Blitz—there was no stopping this madman. Finally, the invasion of Normandy opened the possibility of an Allied victory. Finally, in May 1945, as Dad, Harold, and I were sitting in the living room we heard President Franklin Roosevelt announce VE Day. We froze as the familiar voice intoned, "FELLOW AMERICANS. THE WAR IN EUROPE IS ENDED!" Mother rushed in from the kitchen clutching a dish towel, and Harold's head jerked up. Dad leaned on his knees towards the radio speaker with an incredulous expression. We looked at each other excitedly as the voice droned on with details of the Allied victory, caught up in the knowledge that our fears were over and our boys were coming home. The exhilaration circled the room, linking us in joyful giddiness. We felt the same pride. We were American. We were family.

Now began the post-war drive to normalcy, an attempt to reconstruct regular everyday life, to conform to family ideals. Women

Dad, Judy, Susan, Mom, and Harold in Tyrol Hills. Circa 1947.

dropped out of the workforce and returned eagerly to the home. People rushed to marry, have children, and patronize the church. The atmosphere was positive, and the economy radiated confidence. Prosperity driven by the manufacturing requirements of the war effort had penetrated every home and in a rash of optimism and unity Americans took up the good life.

Thus began the age of conformity. A conformity that a generation of young people two decades later would find stifling and strive to break out of, launching a cultural revolution to which I would be irresistibly drawn.

✦

WE VISITED WEST VIRGINIA often in those early years, primarily Pennsboro and Wheeling where the two sets of grandparents lived. While Pennsboro was laid back and leisurely, full of swimming holes, small-town picnics and country fairs, Wheeling was a grand city of majestic parks, country clubs, and corniced old downtown buildings.

Wheeling was Granddad Fought's domain. Flamboyant, debonair, and domineering, he appeared to know everyone in town and greeted doormen and waitresses by name. When he took us to dine at the Oglebay Country Club, people stood up as we walked by and introductions circled. Of course, some of this was no more than the typical effusive Southern greeting. "How *are* you?" Chatter over chatter, kisses all around, accompanied by bright laughter. At the sight of Granddad maneuvering through a room, remembering each person's name, everyone broke into smiles.

"Hey, there, Bob, you look lively. Been doing too much lovin', I expect."

"Margo, I heard the good news, and I hope it will be a nice fine boy with one upper lip."

"I'm notifying you right now that I'm having a party on the 27th from 3:00 to 6:30—that's all the time I'll allow my guests to talk love and romance."

"Emily, where were you on Friday? I suppose you would rather be with that ugly boyfriend of yours than with your loving friends."

No one seemed to mind his acerbic remarks. His deflating skill was coated in bonhomie and charm and his friends loved it. Whether it was at his box at the Wheeling Race Track or at the restaurants he frequented, people would beam and address him by name. He dressed as jauntily as he spoke, in brown gabardine suits with matching vests strung with a gold watch chain, and colorful spats. His trademark was the selection of hats he had for all occasions, especially one wide-brimmed number with the brim tilting up in a side sweep that lent him a handsome, devil-may-care look.

Granddad's business card read GORDON P. FOUGHT. A member of the Freemason, Elk, and Moose clubs, and an active supporter of the Democratic Party, he was elected mayor of Wheeling, which was no simple job given the corruption that permeated local West Virginia politics in those years. His was the last "strong hand" mayoral term of the city; records show that after his tenure a management team was selected to run the city government.

When he died at age eighty-seven, his cane collection was distributed to family members. One still sits in an umbrella stand in my front hall—a black wooden cane with a screw top concealing a glass tube that holds several cigars. The brass spittoon that sat at the foot of his leather chair in the Hotel Windsor in Wheeling where he spent his last years stands next to the fireplace in my family room

He loved to visit his only child, my mother. On visits to Minneapolis, Granddad sat on his favorite arm chair in the den sporting a plaid vest, cane resting between his legs, square diamond ring gleaming on his manicured hand. I never saw him dressed casually. Even long after dinner, when the rest of us had slipped into pajamas and bathrobes, lazing comfortably in front of the television, he remained upright and suited. All during the hot Minnesota summer, he wore a suit. He once swore he would never visit Minnesota in the summer due to the mosquitoes the size of crows, but I thought it was really because his suits were too hot.

Granddad Fought, when I caught him alone, told stories of his multifaceted and varied careers. He had been, among other things, owner

Susan, Granddad Fought, me, Mother, Dad, Harold.

of an airplane company, a newspaper owner and publisher, an auto dealer, a druggist, and a realtor. But I always suspected he left out more than he revealed. His political experiences in West Virginia politics included harrowing episodes with shady characters, one of whom came to his front door one night and threatened him with a gun. (Granddad told him to make an appointment.) He never spoke of his teenage years, of how he ran away from home at thirteen, fleeing an alcoholic father and abusive stepmother, and the hardships and scrappy jobs he endured. Regretfully, much of his story went with him when he died.

Granddad loved the ladies and they were clearly attracted to him. At one point his wife, Grace, divorced him for philandering. Since divorce was a stigma in those days, he must have committed unpardonable offenses. It seems he repented, she relented, and they remarried and stayed together until her death from cancer at age forty-three.

My grandparent's divorce was a dark family secret I didn't learn until many years later when my own divorce loosened my mother's tongue. After his wife's death, Granddad married a wealthy widow named Bess Dancer and moved into her house in Forest Hills. When her first husband died, Bess managed Dancer Wallpaper and Paint, a successful business he had founded. On marriage to Gordy she sold the company and put herself in his hands. Granddad wouldn't hear of his wife working—no one would claim he couldn't support his own family.

Charming and attractive as he was to the outside world, at home Granddad Fought ruled with an iron hand. He wouldn't allow Mother to ride a bicycle—too dangerous for a girl. He insisted she reject the prize for a local beauty contest, as well-bred girls weren't to display themselves. Nor was she permitted to work. Females didn't draw paychecks, fix sinks, use big words, smoke, or venture out in public alone. Their roles were limited to that of mother and homemaker, a caregiver who provided light relief from serious concerns. Nurturing, teaching, and keeping house, that was their realm.

Education was considered unnecessary for a young Southern woman. Marriage would take care of her future, although college would add a layer of polish. Mother attended Mary Baldwin Seminary, a junior college in Staunton, Virginia, for a year before moving on to Goucher College in Baltimore, Maryland. At the age of twenty she dropped out of Goucher to marry Dad.

Faced with a dominating father, Mother grew up compliant and obedient. She and her mother walked on eggshells to skirt his criticism. Although he doted on his daughter, his temper sent fear throughout the house. The fear of male fury that sent me shriveling into the corners must have shaped her as well. Maybe like me she detested her own timidity, a tendency to flinch at the mere echo of an angry word. Maybe, despite our different reactions—she became pleasing and crafty in the face of danger, whereas I became private and confrontational—we were more alike than we knew. Maybe, sensing the trait in me that she abhorred in herself, she couldn't help turning her rejection on me.

❧ ◆ ☙

WHEN I WAS NINE, Mother and Aunt Harriet, Dad's sister-in-law, and I struck out for a week's vacation in Oglebay Park. Created under Granddad Fought's tenure as mayor of Wheeling, the park was a crown of the Wheeling landscape in the 1940s, covering 1,650 acres of rolling countryside. We stayed in a suite overlooking a turquoise-blue swimming pool surrounded with colorful umbrellas and white cabanas. Mother and Aunt Harriet lunched poolside, played golf, and took me to visit nearby beach shops, where we purchased white shorts and yellow and rose tops with thin straps.

One fine summer day, Granddad Fought, looking spiffy in a freshly cleaned suit and vest, picked up Mother, Aunt Harriet, and me in his new Pontiac, a long, crimson affair with black velveteen upholstery. We approached the Oglebay Country Club through a one-way drive bordered with tall hedges and drove around a tree-lined lawn until an imposing building burst into view, tall and dazzling white in the southern sun, framed against a cloudless blue sky. The wide steps led to a colonial style porch emboldened with white carved Grecian pillars. The lobby was moist with hints of fresh cotton and mint, and the curved ceiling was crossed with ivory trim.

The dining room was humming with the soft sound of low voices. Granddad teased the waiter about his bow tie and ordered a round of drinks and a Shirley Temple for me.

"Don't you like your salad?" Mother asked as she watched me slide a lettuce leaf from one side of the plate to the other. She tried her usual tactics: quoting the doctor, appealing to my health, bemoaning the waste. The conversation focused for some time on my eating. Aunt Harriet was looking into her soup with a disapproving frown. She just won't eat, Mother kept repeating. There were awkward glances in my direction. I felt a growing desire to shoot from my chair. Finally they gave up and resumed their pleasant Wheeling gossip.

I was used to being the fifth wheel. Children were to be seen and not heard. The adult world was not gained easily; you had to grow up. It wasn't so bad, though. I was part of a family unit where I enjoyed physical well-being and security. But I couldn't wait to be up in the world, at a grown-up level, a world made up of fun and activities with friends and stories and country houses and freedom to go wherever I pleased. To be a major player, enjoying the full range of privileges—that's what I wanted.

I sucked on my straw and looked out the window at three statuesque Eucalyptus trees drinking in the sun in the distance, like a performing trio about to burst into song. I imagined myself floating over the white-covered tables and out the window, following an arc out over the rolling lawn where clumps of trees hummed sunshine songs and frothy clouds dozed on the edge of the sky. Out where I drifted under a blue quilt past the circumference of the earth.

Finally Mother turned to me. "Oh, for heaven's sake, go ahead and run around. I can't stand all that twisting in your chair." I resisted an urge to touch her arm, draped in baby blue toile along the arm of the chair. I watched as she picked up her crystal water glass, ice tinkling as she brought it to her lips.

I wandered outside, across the wide lawn to the Eucalyptus trees. From the clubhouse I could still hear the chatter of voices, the tinkling of glassware, soft laughter. The sounds seemed to be coming from inside a drum and they beat in my head like a buried memory. I wondered if I'd made it all up: Mother, Aunt Harriet, Granddad Fought, the lofty dining room, the lawn, the distant voices, it all melted into vagueness. I leaned against the tree trunk, hands behind my back, and gazed at the feathered clouds overhead, white egret wings banked against the sky. So far away. Much too far for me to reach.

Back at the hotel, Mother, Aunt Harriet, and Aunt Dorothy, Dad's other sister from Pennsboro, were preparing to go out. It had been an active morning. I had stained Aunt Harriet's new polo shirt, refused to eat my stewed tomatoes, and tracked dog doo across the white throw rug. I had even kicked over a Chinese pole lamp while flipping cartwheels.

As the women put on their hats, I tore around the room monkey fashion, chasing a white soccer ball, falling on it and lifting it high in the air with my ankles in a shoulder stand.

"Stop! Not in the house." Mother sighed. She apologized to the others. "She's high strung, you know." They assumed a passive look.

At nine I was a handful. That was Mother's word, *handful*, and she invested it with a tone of distress and resignation. Aunt Harriet and Aunt Dorothy looked on as she bundled me into a chair and stood for a moment beside the coffee table, wringing her hands and gazing out at the hills as if a large hand might emerge from the vastness and save her.

"I don't know why she carries on so," I heard Mother say as the door closed behind them. I ran to the adjoining porch and flung myself on a cushioned chaise, letting the heat of the summer air dissipate my feelings until I lay still and felt nothing.

The next afternoon was hot, and I was sent to the pool to cool off while Mother left with Aunt Harriet, and Aunt Dorothy to explore the antique shops, leaving me under the eyes of the lifeguard. I spread out a towel on the chaise, rubbed cocoa butter over my body, and stretched out.

The pool was packed with bobbing heads, the girls in white rubber bathing caps strapped under their chins. Several kids were throwing a red rubber ball back and forth in the water, yelling and laughing. A boy and a girl in red and navy swim suits clamored up the ladder and leapt as far as they could from the side of the pool and emerged side by side, sputtering. I opened my book and read a few chapters while the sun burned into my skin. When I finally looked up, my eyes were arrested by the sight of a red ball reeling high into the air. It spun quickly until it reached the apex of its flight, where, pressed against the blue sky, it became immobile for a long moment as if in a time warp.

During this pause I could see the red ball actually consisted of several sections resembling a torso, with a head and clusters of arms and legs. As I looked, the cutting blare of the sun charged it into a round, bubbly girl in a red dress, her mouth laughing with glee, sailing through the air and falling, finally, back to the arms of the kids. When it touched the water the mass curved back into a ball and the image vanished.

I wanted to leap into the pool, to catch the ball and hold it. I wanted to fly through the air to the cheers of the young bathers like the balloon girl in the red dress, wanted to know that girl, laugh with that girl, be that girl. I watched the flight of the ball from the chaise, arching from person to person, until the sun started to sink and the ball was lifted from the water, the pin removed, and the air pumped out by many hands. The last I saw was a red patch being placed in a picnic basket and carried off into the hotel.

THE SUMMER I WAS TWELVE I became a cripple. I had broken my ankle at camp, but the grown-ups decided to go ahead with my month-long trip to West Virginia. When I arrived at Granddad Fought and Grandma Bess' house in Forest Hills, set high in the hills outside of Wheeling, they expected a low-key visit with me resting my cast on a pillow, reading to my heart's content and hanging around the house. Kids were not entertained in those days, but expected to fend for themselves. There were no playgrounds or jungle sets, no extra-curricular field trips or soccer schedules. There were curfews, rules and expectations. There was nowhere to go. Families listened to the radio, read the paper and played cards.

Every morning Grandma Bess and I sat in the built-in breakfast nook, drinking juice out of opaque red glasses and looking out at the woods together. She handed me a red napkin, kept my glass filled from a rose bubble-glass pitcher, and sat quietly, smiling at me. Her gray hair lifted off her face in short curls, and the light from the window softened the pale, translucent white of her skin. The deep lines that gathered under her eyes gave her a wise, weathered look. Gentleness radiated from her short figure, and I was fascinated by the studied way she moved her hands.

Grandma Bess stood at the door as I set off to explore the neighborhood. I swung on my crutches into the woods and through the yards, climbing any accessible tree and becoming adept at dragging my broken ankle over the branches. The neighbors called Grandma Bess in horror, reporting they had seen me swinging up in the tree tops, brandishing my leg with the plaster cast. In a tentative voice Grandma warned me to take it easy. With no children of her own she was unused to administering discipline. I paid no heed. No disrespect, but I had to do *something*.

My bedroom was upstairs next to Grandma Bess's room. One day while she was dressing she asked if I wanted to see the scar where she'd had a breast removed. Curious, I nodded. She pulled open her robe and there, where a breast should have been, I saw the flat surface of her chest, almost concave, crossed with bumpy pink and blue streaks that looked like a dried mud bed after rain. Shocked, I tried to imagine the knife slicing through her body to remove the white lump of flesh, like sawing through a plump turkey. I couldn't conjure it. Grandma was regarding the scar gently. She didn't seem at all disturbed.

I tried to find something to say. "Does it hurt?"

She smiled. "Not anymore." Seated on the bed in her violet robe and matching feather slippers, she described the trip to the hospital and flowers that filled the hospital room with spring perfume. "The surgery saved my life. I had lots of good care from the staff to see me through."

"What's it like missing a breast?" I ventured.

"Oh, I'm used to it. It had to be done, that's all. I've got another one. That'll do me."

"What does Granddad think?"

"He's glad I'm alive."

I was thrilled that she showed me her scar, her marred body. The interest she took in me, in her soft, unobtrusive way, and her confiding openness felt like a great compliment. Instinctively, I related to her. As Granddad's second wife, she was an outsider in the family, a latecomer, excluded from childhood memories of the other relatives and kept at bay by Granddad's unrelenting harshness. The two of us formed an instinctive understanding. But I didn't get a chance to know her. Her sojourn in my life was short and she remained in the background, a mild, solitary figure.

One morning when the threat of a summer rain was darkening a low, striated sky, we set off to visit Grandma and Grandpa Bradford in Pennsboro. The two sets of grandparents had been friends for years, since the days when Granddad owned and ran the *Pennsboro News*. Granddad Fought loved visiting his old homestead and was eager to inspect Granddad Bradford's new Graham Page automobile. The three of us sat in the front seat of the car as it weaved steadily along a two-lane road winding through the green West Virginia hills, Granddad at the wheel and not another car in sight.

Grandma Bess chattered on about some altercation she'd had with one of the neighbors and how she'd invited the woman to tea to work it out and the woman had stormed out in a huff.

"That was a poor way to handle it," Granddad scoffed. "What's in that empty head of yours? You should find some way to get a brain inside it."

Granddad kept up a barrage. She had blundered, as usual. She was inept, a fool. He was sick of it. He resurrected other occurrences of her stupidity. The criticisms continued without letup. Grandma's low-voiced explanations fell ignored into her lap. She became silent as his sharp voice continued to reverberate through the car. Would he never stop? I was frozen to my seat between them, unable to move. I glanced over at Grandma. She was staring straight ahead, her lower lip dangling, her hands clutching each other in her lap. She didn't say a word or move, or acknowledge the tears inching silently down her cheeks. The anger in Granddad Fought's voice filled the car like a black cloud.

A sickening chill ran down my back and I grew rigid, straining against the back of the seat, frozen into silence. I couldn't think or rationalize what was happening. It wasn't the first yelling I'd heard, but I felt it the most, his voice close to my ear, with me sitting between them like a conduit. I leaned closer to Grandma until I felt her warm shoulder, until it seemed I was sitting in her place, a part of her, disappearing into her and I felt her silence in my own heart.

I was sad when Grandma Bess died of a heart attack a few years later. Her interest in my stories encouraged me. I let her read one. "Keep it up," she'd said with warmth. "You're doing something special." The word special resonated. She understood, had some knowledge of what it was like to be me.

Chapter Five

Neighborhood Antics and Learning to Love Cows

W HEN I HEARD THE WORDS "we don't hire girls," I hung up meekly. But as the words sank in, I felt a surge of angry protest. What? How could that be? My older brother had carried a paper route for two years; now it was my turn! I was tired of my brother flaunting his five-year advantage over me, always way ahead, always older and a boy. My mouth tightened—something must be done! A sudden fury locked me into place and I stared out the kitchen window where the ground lay flat and barren under the gray autumn sky. I craved a real paying job. The idea of prowling outside in the semi-dark cover of early dawn was enticing. Digging a paper and envelope from an upper drawer of Mother's desk, I trotted upstairs, settled myself on my bed and composed a letter to the *Minneapolis Morning Tribune*. The idea was to be straight and businesslike so it wouldn't sound like a twelve-year-old's letter. I introduced myself, gave my address, and stated that I was seeking a position as a paper carrier and would appreciate an answer as soon as possible, signing it Paul Beckman. The next morning I slipped the letter in the mail slot in the front door, careful not to be observed.

Five days passed, six, ten—no reply. The rush of expectation slowly ebbed. I had nearly forgotten about it when one day my mother's distant voice floated up the stairs. "Judy, are you in your room? Someone is here to see you." I skipped down, bursting with curiosity. Standing at the door was a middle-aged man with cringing eyes and a bulging overcoat, carrying an official-looking brown briefcase.

"Hello," he said. "I'm from the *Tribune*. Are—are you Paul Beckman?"

My mother was looking on, a combination of puzzlement and wariness on her face.

"Yes, that's me!" The man hesitated. "But you got it wrong," I added. "My name is Judy."

The rep from the *Tribune* looked confused. I assured him I would have no trouble walking up to the bus shelter on Highway 12 or pulling the wagonload of newspapers up and down the hills, even when the days shortened, and I would have to find my way in the dark.

After a series of questions, he gave me the route. I ran upstairs and threw myself across the bed, kicking my legs and thumping my chest in glee. The crafty plan I'd carried out without any outside intervention had worked. I was a working girl!

Heady with success, I felt my blood racing through my body. I didn't know if my height or eagerness or craftiness won the *Tribune* rep over, or the fact that Harold had carried the same route. What he didn't know was that I had two buddies, Mike and Smitty, to keep me company. After the first two days of responding to whistles, they showed up at the back door at 5:00 a.m. every morning when I emerged into the darkness, prancing with impatience. The only visible creatures alive, we traipsed along accompanied by the odor of moist grass and tangy autumn flowers. It was a human-less world, just the three of us. I folded each newspaper into a bundle and tossed it against the garage doors, while Mike and Smitty streaked across the lawns with their tails lifted, poking their noses into every bush and crack.

After six months boredom set in. I kept the job awhile to try to win a free helicopter ride by ringing doorbells and drumming up more subscriptions, but I didn't get enough to win. Without protest from any quarter, I quit.

❧ ◆ ❧

IN SEVENTH GRADE I acquired a best friend. Jean McIntyre joined our class of ten at Meadowbrook. At last someone my age within walking distance! It wasn't long before I was at her house constantly. Not allowed to bike on Highway 12, I walked along Highway 12 and just before Highway 100 turned left and continued past the fenced Wilhelm Held farm and on for another half mile to the small bungalow where Jean lived. She balked at coming to my house, preferring to stay at home with her parents and little brother. She thought the two-mile walk to Tyrol Hills was too far. This attitude was baffling, as all I wanted was to escape my boring existence.

Jean and I were opposites. She moved deliberately, sat quietly in her chair and looked at me with calm brown eyes. Part Irish, with a dash of Mexican thrown into the pot, she wore her black shoulder length hair pulled back from a wide forehead. Sensible but fun-loving, her twinkling laugh rang out easily, especially when her dad cracked one of his jokes. We listened to the radio in the living room, with her dad relaxed in the easy chair smoking Pall Malls and her mother sewing on the couch.

Jean's parents rarely went out, except sometimes on Saturdays nights to an aunt's house. The bedrooms circled off the living room so that family members slept close to the main hub of the house. There was always the resonance of something going on at her place, the comforting sensation of having people around. When I spent the night we played marbles in the dirt in her back yard and gin rummy at the kitchen table and bossed her little brother around. Or we listened to records lying on our backs on Jean's bed, feet propped against the wall.

A favorite game was dialing random numbers from the phone book and pretending we were marketers and had a great deal on Hoover vacuum cleaners. Or we might claim our target owed us insurance money and there would be consequences if they didn't pay up. The reactions of our victims, incredulous, worried, then skeptical, caused us to roll on the bed, hugging our sides with muted laughter. We ended the calls on a vague note, assuring them we would do nothing now, but they had better do some thinking.

One call was answered by a young boy.

"I'd like to talk to one of your parents."

"You can talk to me."

"How old are you?"

"Old enough."

"You're not more than eight or ten."

"So? I take all calls of this nature."

"You don't know the nature of this call."

"Just tell me what you want."

"I want to talk to your mom or dad, kid."

"I'm an orphan."

"Go back to your blocks, kid. Goodbye."

After dinner we shut ourselves in Jean's room and gossiped about the kids at school or some strange thing Timmy had done—Jean had replaced Timmy as my sidekick in school. Once he brought a pubic hair of his to school in a jar, which we found disgusting and refused to speak to him for a week. But we were getting interested in male/female functioning. Putting our noses together, Jean and I tried to figure out how sex worked. We decided that if a man and woman kissed long enough, the seed of a baby would be produced. Then without an explanation, Jean said she wasn't interested in that junk and didn't want to talk about it anymore.

Once settled in her double bed with the lights out and kissed good night by her mother, we played "guess-the-movie star." This consisted of one person outlining with a finger two initials representing the name of a movie star on the other's back. The receiver would guess what movie star the initials stood for. When I drew DD on Jean's back she correctly guessed Deanna Durbin. I fooled her with the initials BK, as she didn't know that Boris Karloff played Frankenstein—I wondered how could she be so ignorant, but she stumped me with Buster Keaton. The beauty of this game was that it didn't require much talking, so we weren't in danger of hearing a reprimand called out from the other room.

Mornings we were awakened in bed by the voice of Patti Page crooning *The Tennessee Waltz* from the gramophone in the next room, and I could hear Mrs. McCollum's high voice singing along.

> *I introduced him to my loved one,*
> *And while they were dancing,*
> *My friend stole my sweetheart from me.*

I lay on my back, waiting for Jean to wake up beside me, staring at the wall streaked with golden slivers from the window blinds and the patches of errant sunlight flickering on the mirror. It felt good to hear the familiar household sounds beyond the door, the smell of bacon, a soft voice, the raising of blinds, the signs of breath and movement close by, waiting for her mother to call us in to breakfast. I relaxed into a lazy feeling of contentment.

Once up and about I was consumed with an itch to make things happen. On one occasion I talked Jean into sneaking out to roam the neighborhood after dark. She was hesitant, but I assured her I had done it many times and that there were wonders out in the darkness she couldn't imagine.

"I'm not sure. It's winter. What will we do?"

"The temperature's not bad—over twenty degrees. Look, I've some great ideas. I'll tell you everything tomorrow. I'll be at your house at six."

That's how it began. I showed up at her door, and as dusk descended we announced we were going for a walk. Slipping on our parkas we made our way down the back road that connected to Highway 12. On one side a row of houses crouched in the dark and on the other a wooded area gradually faded into a deepening blackness. Once it was dark enough that we blended into the shadows—crucial to our plan—we prepared a pile of snowballs, rounding them into smooth, hard bullets. When a car approached we'd rip out of the woods and pelt it with snowballs as it passed and retreated down the road. Our aim improved with practice, and we got some pretty good hits directly on a side window. Sometimes an irate car screeched to a stop and a man leaped out, jerked his head in all directions, then popped back in and roared away. But most cars didn't slow down, even when we hit a front window straight on. When a car did stop, we disappeared into the underbrush.

There were variations. With a moon throwing a yellow haze over the ground, one of us would lay on the roadside, just far enough out of the lane to be missed by a passing car, hands spread-eagle over our head, sunk face-down into the dirt, motionless. A few heartless souls would pass right on by, but most often the car would continue a few hundred yards and slam to a halt. We would hear the brakes squeal and the car door open, and by the time the frantic figure had emerged from the car and panted up to investigate, we had both fled into the trees. Occasionally we heard mumbled cursing as the driver reentered the car, or a yell would follow us, "You creeps should be sent to reform school!"

But after a while Jean lost interest in these diversions. I think she was afraid of getting caught, although she wouldn't say so. I was disappointed. Too bad Timmy wasn't available, but the tight construct of his home life, where he lived within a strict schedule, didn't allow such capers, as I was soon to find out.

≈✦≈

NOT LONG AFTER THE END of the eighth grade, my nocturnal escapades came to an abrupt end. It all started when I got permission to sleep in the vacant maid's room. This became my private hideout until the night of my downfall. The maid's room was on the first floor, a tiny room next to a half bath, set at the end of a short hall between the kitchen and the door to the garage. These three doors, bedroom, bathroom, and garage, clustered at the end of the hall. By commandeering this corner, I could escape to my own never-land. My parents gave in to my whim, probably figuring I wouldn't last long downstairs by myself. I immediately snuck a willing Debby from the basement into the single bed with me—not allowed—and snuggled under the covers close to her warm body, her angular legs and paws thrusting in all directions. Eventually we settled in,

Debby's yellow head resting next to mine with an air of patience and a "I know a good thing when I've got it" look on her face.

As soon as I heard the newscaster's voice clicked off in the living room and my parents' footsteps thumping up the stairs to bed, I turned on the small radio on the night stand—not allowed—and snuggled in for a delicious hour of listening to *Inner Sanctum*, *The Shadow*, *Dr. Kildare*, *Hallmark Hall of Fame*, or *The Lux Radio Hour*. A thrilling shiver passed through me when I heard the slow, squeaking door and Orson Welles's deep, breathy voice intoning, "The Shadow Knows." I hugged Debby close.

The rush of being scared lifted me into a delicious alertness. As my nervousness dissipated, I began to enjoy the freedom of being alone and doing exactly as I wanted, singly responsible for my own little ship. Closing my eyes I imagined commandeering a winged craft and streaming full sail out into the ocean into black waters teaming with monsters that I easily subdued. After a while Debby got hot and wiggly, and her lumpy body became a bit of a nuisance. The next morning I found her lying on the oval throw rug next to the bed. Whether she had needed her space or I had pushed her out, I wasn't sure.

One night, instead of pulling on my pajamas, I turned out the lights and sat down on the bed. I wasn't sleepy. My eyes moved past a frayed arm chair and pine chest of drawers, over to two corner windows. Beyond the windows a dark wilderness beat in shafts of moonlight, hinting of intrigue and mystery. I waited until 10:30 when my parents' room upstairs became quiet. I waited some more. Then I went over and raised the sash of the back window, jimmied out the screen, and slipped through the opening into the night.

The grass was soft underfoot. I looked around. No sound. Outlines of houses emerged from the darkness as my eyes adjusted, and I could see the shape of trees on the lawns, of cars standing in driveways, and smell warm whiffs of honeysuckle and pine oil. The woods, a black mound in the background loomed as a mysterious but strangely collaborative presence. I started off down the hill, then, to avoid the street lights, moved off into shadows that gathered around me as I melted into their world. I became part of the dark, integrated into a symphony of shades and forms, where no one could see me but I could see everything, where I was secret and safe. The fact that I was on a clandestine venture, unknown to my parents or to anyone, created a thrill and charged every nerve with anticipation.

My parents were baffled. I couldn't wait for bedtime. Every night I roamed the neighborhood under cover of darkness until I knew by heart the shapes of the houses and the layout of each yard. Cars turned into driveways, headlights shooting ahead of them. Garage doors were opened and closed, bedroom windows raised to let in the air, and I could hear low voices, bed-time voices and sometimes crackling radio sounds. I was drawn to the bustling houses where closing-of-the-day activities were going on.

One night, I came to a white house set at the top of a hill and heard loud voices mingled with laughter and tinkling music coming from an open basement window. It was the Gibbons' house, where they were hosting one of their Saturday night parties. I tiptoed up and peered into an amusement room thronged with people holding glasses and chatting in small groups, some sitting on stools lined up in front of a bar. To my surprise I caught a glimpse of my mother at the far end of the room, standing in front of a tall man in a plaid shirt, laughing. I watched, fascinated. An obscure impulse arose in me to do something, but I couldn't think what.

Here was an opportunity not to be missed. Finally I moved to an unopened window a few feet away and scratched my finger nails across it. Nothing happened. I continued scratching, loudly, insistently, then knocked with my knuckles. Suddenly I heard a man's voice, breaking through the party noise, yelling. I leapt up and ran with all my might through the long yard and into the trees, followed by strident clamor and door slams from the house. I was panting heavily. Thank heavens I hadn't been seen! All of a sudden I was no longer a happy meanderer, investigating the world. I had become an intruder, a fugitive. I moved deeper into the obscurity of the darkness. My heart pounded, I could feel thumps heaving in my chest. I was electrified. Running back to the maid's room, I climbed into bed and lay still, clutching Debby. The next day there was no sign of suspicion from my parents. I was home free.

With each foray I became more daring. It was fascinating to observe what was going on inside the houses, with people stretched out next to the radio console or sitting at a table over notebooks or coming in from the garage, talking with voiceless mouths. Since most of the homes were two-story, I saw only the downstairs rooms as I lurked under cover of a moonless night.

I decided Timmy Olson would be a fine collaborator in these nighttime forays. He was hesitant but agreed. I told him I would be at his house on a particular night and to be on the lookout. At around ten o'clock I arrived and crouched behind the lilac bushes as planned. A pool of light from the moon glared on the lawn next to the house and the odor of moist grass stirred around my jeans. Finally the upstairs lights went out, one by one, until the windows disappeared and the house quieted under the dark brow of the sky.

After some minutes had passed, I approached and threw pebbles at Timmy's upstairs window. No response. Strange. After several tries a flash of light and I caught a brief glimpse of Timmy's figure silhouetted against the background before the light was extinguished. I took it as a signal and retreated to my hiding place to wait for him to come down.

Suddenly, without warning, a glaring light flashed in an upstairs hallway. I heard voices and doors closing, and the windows of the house lit up like flares on a birthday cake, one by one. I watched, frozen. After some time the back door opened, a blinding floodlight was thrown out over the yard, and a male voice rang loud and stinging through the darkness.

"I know who you are, girl! You get out now! Don't ever come here again, you peeping Tom!"

Terrified that at any moment he would burst out of the house and right for me, I broke out of the bush and fled, his words stinging my ears. I didn't stop until I was blocks away, well hidden in the black underbrush. Scurrying home I slipped into the maid's room and under the covers, afraid the thumping of my heart would never stop. I only wanted one thing: never to see Mr. Olson or his anger again.

The next day my fright gave way to anger, then to rage. Mr. Olson knew it was me because Timmy had told him. Timmy had revealed our plot, the milk toast! I was sure he had blabbed everything on the spot. Why couldn't he keep his mouth shut? I would never forgive him. I would never speak to him ever again.

Timmy wasn't allowed to play with me for the rest of the summer. By the time school started in the fall we'd both forgotten all about it.

My night wanderings were about to come to a final, crashing end. A plump teenager started showing up three nights a week to baby sit at the Meeker house. From my post outside the living room window, I watched her play with the baby, talk at length on the phone, and traipse around the house looking in drawers. Some nights she collected a bag of cookies from the kitchen and sat munching, every once in a while poking a few crumbs into the baby's mouth as it lay in the playpen. The baby spit them out and started crying, stabbing its legs in the air until she plunged a bottle in its mouth.

One night, after the baby was bedded down, the sitter sat in the living room reading a magazine. I scratched on the window and saw her look up, startled. She hesitated a moment before coming to the window and peering out. The next night I tapped on the window again. The girl came over, peering out into the darkness, her face scrunched and curious, looking to the right and left. Then she moved over to the telephone, dialed, and talked into the receiver for a few minutes, obviously telling someone what had happened. I waited around but nothing happened.

This went on for several nights.

Finally, as I was scratching my nails across the pane one evening, suddenly three men with flashlights leapt into the living room from the hall and dashed out the front door. They must have been wearing track shoes and they meant business. I fled across the open lawn and behind the house next door, desperate for cover, not daring to stop to look back. They were close behind. I could hear the stamp of their steps pummeling the ground. Instead of heading directly home, I sprinted up to the highway, my chest pounding, and circled back to my house, carefully scrutinizing the terrain for signs of the men before crossing the street. Somehow I had lost them.

My prank at the Meeker house had taken on serious tones. It was too close for comfort. I decided it would be my last trip to that house.

It wasn't.

The next day my mother called me into her bedroom for one of those serious talks, and I knew I was done for. I had been identified. She and Dad were horrified. How could I be so sneaky? How long had this been going on? What do you mean you were just exploring? In the middle of the night? *What will people think?*

I had to return to the house and apologize to the Meekers. I dragged myself over and rang the front bell. Mrs. Meeker answered the door with an irate look, accepted my hang-dog apology, and told me I had frightened the sitter a great deal and how would I feel if I were in her place? I felt sheepish, but I couldn't sympathize with the sitter, who was so spooked over a little scratch that she had to call in the National Guard. People with sinister intentions don't scratch on windows. What was she thinking?

There was no more sleeping in the maid's room. Debby went back to sleeping alone in the basement. I had become the bad girl of the neighborhood—word got around. I missed being out in the dark among the houses and the breathing shapes, where I was invisible and felt safe.

➤

BREA NELSON LIVED across the street with a crazy mother. She was fifteen, two years older than I, and she was my idol. Not only was Brea beautiful, with even features and graceful Scandinavian cheekbones, she was accomplished. She could draw human figures in charcoal, design stylish dresses, and write lyric poetry, some of which she let me read. I was fascinated by her talent, her confidence, and her sophisticated ideas. She aspired, in the privacy of her isolated room on the top floor, to attend a private high school, to study art, and to leave home. She eventually attained them all.

Her mother was a dark force not to be thwarted. She moved about sphinxlike, seeing to the household while Mr. Nelson, a taciturn dentist, read quietly in his straight-backed chair. She saw no need for laxness or frivolity. A short little woman with clipped black hair, a tie-clip mouth, and darting eyes, she ran the house with a stern grip. I never heard her laugh or make an amusing remark. She seemed plagued and did nothing but complain. Brea didn't do her chores properly. The house was a pigsty (there was never a pin out of place). No one did anything but her. Every little thing rankled the woman.

Mrs. Nelson closely supervised her daughter's trips out of the house. Brea was not allowed to have girlfriends over—not that she had any girl friends—or come to my house. It was out of the question. She spent most of her time cooped up in her room upstairs, drawing, composing and looking out the window.

Mrs. Nelson didn't miss a trick. She watched Brea's every move and tore into Brea or Mr. Nelson when she was overwrought, yelling so shrilly that Brea stayed put in her room most of the time. Brea told me she coped by showing her mother total obedience and keeping her longings and bitterness hidden, her every track covered. Brea's father was usually in the back room, deep into his paper. I don't think I ever spoke to him, other than to say hello. Like he wasn't there.

I dashed over to Brea's house at every opportunity. When I knocked on the back door, Mrs. Nelson would look at me stonily through the screen. I had nothing to recommend me, but she let me in. I think she tolerated me because I lived across the street and could be released back to my own house at a moment's notice. Once she discovered I was willing to help with the chores—Brea's clever ploy—Mrs. Nelson allowed me over for brief periods of whispering up in Brea's room. I did some vacuuming and dish washing, but this didn't last; my feeble efforts at housework didn't meet her standards—I hadn't dusted thoroughly or I tracked dirt on the kitchen floor.

One Sunday Mrs. Nelson invited me to church. I suspected it was an effort to shape me up. After dutifully joining in the service in the main chapel, I sat with Mrs. Nelson and Brea at a long table for lunch.

Mrs. Nelson conversed with a woman friend while Brea sat immobile as if she wanted to stay out of the line of fire. She had one aim: not to set off her mother. I must not have shown much promise, with my lack of religious enthusiasm, for I wasn't invited again.

After that the reins tightened. Now Mrs. Nelson didn't want anyone near the house, period. If she found me at the door, even if I had just come to get a book, she would dismiss me curtly, and Brea would have to endure a litany of rage that sent her to her room in tears. From then on I could only visit when her mother was gone, which required a bit of maneuvering, and I snuck hurriedly out the back when we heard her mother's car grind into the garage.

And then came the disaster that banished me from the house forever. Brea and I were sitting in the kitchen one afternoon. Mrs. Nelson was out. Just that morning a delivery of a half-dozen, hand-painted Easter eggs had arrived from Russia, finely drawn in rich Byzantine colors. They were set on the kitchen table, carefully arranged in a robin's-egg-blue China bowl lined with a mauve velveteen cushion. The direct light from the window picked up the rich hues of ruby, saffron, citron, emerald, azure, and vermillion and splayed purple and gold sparkles onto a nearby wall. Fascinated, I lifted one of the Russian eggs and held it gently.

"Be careful," Brea warned, "If anything should happen to one of her precious eggs, there'll be hell to pay."

Where do thoughts, or rather impulses that are contrary to every sense of reason, come from? Without thinking I tossed the egg I was holding into the air. Was it a contorted dare from the subconscious? A foolhardy attempt to thwart fate? A reckless abandon, a warped humor? The egg didn't go up very high, but a nervous twitch or a gust of air must have intruded, for the egg flew past my outstretched hand and landed on the floor, smashed into a hundred brilliant pieces.

Brea refused to allow me to apologize. I could never set foot in the house again. Her beauty, talent, and carefully crafted dreams, her celestial world of escape that soared way beyond my little portion of childish games and scuffed knees was lost forever.

ONE MILD SPRING DAY, Debby and I emerged from a long afternoon in the woods and headed home across Highway 12. The gutters were full of morning rain, and I sloshed along listening to the splat-splat of each step. Going through the garage I entered the house, Debby bounding ahead of me. Debby was not allowed upstairs with wet paws, and I was about to order her to the basement when a figure appeared at the far door of the kitchen.

"Hi. I'm Luanne. I'll bet you're Judy." The strange figure smiled, pulled a towel from the drawer and set about rubbing each of Debby's paws with a brisk back and forth motion. "You two are as wet as kittens. Better get those soaking tennis shoes off, honey."

"It's wet out there," was all I could find to say. *Who was this person with mother's towel in hand, making herself at home in our kitchen?* I knelt down beside her, enjoying Debby's curiosity. Debby, a good-natured yellow Labrador, watched her paw being bounced around in the air by this stranger, then she twisted full around and stuck her nose in Luanne's face, sniffing, and started to wag her tail.

When the dog was dried off, Luanne led me into the maid's room and showed me photos she'd already set out on the bureau of her family: her mother, father, and two brothers were standing on the front porch of the small clapboard grey farm house, with stretches of rich fallow land in the background and three spotted cows standing by a wooden fence.

Mother often hired girls who came in from the country to attend cosmetology school in Minneapolis. In return for helping around the house, the student received a small salary along with room and board. Luanne Johnson explained that she had arrived just that morning.

No one had said anything to me. To tell the truth, I didn't care to have maids in the house—wasn't there enough to take care of without having to be always fussing with the maid, telling her what to do and seeing that she was doing it? I resented all maids and found little ways to plague them, to Mother's frustration. I would rather have Mom to myself, and the fact that I didn't have her anyway didn't matter. Mom said I had an attitude.

But Luanne was different. Nineteen, with soft brown hair falling to her shoulders and a sweet open smile, Luanne took to me from the first. I began to spend time in her room or sit in the breakfast nook with a book while she stood over the sink doing the dishes. On weekends she usually went home to the country to see her boyfriend. Sometimes we went for a walk along the dirt path to the railroad tracks. We'd sit on a rock and look up through the trees and watch the clouds form patterns, or listen to a bird caroling from the underbrush. Then Luanne would begin to sing. She taught me a tune about a cowboy named Jack:

> He was just a lonely cowboy
> With a heart so brave and true.
> He learned to love a maiden
> With eyes of heaven so blue.

And another:

> Bill Grogan's goat, was feeling fine
> Ate three red shirts, from off the line.
> Bill took a stick, gave him a whack
> And tied him to the railroad track.

My favorite was "Ole Shep":

> When I was a young lad and Shep was a pup,
> O're the hills and the valleys we'd stray.
> Just a boy and his dog, we were both full of fun,
> And we grew up together that way.
> I remember the time at the old swimmin' hole
> When I would have drown without doubt
> But Shep was right there, to the rescue he came,
> He jumped in and helped pull me out.

The song went on about ol' Shep growing old and blind, and the boy had to put him down, holding the gun with trembling hands. "No more would I roam with ol' Shep."

I sang the verses during my lone treks through the woods on summer afternoons, breaking dead limbs from tree trunks. It never failed to make me cry. For some reason I cried at sad songs and every sappy story. Mother used to chuckle to see me weeping as she read *Ferdinand the Bull*.

"Why is she crying?" Dad would ask. Mother explained that I felt sorry for Ferdinand.

As she sang, Luanne would stroke my hair. She could produce the prettiest, clearest yodel, and she tried to teach me, "Yodel-let-tee," but I never mastered the ripple effect of the throat turning over.

Once Luanne invited a girl from the beauty school over on her Sunday off, and I sat in the maid's room with them until they took off on a downtown bus to see a movie. I watched them as they climbed the hill to the bus stop. I was hooked. I became her shadow.

One night after dinner when I was helping Luanne dry dishes, she invited me to visit her family farm. My parents agreed—they saw her as a treasure, a saint—and so it was arranged. Dad drove us to the Greyhound bus depot downtown and off we went. I carried a tote bag holding a Kleenex packet, a book, a hard-back glass case, a Fuller brush, and six packs of Juicy Fruit gum. Mother gave me a small bunch of nosegays for Mrs. Johnson.

I peered excitedly out the bus window as we drove into the thinning landscape—I was off on an adventure with Luanne! I almost put my hand through her arm, but instead leaned ever so slightly against her shoulder. The fact that she had a fifteen-year-old brother at home intrigued me—but not for long. What interest had I in boys? All they could do was throw balls to each other and stare at you from a distance.

The bus streaked deeper into the country, racing by boxy houses, billboards flashing Hamm's Beer and Rolaids, and filling stations with two pumps. Gradually we saw nothing but massive fields of black farmland and stretches of pine woods.

Luanne's brother Calvin spent summers working the farm but was bent on becoming a surveyor. I had never heard of anyone named

Calvin; the name must have come from the Bible, like those other strange names, Caleb, Cain, and Noah, names I didn't think existed in real life. I wondered if Calvin would be wearing a stiff, white priest's collar. *A boy. Hmm.* I nestled my head against Luanne's coat. It was hard to think about anything in the proximity of Luanne's smile.

Mr. And Mrs. Johnson gave me a warm welcome. Mrs. Johnson, a slender woman in a calico skirt and long, water-soaked fingers, led me to a room in the back of the house that Luanne's oldest brother Jeremiah had occupied until he left for a job at the iron-ore mine in Duluth. At supper Mr. Johnson sat at the head of the table, eating silently. When I asked if they had any dogs, he explained that the dogs they kept were not pets. They were never let into the house. Their job was to keep out the coyotes, and when a dog got sick he took it behind the barn and shot it. When I suggested contacting the vet he just laughed—such an expense was out of the question for creatures more prolific than rats.

Calvin sat across from me, listening. He wore a brown t-shirt and sat up straight, like someone who was used to upright, weight-lifting work, instead of slumping over books all the time like me. I snuck a look at his thin arms lying casually on the table and his hands bronzed from the sun. Strands of straight black hair drooped over his forehead and his ears were shaped like mushrooms, but his face was darkly handsome and he held a serious look older than his years, along with an impish laugh and sparkling brown eyes. He looked at me a lot and asked me if I had a dog, as Luanne had told him I was dog crazy. I told him about Debby and described our games of hide and seek in the woods and how I'd run off and she ran around excitedly looking for my hideout.

My ideas about boys were contradictory. On one hand they did all the fun things and inhabited a world I clamored to share. I saw them as creatures apart, doing things that were rougher and harder, like flying airplanes, shooting guns, and leaping on an adversary. On the other hand, they thought only of themselves and rarely looked at girls, as if girls weren't worth noticing. They weren't even nice. I couldn't see much point in boys. Well, Timmy was a boy and he was all right, I had to admit. Once, a strange boy looked straight at me, keeping his eyes glued on mine, and I'd felt a piercing twinge of pleasure. I decided to keep an open mind.

At the crack of dawn, I found myself seated at the breakfast table with Luanne and Calvin, while their mother served us fried eggs, thick slabs of bacon, and grease-soaked potatoes. "Eat up. It'll put spin on your bones," she said. Mr. Johnson was already out in the shed repairing the tractor.

While Luanne took up household duties, I was sent to explore the barn, where I sighted a score of bedraggled cats sweeping around corners and disappearing. The odor of dank stalls, animal sweat and hay was everywhere, imparting a not-unpleasant earthy richness. When I stepped outside, pulling the heavy barn door closed, I was met with the pungent odor of fresh hay mixed with whiffs of manure.

The farm was fresh with life. Fields of corn stretched to the horizon. At the far edge of the wind-swept woods, a cluster of black-and-white cows rotated their mouths as they basked in the early morning sun. Mr. Johnson showed me how to reach under fat chicken bottoms for eggs, and Luanne gave me a ride on the tractor. We threw sticks for the mutts that lived behind the tool shed. Life here was natural and outdoorsy, and I was entranced with the novelty of it all. The odors were intoxicating, the scrambling of life at all sides invigorating, and the sight of Calvin's thin form bent over a backhoe sent a flutter down my back.

That night Calvin volunteered to show me the farm after dark. He couldn't believe I had never been in a barn before or seen a live mouse and laughed when I worried the cats hadn't been fed. The cats kept the mouse population down, he explained. They were not interested in humans and went their own way.

After supper we explored the barn. Calvin's flashlight caught a mouse darting across the floor, the beam highlighting its uplifted rump and toothpick tail. As we inched across the floor my bare arm brushed Calvin's.

"I don't guess there are any animals about, maybe it's too early," I whispered idly, intensely aware of the figure next to me.

"They're here, for sure. We have to be quiet."

We stopped. I heard a flitter of movement from the rafters and the sound of Calvin's breathing. "Come on, there's something else." He led the way to the barn door.

I followed him across the bumpy ground towards an enormous silo, so tall I couldn't see the top. Inside we were hit by the sharp smell of fermenting grain. I clamped my hand over my nose.

"You'll get used to it," Calvin laughed. We followed the path of his flashlight over to a wall ladder that stretched up the side of the curved wall and straight up into an endless darkness. He turned towards me.

"We'll go to the upper platform," he said in a low, soft voice into my ear. I moved closer. With the flashlight off, his low voice was my only point of contact. I liked the feel of his breath against my ear and decided to stay next to him. Sensing my apprehension he indicated that he would stay by me no matter what unknowns were lurking in the dark. Despite the fact that he was not much older than I was and that I hardly knew him, for some reason I trusted him completely. I turned and looked straight into his soft blue shirt illuminated behind the flashlight. His shadowed face smiled down at me and a strange stirring crept into my chest and filtered into my fingertips. I straightened up with a new alertness.

I was also aware of a delicious sense of daring.

"You first. I'll be right behind," he said.

Up I went. The flare of the flashlight slashed through the dark like a knife as it bobbed up and down in Calvin's hand. The rungs of the ladder felt slippery, and I hung on to each rung tightly. There was no trace of life as we know it, only the tall outline of the silo reaching stories high into the sky. Down below, getting further and further away, a vast nothingness. I was suddenly frightened.

"Keep going," he prompted from beneath me.

We must have been higher than the Empire State Building when we finally reached the top. I could smell the odor of sour hay rising from the pit below. Calvin asked if I want to sit on the edge of the platform and dangle my feet over the side. I looked down into the black bottomless pit from which I was sure no creature would ever return. I didn't think so. He laughed—he was always laughing at me—and we sat back on the floor, encircled by the damp walls, until finally he said his mother would worry and we'd better go back.

The Johnsons saw Luanne and me off at the bus stop. They had treated me as an honored guest. To Calvin, I guess I was the big city girl. He asked if he could write to me. I said yes. Why would he want to write to me, I wondered? But the idea seemed jolly and I waited for his letters. Calvin was not such a bad name—had an exotic ring, much more interesting than, say, Timmy. He signed his letters, "Your faithful Calvin," and I signed mine, "With friendly regards, Judy."

The boys in school were old hat, boring, and preoccupied with roughhousing. But Calvin was different. He liked the fact that I was a girl, he even liked me. I tore open his letters, then hid them from Mother and her condescending laugh. It was delicious to have a secret involving a boy and to be venturing into unknown territory.

A year later, Luanne had completed beautician training, found a job as a hair dresser in Minneapolis, and obtained a room of her own. The following year she married her long-time boyfriend and moved back to her home town and she and Calvin dissolved into a forgotten dreamland of the past.

Chapter Six

❧ Boys and Shadow Nights ❧

ℐT WAS THE BEGINNING OF JUNE 1948, and the entire school was
gathered at Meadowbrook for the big event—our eighth grade
graduation. For eight years I had worked my way from classroom to
classroom, first across the hall, then up the wide cross-back stairway to the
second floor containing the fifth/sixth and the seventh/eighth grade rooms.
Now I waited in the basement sitting in a line of folding chairs with my
nine classmates. Around the room flowers burst from bowls and chartreuse
vases and parents flowed in through the door and slowly filled the folding
chairs.

Mr. Williams, standing by the door in a charcoal gabardine jacket and
tie, looked strange without his usual white collar shirt and grey slacks. Mr.
Williams, a tall man in his forties with rumpled hair and a smooth tan,
taught seventh and eighth grade and doubled as the school principal. Mr.
Williams ran the classroom with an unassuming nonchalance. The
anticipation of his speech, which we knew would be loaded with respectable
words—be good, be grateful, be prudent—kept us lined up neatly in our seats.
An excitement ran down our row of ten targeted students. We were finished
with one phase, moving on to something bigger, better, older. We'd used
up the space here. I couldn't wait to get out.

I glanced at my fellow eighth graders lined up next to me: Snookie
and Jean, then Nancy Krech, Betty Farendorff, Bob White, Colin
Campbell, Ken Woodburn, Timmy Olson and a recent transfer named
Joyce. Most of us had been together for years. Betty was quiet and

withdrawn. Nancy, the fat one, was so hang-dog and supplicating that everyone avoided her. Snookie, small and perky, joined Jean and me during recess periods, but she lived out on Olson Highway, too far to hang out with on weekends. As for the boys—aside from Timmy I hardly spoke to them. Despite the close day-by-day proximity, I didn't know much about any of them except Jean and Timmy. Even Timmy and I hadn't spent much time together in recent years. Except for a hayride party his mother hosted for his thirteenth birthday, I didn't see him outside of school. At the end of the day, we all piled in buses, dispersed across the wide reaches of Golden Valley, and disappeared into our separate houses. The only person I saw on weekends was Jean. I was at her house constantly.

Besides, I was shy. Those embarrassing or awkward episodes that accompany the growing-up process crumpled me, the details haunting my thoughts for months. One day I forgot to get off the school bus at my stop and flew up the aisle, blubbering indecipherable nonsense at the bus driver, then tumbled down the steps and ran. Behind me I heard the bus explode into hysterical laughter. For months my mind replayed this episode in a loop of shame that began its frightful roll whenever my guard was down.

I caught Timmy's eye but quickly remembered I was mad at him and turned my head. No way would I forgive him. He had ruined the plan of a lifetime. When the lilacs were starting to show a flash of purple, Timmy and I decided we were fed up with parents and rules and school. The sole purpose of parents was to keep us penned in. School was just as bad. The classrooms were so close together and the rooms so small we couldn't get away with anything—adult eyes were everywhere. In the classroom we behaved with modest and obedient decorum—to challenge authority head-on would have been unthinkable—and we longed to try something new, something fascinating and out of bounds.

Here was the plan.

We would run away together. We would leave it all behind. We knew all the popular songs of the day and would become singers . . . or something. Plans were vague. Our first step was to get safely away and things would fall into place from there. Friday after school we would skip the bus and link up after the grounds had cleared and the building was deserted. We worked out alibis. (I was going to Jean's; Timmy's was going to his aunt's.) We would not be missed until we were safely away and out of reach. Each of us would bring one small suitcase and five dollars. We would hitch-hike. People were sure to pick up two innocent-looking kids. We were brother and sister, going to visit our grandmother who lived wherever the car was going. It was foolproof.

Our plan was in order, but first we had to learn *"Besame Mucho"* by heart. For days we practiced, cloistered in the copy room at the end of the hall. Finally we set up a time and place to meet for the big day of departure.

At the last minute Timmy backed out. On Friday afternoon, just as the yellow bus pulled up in front of school, he informed me it was off. He couldn't do it. *Why not?* He wasn't ready. *What?* I was furious. That was the end of Timmy. He was not to be trusted. I wouldn't be speaking to him any time soon.

Drawing my patent leather shoes under the chair, I looked around the large basement room, the all-purpose setting for meetings, assemblies, and entertainment. For years, Friday night bean suppers had been served here, presided over by the four Meadowbrook teachers. We showed up with our parents and sat around long lunch tables spread with white paper tablecloths. Bulging women in print wrap-around aprons handed out hamburgers and dipped ladles of small brown beans spiked with ham onto the plates, along with warm butter-soaked white bread that melted in your mouth. Supper was followed by sing-a-longs, performances of student musical talent, or an excerpt from a play.

At one of these suppers, our class performed a skit that revolved around a popular song of the day called "Pass That Peace Pipe," a ditty about Indians that spoke of burying the hatchet, punctuated with "Ugh, ugh, ugh." The boys were dressed in feather headdresses and Indian leather, while the girls pranced around playing young Indian maidens. While singing we marched in a circle, bobbing our heads up and down in floppy imitation of an Indian campfire dance.

When you quarrel it's grand to patch it
Pass that peace pipe and bury the hatchet
If your temper is getting a top hand
All you have to do is stop and
Pass that peace pipe and bury that hatchet
Like the Chocataws, Chickasaws, Chattahoochees, Chippewas do.

Since everyone in the audience knew the song, we didn't have to be polished. Those were the days when "cowboys and Indians" was a popular kid's game. The good-guys—the cowboys—chased the murderous Indians with bows and arrows while yipping and flapping their hands over their mouths in loud whoops. There was something wild and dominating about the process and the conquering of righteousness over the evil enemy. No one gave the racial implications a second thought.

The auditorium grew hushed as Mr. Williams walked up to the podium. Today was the big day. Today the eighth graders were to be honored. It was over. Mr. Williams was about to tell us what it meant.

"Boys and girls," began Mr. Williams, his eyes scanning the front row of listeners. "You are to be congratulated. You have completed your first eight years of school. You will be launched out into the world, a world of challenge and reward. You will be faced with opportunities. You must take them." Mr. Williams cleared his throat. "You are leaving the safe shelter of your young years. From now on more will be expected of you. If you apply yourselves at St. Louis Park High School your years will be fruitful, and like a small fish in a big bowl, you will learn to swim in a swifter current." We listened obediently, the odor of glazed sugar and sponge cake wafting by our faces. To us the future meant only one thing: high school and the coveted world of football teams and dances.

After the ceremony we grabbed plates of food and passed around autograph books. Mine, which I still possess, ratty and faded, contains verses like, "You might be on end, but I want to be your friend" and "Roses are red, violets are blue, skunks stink and so do you."

And so ended my days at the little red-brick school house. There would be no more watching the Lilac Day queen receive her crown on the hill behind Meadowbrook. No more sneaking copies of *National Geographic* from the hall bookcase. No more production sessions in the upstairs copy room where Timmy and I wrote the one-page school newspaper. No more dropping spit balls on Mr. Williams's head from the upstairs lavatory. It was time to leave and I was ready.

Exit pranks. Make way for a new inspiration—boys!

IN THE MIDDLE OF NINTH GRADE, Dad moved us to a larger prairie style-house on Lowry Hill in Minneapolis. We could look out the front windows rising above Groveland Terrace and see the dome of the Basilica on Hennepin Avenue beyond the parade grounds. The front entrance led through a second door into a central hall that branched to other sections of the house. A wide stairway ascended halfway up to a landing and then made a U-turn to the second floor. A push-button intercom system was linked to wooden wall phones that hung in each floor, but it was no longer in operating condition.

We now had four bedrooms. My room cornered on Groveland and Dupont avenues and Susan's room was behind mine. Harold occupied the former maid's room in the back, which boasted windows on three sides and had its own bath and stairway descending to the kitchen. Dad fitted the amusement room in the basement with a pinball machine, a record player, and a dry bar with three stools and stocked the separate kitchenette with cokes, ginger ale, and bottles of Miller Highlight beer. A long driveway entering from Dupont Avenue ran behind the house and down the hill to Groveland Terrace on the other side. Beyond two stone pillars framing the driveway stood a detached, three-car garage. An elderly couple, George and Pearl, lived in the apartment above. George mowed the yard, did odd jobs, and tended the *pee-own-ees*, as he called them, which lined either side of the driveway. Pearl cleaned the big house.

I joined the Church of Youth choir at the Hennepin Avenue Methodist Church, one block away. On Sunday mornings I marched up to the choir rosters in a black robe and squeezed in among of the

57 Groveland Terrace in Kenwood—1949.

altos. I could hear the tenor voice of the choir director's knock-out-handsome son, Steve, several heads down the row. My crush on Steve was provoked by my habitual lateness. One morning I came rushing in the side door of the church, down the stairs, along the hall, and burst breathless into the choir chamber where the others were putting on their robes. As I rounded the corner I crashed smack into Steve, knocking his music book to the floor. We exchanged confused glances. Two weeks later I charged into him again, slamming my nose against his chin. He started glancing at me from the tenor section, no doubt plotting ways to avoid me.

I stole looks at Steve constantly; in fact I couldn't keep my eyes off him. His mother, the choir director, began to notice something from her vantage point at the front of the choir, and I tried hard to restrain my wandering eyes. At least Steve knew who I was, I thought. I guessed this was an advantage, although what advantage wasn't clear. He watched for my arrival and we exchanged surreptitious glances when we happened to pass. I never missed a rehearsal or performance.

He showed up at many of the Church of Youth picnics and Friday night sing-a-longs in the church auditorium. With plates piled with hamburgers, Gedney pickles, and baked beans, we crowded around long tables and sang "Cruising down the River," following words printed on a white screen. I caught him staring at me but would have died rather than approach him. He was so far out of my league that any actual encounter would have thrown me into confusion. What could I have said, with my skinny figure, stringy hair, and slumped shoulders? Girls with opulent bright hair and vivacious laughter loomed everywhere.

❧ ♦ ❧

ONCE WE OBTAINED DRIVERS' licenses, we began boy-chasing in earnest. That summer Jean, Snookie, and I took to cruising the town in Mom's yellow Studebaker, prowling along Lake Street and down Hennepin Avenue. When we spied three guys in another car, one of us would lean out the window and yell.

"Hey, where ya goin' with that green hearse?" we hollered. The boys waved, yelled back, and then motioned us to follow them around the corner where they pulled up to the curve. Our car slithered up behind theirs, an older model rusted along the fender. We jumped out and angled along the curb, looking each other over.

The boys wore jeans and close-cropped hair cuts. They shuffled their feet or leaned against a car fender.

"So what are you girls up to?" one of them asked.

"Just out for a drive."

"Want to do something?"

"Probably."

"Want to go over to the Creamery for a coke?"

If we liked their looks, we agreed and followed their car to the café where we slid into a booth while the miniature jukebox on the wall above each table blared out the harmonies of "How High the Moon." Sometimes we agreed to join them afterwards, and after grabbing a couple of six packs, headed to a hidden parking spot in a secluded park. Piling into one car, we opened the beers, and exchanged information about schools and background. We fabricated yarns about who we were, supplying no last names, no addresses, and no official facts.

Necking became a favorite pastime. We never went beyond kissing. Nice girls did not go "all the way." It was the girl's responsibility to enforce this iron-clad rule and mostly the boys understood this. Some daring girls allowed petting and would let the boy get into her blouse, especially if they were going together.

Naturally, we couldn't bring these guys home. At the end of the evening Jean, Snookie, and I drove away into the anonymity of the city, waving a vague good-bye. Since we had to cloak our identities, there was no way we could see them again.

Sometimes the boys had no expectations, considering how we'd met. Sometimes they wanted to see more of us. Once or twice I broke down and let a boy drive me home. I would direct him up to the carriage apartment above the garage and run up the steps to the front door. I hid underneath the overhang until his car had driven off before scampering across the lawn to my own back door. I wanted at all costs to avoid being identified with a house in Kenwood and the suggestion of affluence. This identification would, I was certain, set me apart and create a barrier with any of these boys.

Once I carelessly let a boy I liked drop me at the big house. Several nights later I heard loud beeping outside my bedroom window and looking down saw a rusted-out olive-green car filled with boys, their faces peering up at the house. I ducked out of sight and hid on the bed. The honking persisted interminably, until Mother finally knocked at the door. "Do you know anything about that strange car?"

"Don't know a thing."

The car finally drove off. It taught me a lesson.

&·♦·&

ONE SATURDAY NIGHT at the ebb of a long, sultry August summer, Snookie and her two older brothers threw a party. Mrs. McIntyre dropped us at a small bungalow in Bryn Mawr on the north side of Olson Highway. Jean and I, freshly made up in Spice Pink lipstick and a thin streak of eyeliner around our eyes, walked up to the house and rang the bell excitedly. A soft breeze stirred the air and wafted around our striped sundresses. The door opened and Snookie stood there in her green-and-white shirtwaist dress with patch pockets and a forest green scarf tied around her pony tail.

Small and agile, Snookie combined a freckled mouse-like face with the deliberate movement of an aardvark. But she could be quick when inspired, and with her short skinny legs could run the fastest of any girl at Meadowbrook School. Quiet in her early years, by ninth grade Snookie was learning to enjoy herself and a squirrelly grin lit up her face when she was having a good time.

We followed Snookie into the basement where strings of blue lights hung along the ceiling, and a long table set with cokes, beer, mixed nuts, and pretzels was pushed against one wall. Young people lounged on couches and chairs that lined the edge of the room, played dart-board, and munched popcorn from a large orange bowl Snookie's mother kept refilling. The dog, Blackie, trotted down the stairs and sniffed his way around the room, tail beating, searching out attention, although when he showed a persistent interest in the Polish sausages he was banished upstairs.

The guys hung around the food table and, as the night wore on, pulled the girls up to dance. Someone switched off the main lights and a single brass floor lamp in the corner cast a golden gaze over the floor, while the overhead bulbs lent a purple aura to the darkened room. A Victrola plopped down 33⅓ rpm records from a stack perched atop a spindle: *Buttermilk Sky, Blue Skies; Blue Moon, My Darling, My Darling, Maybe, Golden Earring, Mood Indigo.*

I sat in my blue-and-white sundress with matching jacket and ballet slipper flats and watched the guys mull around the room, popping Old Dutch potato chips into their mouths as they eyed the girls. One or two asked me to dance, guys dressed in Levis with tapered legs and crew-necked polo shirts, or button solid-color shirts with open collars. Dancing was effortless; precise steps were not required, scooting one foot at a time to a spot on the floor a millimeter away was enough. The music played slow and languorous, as the couples now merged into single silhouettes in the dark. I felt my partner's breath against my cheek and his arms tighten slowly, languidly around my back.

The door at the top of the stairs opened.

"It's awfully dark down there," said a male voice.

"Oh, Frank, let them have some fun."

"I'm going down."

"No, no. Here, I'll send Blackie down. That will amuse them."

"What? What good is it to send a dog down? Is he going to give us a report?"

The door closed, no sign of the dog.

Someone turned up the music. Mel Tormé's voice crooned, "*I'll cling to him, each spring to him, and long for the day when I'll cling to him.*" My partner drew me closer, drawing my arms around his shoulders, and my cheek tipped against his bent head as we warmed with the rhythm of the song. The closeness banished all thought or talk. We swayed, buried in each other's movement. Other couples drifted like shadows around us.

The upstairs door flew open again. "Snookie? Are you down there? Do you want more popcorn?" No response.

"Snookie, I'm coming down. I'm going to turn on the light. Snookie?"

The record scratched to a stop and the couples broke apart.

"Come on down, Mom."

"Frank, you go down."

"All right and there'll be hell to pay."

"I'm going. I'm going myself. Never mind." With that we heard the click of heels descending and Snookie's mom came into the room, looking inquisitive and sheepish. Her short hair was streaked with gray, the side pocket of her beige print housedress bulged with Kleenex. "Don't let me disturb you. Keep right on doing what you were doing. Do you need me to fetch more lamps so you can see?"

"Mom, it's more fun to dance in dim light. It's not so embarrassing. It helps us relax."

"Well, of course. Your father . . . Just don't sit down too much. Stay moving. Dancing is such fun. I used to love it when I was a girl. We had big dances you wouldn't believe, with full white dresses and flowers . . . not quite like this."

"Thanks, Mom. You can send Blackie down."

"All right, dear. I'll see if he's available."

The music started up and the couples recommenced their swaying. No one talked. It was a relief. Nothing to do but feel the warmth and listen to the songs that recounted love and happiness and loss. Here was a way of connecting to boys that felt comfortable. With the sweet odor of peppermint breath brushing my ear, I lost myself in the music and the blue night.

LATE ONE AFTERNOON as the sun lowered over the lake, Snookie, Jean, and I sat on a wooden bench at the Calhoun Beach pavilion drinking Dr. Peppers. Three good-looking guys ambled by, gray blankets tucked under their arms, looking idly at the women in shorts trailing dogs and the pre-teens whizzing by on roller skates. We surveyed their dark jeans and colored sport shirts. They slowed, turned, and ambled over to the bench. "Hi." They explained they were from West High and lived in the neighborhood. Did we want to walk with them? When we reached the other side of the lake they invited us to a group picnic with promises of baseball and bonfires. We agreed.

At the park the boys spread out blankets over the grass. Shouts came from a nearby baseball game and a thin odor of charcoal fanned over the field. A crowd of picnickers from West High were enjoying the soft twilight air, lounging on blankets, sitting on blue-and-white coolers, or standing around a steaming grill. Jean, Snookie, and I settled ourselves on the blankets with the boys and watched the ball game between spurts of talk. The tall, dark boy, whose name was Jack, looked directly at me as he spoke.

The boys brought us grilled hamburgers on paper plates and large paper cups of beer. Our made-up stories were no good here; these guys were too open and generous to fool. We talked about the Calhoun beach boat rentals, the new popcorn shop on the corner of Hennepin Avenue, and the second-hand car the blonde boy had just purchased. Jack, leaning elbows on knees on the blanket next to me, darted a smile my way every so often. I was intrigued by the wry smile that crossed his face at some remark, the way his brown eyes turned to me to see if I'd caught a joke, and his rugged, good-looking face.

As a yellow pool of moonlight crept over the grass, the others wandered off. Jack and I turned on our backs and watched the orange fringe around the tree branches overhead fade into darkness. The nearby activities died down, revealing a murmur of rustling leaves, and the rolling of hushed voices issued softly from the nearby bonfire.

I breathed softly as the shadows faded into the underside of the night. The ground gave off a faint scent of lavender. Then Jack was pulling me to him, holding me close. As I lay in his arms I breathed in the musky smell of his leather jacket against my face, an odor that would remain intoxicating long after I was away from his breath and his kisses.

❧ ◆ ☙

THE NIGHT NANCY KRECH came to my house brought an end to my innocence and a stop to unchaperoned parties in the basement. Nancy's heavy weight made her something of an outcast. The angora sweaters with matching socks she wore to school rather than camouflaging only emphasized her elephantine shape. Her manner was hangdog and pleading. Neither pretty nor clever nor confident, Nancy coasted in the background of the class. In the Meadowbrook graduation picture she loomed in the back row, an unfocused though dominant figure. The candy and other treats she distributed at school proved a hopeless appeal, for the attention of her classmates evaporated as soon as the offerings were gone. Once her parents invited the eighth-grade class to her large brick house for outdoor grilled steaks and lemonade, which improved her status for about a week.

The Saturday night of my party, Mrs. Quady, a matronly widow, was staying with us while my parents were cruising the British Isles. Nancy unexpectedly showed up. She had burst in when we were discussing the party and there was no was polite way to avoid including her. As Jean, Snookie, Betty Farendorff, and I were mixing in the basement with a group of friendly young soldiers, we spied her swaying down the stairs. Eying the large swivel armchair, she arched her back and sank into the cushions, smiling at the uniformed boys standing nearby. Jean's boyfriend Mickey had recruited them from the airport military base where he was stationed. Most were from other states and glad to be entertained in a private home.

The record player blared "How High the Moon" as people bent over the pin-ball machine or sprawled around the room guzzling beers. Snookie and I sat on stools at the bar talking to two soldiers. Finally the overhead light was switched off, someone put on a slow ballad, the coffee table was pushed against the wall, and couples formed to dance. From the corner of my eye, I saw Nancy seated in the lap of a rather slight guy, and it flashed through my head that the boy, and possibly the chair, would not long bear up under her. The snaps of the pin-ball machine balls lurching back and forth faded until the only sounds were beer cans popping open and records beings slipped into place on the phonograph. Shadowy couples moved about the room and blended on the dance floor, indistinguishable, obliterated by the magic of the music. I felt the warm pressure of a boy against me and melted trancelike into his arms.

Mrs. Quady's voice rang from the top of the stairs that it was midnight and time to close up. The lights were switched back on, the music silenced, and people stood up or broke apart.

But where was Nancy?

We searched the bathroom, the kitchenette, the laundry room, even Dad's tool room on the far side of the basement. Finally I approached the furnace room, a small enclosure directly behind the bar. When I opened the door, I heard scrapes in the darkness. Groping for the light, I pulled my palm over the switch, and there on the floor under the stark glare of an overhead bulb was Nancy Krech. She lay there on her back, legs spread, with her naked thighs flushed out on the bare concrete, the slight boy stretched over her on his elbows.

The sight of them spread out next to the dusty furnace was so incongruous that I couldn't speak, I stood stark still, my throat clutched, my eyes riveted to the two figures on the floor. Then I looked away, hoping the vision of her with this soldier she had never met before would lose its intensity. Nancy and the boy scrambled to their feet, blinking. Nancy tugged down the side of her chemise dress that was matted with charcoal and beer, and the boy whipped his army pants up and fumbled with buttons, all the while twisting his head away from the naked bulb. Neither looked at me as they passed through the doorway. We didn't exchange a word. The people crowding around stood uncomfortably, looking at their shoes and each other.

I flew up to Mrs. Quady for refuge, unable to conceal my shock. I hadn't intended to tell her the details, but as soon as she demanded to know what happened, I spilled. There was no getting around it, no other way to explain my distress. I begged her not to tell my parents when they returned, but she had her duty. I think she was more distressed than I was, for she had a worried frown on her face all the next day.

The next morning Jean and I commiserated on the phone. We agreed that what had happened was shocking and that Nancy's desperate bid for male attention had led her to degrade herself. We wanted nothing more to do with her. Later Snookie added that Nancy would do anything to get boys. I couldn't shake the squalid sight of Nancy and the soldier on the furnace room floor and feared the image would spring to life every time I looked at her. Something I hoped never to have to do again.

Mrs. Quady continued to stay with us on future occasions, but there were no overnights, no parties, and above all no boys within a mile.

I did see Nancy once more, several years later when Betty Farendorff talked me into visiting the apartment where Nancy lived

with her husband and baby. She had changed, Betty assured me, become
a solid homebody, enveloped in happiness. One afternoon we paid her
a call. I spent an uncomfortable hour in the messy apartment with rows
of dying plants crowding the counters, sticky fly bars hanging from the
ceiling, and a screaming baby in a high chair spitting mashed apples
down its chin and onto the floor. Nancy lumbered around the kitchen,
rotund as ever in a torn cotton chemise. The smell of dead fish hovered
over the sink. The scene left me depressed. If Nancy had found happy
domesticity, I wanted no part of it.

I'd like to reveal that I felt compassion for Nancy's position as
underdog, that I could sense her loneliness, but such was not the case.
It would be a long time before I could see into people and grasp their
misery. In those days I saw no further than my nose.

Part II

Fitting In

Chapter Seven

❧ Taking On High School ❧

I T WAS A SHORT WALK from the house on Groveland Terrace, past the stone wall of the John Rood property and down the steep grade to Northrop Collegiate School at the foot of Lowry Hill. I entered the doors fresh and neat in my new school uniform, little dreaming what was in store.

I stood in the dark entrance hall that loomed like a cathedral above me, imposing and untouchable, gazing at the square-patterned chestnut paneling and the green and mahogany marble fireplace that was circled by a low three-sided, spindle railing. Against one wall a polished bronze circular stairway rounded up to the second floor. There didn't seem to be a smooth wall or unadorned corner anywhere. The entire school, from the ivy-covered red brick exterior to the heavy wooded interior, exuded tradition and regulation.

I felt raw. Here I was, entering my sophomore year tested, uniformed, and totally out of my element. The tenth and eleventh graders gathered for homeroom on the second floor, and I soon found myself seated alphabetically at my desk, flanked in front and back by Nellie Atwater and Sue Brockman, listening to Miss Grey at the front desk deliver a formal orientation.

It took me awhile to figure out the shape of the Northrop class structure. My classmates were located in three main neighborhoods. One set lived, like me, in Minneapolis, in the Kenwood area that included the chain of city lakes. A second group was sprawled through

Hopkins and Edina and carpooled to school together. A larger group traveled to school from Lake Minnetonka, driven down Highway 12 by fathers on their way to work downtown. These families were part of the Minnetonka social scene; they belonged to the Wayzata Country Club, the Minnetonka Arts Center, and various bridge clubs and included among their ranks prominent names like Whitney, Pillsbury, and MacMillan. The girls in these groups led a contained social life outside school. During the week they congregated in the halls and over lunch, swapping anecdotes about weekend parties, overnights, vacations, and ski trips.

The number of years you attended Northrop mattered; your degree of Northrop-ness and the depth of your background was judged accordingly. Most of the girls had been at Northrop since grade school and moved in a close-knit clique that was sufficient unto itself. I watched my classmates cluster around the desks of the Lake Minnetonka crowd. These confident, laughing, breezy girls lived in lakeside mansions, got high marks, were groomed impeccably, had postures like flag poles, and behaved with intimidating composure. I sometimes wondered what it must be like to be so self-possessed. I held back from stepping into their space, unable to summon any language that could introduce me.

As a newcomer with a rural-like Meadowbrook background, I occupied the bottom rung. I had no confidence and no talent and fancied that I personified all the reasons the levels of superiority had evolved in the first place. Plus I was quiet and passive. I wasn't pretty and was accident prone. I had nothing to recommend me. I legitimized all apprehensions.

It was not long before things began to happen. One day I swept into Miss Pease's class and plunked myself at a desk, flustered at being late. Miss Pease was explaining an equation up at the black board. As I attempted to bring her writing into focus, Miss Pease stopped talking. She looked at me in her direct way.

"Judy," she began. "Do you know what class you're in?" My eyes froze. A long silence. "This is math. You aren't in here until next period." No one said anything as I gathered my books and slunk red-faced past the class and past Miss Pease, who looked after me, a slight smile on her face. Burning with shame I longed to hide somewhere in the depths of the school and never emerge.

I wondered what was being said about me behind closed doors. After a series of goofs, I made up my mind I would stay out of the way and become as unnoticeable as possible, preferably invisible.

One afternoon the tenth graders were seated at long lunch tables on the third floor, waiting for the servers to bring dishes such as spaghetti and garlic bread, Sheppard's Pie, or a noodle hot dish, along with vegetables or salad. Each table was headed by one of the instructors, and it was the task of the student seated to her right to draw out her chair. I happened to occupy that privileged seat and my eyes were fixed on the dishes being set on the table that sent tempting odors my way. When Miss Pease appeared she stopped by her chair and stood quietly waiting for me to catch on. Finally the girl across from me shot me a look and whispered, "Pull out her chair!" I hastily jumped up and did so, bumping the chair into Miss Pease's knees in the process. Miss Pease sat and spread her napkin serenely on her lap. Luckily I remembered to pass the serving bowl first to Miss Pease. From then on I watched my every move. No relaxing here!

Just when I thought I had uncovered every taboo and there was nothing left I could do wrong, some new challenge came along. One day during dessert I was sucking on a spoonful of ice cream and slipped it leisurely in and out of my mouth, savoring each taste.

"Ugh. That's disgusting," exclaimed the girl sitting across from me. "You don't put the spoon in your mouth and take it out with ice cream still on the spoon." All eyes were turned in my direction. "We don't want to have to look at something that's been in your mouth!"

A few heads nodded in agreement. I lowered my spoon to the dish, abashed. It didn't occur to me to speak up with, "That's ridiculous. It's more fun to eat this way. It lasts longer." or "Whoever told you that? You lick ice cream cones, don't you?" Stealing a glance around I saw amused smiles around the table and tucked in my wings for the rest of the meal.

Something had to be done. I couldn't be a quivering mouse any longer. Most of the girls were fun-loving, joked, told funny stories, and played tricks on each other—like writing bogus notes from Patty's boyfriend and slipping it in her Latin book. I had to come up with a trick of my own. Finally a brainstorm—it came to me in a flash.

One noon hour when everyone was at lunch, I snuck back early to study hall and placed the lid of my wooden desk in the upright position. On it I taped a piece of yellow paper with capital letters written in black marker that read:

**WHO WOULD LIKE A DATE WITH FRANK SINATRA?
YOU WILL GO DANCING AND A LIMO WILL PICK YOU UP.
SIGN YOUR NAME BELOW AND YOU WILL BE
GUARANTEED THE TIME OF YOUR LIFE.
P.S. FRANK IS BETWEEN GIRLFRIENDS; YOU HAVE A
CHANCE.**

I left an Eversharp pen clipped to the desktop and slipped out to the back of the school to wait in the woods. The class would soon be returning from lunch and hanging out in the study hall until the bell. They couldn't miss the sign if they tried. This would be a hoot.

Twenty minutes later I reentered homeroom and swept my eyes across the desks. Most of the students were piling books in their arms and heading for the door to class. My desk top was still open, displaying the red sign with blaring black letters, but it had not been touched. There was no sign of recognition on anyone's face. I left the sign up for the rest of the day until everyone had left, then I took it down and dropped it into the waste basket.

After that I noticed a few sideways glances in my direction, which were quickly diverted. They must have thought the sign was so stupid they had no words. What was there to say? She had best be left to herself, this weird new girl. How did she ever get into Northrop? What is the world coming to?

It didn't help that I was something of a slob. I was oblivious to personal decor. To me dressing up meant putting on lipstick and combing my hair, which stayed put for ten minutes. Why bother? My looks were nondescript, and except for comments about my blue eyes I was undistinguished. Now that I was attending Northrop, my mother was anxious for me to shape up, to move past scruffy adolescence and into young lady attire.

She enlisted my classmate and best friend, Margo Holt, to get me to wear my creamy new saddle shoes, to make me understand that I must make a good impression. Margo tried: "Those loafers should be *burned*." But I stuck to the well-worn penny loafers that could be kicked off under the desk. After commenting that my shoes were falling apart and my lime-green socks had seen better days ten years ago, Margo gave up.

But Mother didn't.

To this impeccable beauty, who stepped out of her bedroom each morning ready for an appointment with the queen, I was a disaster. Her daughter needed shaping up, academically, physically and culturally. This included manners, wardrobe, and bearing. The challenge was daunting. I was sent to Estelle Stevens Modeling School, where I was categorized as a combined Country (outdoorsy) and Patrician (reserved) type and was taught how to apply the numerous tricks of makeup, how to choose clothing styles suited to my type, and how to walk and pivot on a runway. This, along with the Arthur Murray ballroom lessons, where I learned to fox trot, waltz, and lindy, was supposed to displace some of the freewheeling outdoor flavor I presented. I learned to wear gloves, a cloche or brimmed hat, and carry a purse, all color coordinated with matching heels.

Right after Christmas, Mother and I went shopping big-time. Mother wore the Christmas present Dad gave her: a full length mink coat in deep hues of chestnut, charcoal, and russet brown, with cuffed sleeves and a matching collar—a royal jewel, the crème de la crème. She slipped on the mink and we piled in her Camaro and headed downtown.

The Minnesota sky was icy blue and the air crackled, enlivening our steps as we walked along Nicollet Avenue past Power's, Donaldson's, Dayton's, The Tea Shop, and Young Quinlan's. The two of us weaved through pedestrians in felt and fedora hats, fur-lined boots and overcoats. Behind the Foshay Tower we spied a corner of the Roanoke building two blocks away where Dad was laboring in his office at that very moment.

As we stepped out of the elevator at Harold's, a tall sales clerk wearing an armful of gold bracelets approached. "Good day, ladies."

"We're looking for some clothes for my daughter," Mother told her. "Could you help us?"

Seating herself in a corner chair in the fitting room, Mother watched me try on soft British wools, cashmeres, shimmering taffeta, rich plaids, and Norwegian sweaters. The clerk reappeared from time to time with fresh items. "That's nice," Mother ventured when one caught her fancy. She favored a full black-and-white-striped skirt, topped by an oyster angora sweater with a rolled collar that covered my neck bones. "Do stand up straight," she urged. "You look so much prettier." She fingered strands of hair along my forehead. "A good combing would help." I automatically reached up to smooth the errant strands. She couldn't understand why, with regular permanents and setting my hair with bobby pins every night, my hair looked continually messy.

I eyed my slim figure in the mirror, searching for clothing that would smooth me out or prop me up, willing to go along with anything that might improve my standing in the world.

"We'll take the gold tweed with pearl buttons as well," Mother told the sales clerk, handing her a dress to add to the pieces we'd already selected. "Now we need some matching jewelry. What would you recommend?" We followed the clerk to the display case and peered through at the rows of gold bracelets and necklaces.

"This two-strand will go nicely with the round collar," suggested the clerk, drawing out a gold beaded necklace with a high price tag.

"Oh, yes," exclaimed Mother. "Let's see it." I tried it on. "What do you think?" inquired Mother of the clerk.

The clerk was all enthusiasm. "Oh, it looks marvelous on her. A perfect match."

I became irate. Mother always threw herself on the opinion of the sales clerk, letting herself be talked into the most expensive items. The way she leaned on their judgment was pathetic.

"I prefer the herringbone," I said flatly. Our selections included a wool pleated skirt with two matching sweater sets in red and navy, a wool checkered suit, a black-and-white Liz Claiborne suit, and two belted dresses. My favorite was a flared black skirt and white crepe blouse, which I stored carefully in a plastic dress bag to save for just the right party with just the right boy. It hung in the closet waiting for the perfect event that never happened.

❧◆❧

CLASSES AT SCHOOL presented another challenge. Latin was a drag. After learning how Caesar invaded Gaul and divided it into three parts, I lost track. And the teacher's assurance that knowledge of the Latin vocabulary vastly improved our English didn't help. I guess it was less boring than endlessly conjugating French verbs, with the teacher at the board and the students repeating the imperfect endings. In Miss Chambers's history class at least we discussed the material, which was more interesting. Miss Chambers gave us tips on memorizing dates, like how to recall when Columbus discovered America. "In 1492, Columbus sailed the ocean blue." This was not to be confused, she joked, with "In 1493, Columbus sailed the deep blue sea." After that I could never remember which one was the correct verse.

Because the classes were small—ten to fifteen students—the teachers knew our learning habits inside and out. It was difficult to get through a semester, no matter how dry, without learning something. There were no boys to crowd us out with strong voices or virulent antics. Many of the girls developed strong voices of their own. We could be ourselves without worrying about impressing a pair of bright male eyes.

It was clear the academic emphasis at Northrop called for a revolutionary approach. One had to *study*. Each night after dinner, I sat at my desk with a goose-neck lamp until my homework for the next day was completed—no variations. There were long chapters on history to digest and French verbs to memorize between bouts of blurring out the page, heaving sighs, and staring at the iron-clamped door. I dallied and doodled my way through a few months of homework, wrestling with each page, until a shock one day at school got the message through to me.

The assignment for English, my favorite class, was to pick an author and write a paper on his or her work. I perked up. This I could do. I chose Charlotte Bronte, whom I had already read, and reread *Jane Eyre* and *The Professor*. I took a book out of the library about Charlotte Bronte and read that. I even enjoyed doing it, except that it took ridiculously long. But I persevered. At least there was one subject I could do well, never mind Latin and math. But when I picked up my paper from the front desk, Miss Grey had marked it D. *What? How could that be? What is going on here?*

I marched to Miss Grey's office.

"What's wrong with this?" I wanted to know.

"Too superficial. You need to spend more time on it. Dig deeper."

It took most of the school year before I was able to catch on to studying and writing papers. There was no way but to buckle down and spend hours in my room in total quiet, reading and underlining. Studying for final exams took longer to master: rereading all the chapter underlines I had made over the semester, reviewing classroom notes, copying both into a single outline, and then going over the outline far into the night until I had it memorized. In the morning before the exam I did a final review, crossing out the correctly answered questions and repeating the process until there were none left. This required concentration and a stick-to-itiveness that had rarely been part of my fly-by-night, meandering existence.

By twelfth grade I was studying like a dog. My friend Margo would stop by the house early before an exam so we could quiz each other for a last review, and we continued to cram as we tramped down the hill to school. Margo confessed that she hadn't studied as intended and would have to wing it. I had suspicions that my notes benefited her more than they did me. To my annoyance she invariably received an A or B to my C, which bothered me no end, until I just had to admit that she was smarter. Some people have all the luck.

❧ ◆ ❧

THE HIGH STANDARDS of the school included personal integrity. Ours was fundamentally a prudish class—the term *goody-goody* might apply—although we liked to think of ourselves as daring. We chose as our senior class motto *SAFETY FIRST*, an effort to coat our staid lives with a splash of notoriety. Despite the wild antics in the halls, our moral standards were tight. The Northrop honor code bound us all in a pledge of honesty, and we were encouraged to take this pledge seriously. So our shock was great when Anne Clayburn, one of our less academic classmates, was caught cheating on a Latin final. Our class president called us to a private meeting, secluded from the teaching staff. What to do? Anne needed to be confronted and made to understand that her cheating brought all of us down, as well as compromised her own prospects. When confronted with the evidence and encouraged to grasp the seriousness of her action, Anne burst into tears. After two hours of persuasion by class members and soul searching and promises on the side of Anne, we agreed not to turn her in.

Some months later Anne crossed another boundary that was equally reprehensible: word got around that she was *sleeping with boys*. We couldn't have been more horrified. The grapevine fluttered with whispers. Everyone knew. It was rumored that boys were falling over each other to take her out, expecting to get what was denied everywhere else. The fact that Anne was one of the beauties of the class, with dark hair curling loosely around her head and china blue eyes, made it all the more difficult to understand why she would sacrifice her reputation. Eventually she started going steady with a popular Blake boy and the rumors ceased.

❧ ◆ ❧

I HARDLY KNEW ANNE. The only girl I was close to the first year lived in my neighborhood. Margo and I first met by chance in the school lobby. I'd seen her often but we'd never spoken. Every afternoon at the three o'clock bell I gathered my books, exited by the back door of the school, and strode up the back hill. Often I noticed another girl walking ahead of me, a short girl with blond hair who disappeared by the time I reached the top of the hill. It seemed I wasn't the only Kenwood student who walked to school.

One Thursday, I descended to the lobby to keep an appointment to see Miss Spurr. I'd first been exposed to Miss Spurr on the opening day of school when the student body had assembled in the main floor auditorium. Miss Spurr, in her official role as principal, had delivered a lofty talk on opportunity and responsibility. Her formal Eastern style and prim wavy hairdo, chesty posture and large, looming authority underlined the significance of her words. Her favorite admonition, "A word to the wise is sufficient," was brief and to the point, just as she was. Miss Spurr personified Northrop officialdom: aloof, upstanding. I had never seen anyone like her.

It was the last period before school ended and I was seated on a bench waiting to be summoned to her office. The lobby was deserted. As I was regarding a photograph of Cyrus Northrop hanging above the fireplace, a blonde girl moved into view. I recognized her immediately. She looked over at me and then away, adjusting the leather belt around her navy uniform. Finally, she came over to the bench and sat down.

"You waiting to see Miss Spurr, too?" she asked.

"Yes." Miss Spurr held introductory meetings each fall to connect with the students and launch the school year.

"Nothing to worry about," the blonde girl said, "All she ever wants is to know is how you spent the summer and how you're liking school."

"You don't have to kneel on a stool?" I asked, and she tossed her head to one side and smiled, looking at me with a friendly air. She was almost pretty, with her soft blonde hair, creamy Irish skin, a small, slightly hooked nose, and a lively, intelligent gaze.

"Oh, she barks but she doesn't bite," she said encouragingly. It turned out that Margo lived four blocks from my house. She offered to walk up the hill with me after school. You bet. Little did I know that she would be my best friend and confidante for the next three years and far beyond.

When I entered Miss Spurr's office I was greeted by short woman with a ramrod gaze and the stance of a heavy weight. She motioned me to a tall-backed brocade chair facing her desk. Soon she was expounding on school duties, academia, and Eastern formalities. She focused her smile on me: gracious, direct, and impenetrable. Here was someone you didn't trifle with. But I soon got used to her. The progress and future of the students were her primary concern, and she would back them in whatever way possible. The podium lectures she gave in the auditorium began to sound uplifting I couldn't help but like her, from a distance, hoping I would never have to be alone with her for more than two minutes.

From then on, Margo Holt and I trudged up the hill to my house every day after school, fixed ourselves saltine crackers with jelly, or pulled out a round tin of Old Dutch Potato Chips and a plate of butter to spread on them. Sprawling out on the sun room rug, we listened to *Tom Mix* and *The Lone Ranger* until in our junior year the radio was replaced by a grandiose fifteen-inch TV console.

More often we ended at Margo's house. She was full of invitations. Did I want to do this or that? Her assertiveness matched my shyness. She not only spoke up readily, she didn't take no for an answer. Of course no was not the answer I ever wanted to give. We were at her house almost every day. Margo was not one to appreciate being alone and sought company at every turn. She had no close friends at school, despite moving up the grades and through dancing class with the rest of the "established" girls. Mother readily agreed to my long absences, more than happy to have me in a respectable home with a new classmate and fulfilling her expectations that I would better myself and find friends now that we lived in the upscale Kenwood neighborhood.

Margo lived in an old, inviting three-story Kenwood house with a wooden porch stretched along the entire front. The entrance door was never locked, allowing the five Holt children easy access to the house. Before long I had acquired the same privilege. The minute I first entered the dark hallway I knew this house was different. Mine was airily constructed with tall hallways, light woodwork, sliding doorways to parcel off the dining room and den, and a sweeping curved central staircase, giving it an open, spacious look. Mother had adorned the rooms with documented antiques and Ethan Allen furniture. The Holt house was dark and homey. Solid mahogany furniture, much of it passed through generations, circled around the living room. A voluptuous Viennese tapestry hung over the fireplace. Dark molding circled the ceiling and the heavy brocade drapes were drawn, plunging the room into an old-world darkness. Everything in the house seemed to have taken root, like the oak trees in the yard.

We found Mrs. Holt in the back family room bent over a roll-top desk, working on some papers. When Margo introduced me her mother turned in her chair, held out her hand and gave me a wide, beaming smile. Her flat shoes and loose gray suit spoke of comfort and function. A bookcase stuffed with hardcovers stretched across one wall of the room. People lived and worked here, too busy with projects to put away every notebook or fold every lap robe. The contrast between this home and mine was glaring: the one meticulous with orderly elegance, fashioned for entertainment, and the other casual with purposeful clutter. I thought I might fit in here.

"So you're the Bradford girl? Glad to have you. Make yourself at home."

Mrs. Holt inquired about my family and where I lived. With her square white teeth and thin mouth she looked like an older version of Margo; the two faces reflected the same open expressions and the same alert hazel eyes.

"Margo," Mrs. Holt said, "Take Judy to the kitchen and fix yourselves a snack. There's some ice cream in the freezer." She turned back to the ledger on the desk.

I soon became comfortable with Mrs. Holt. She had the reassuring habit of always *being there*, at her desk or in her recliner. She handled the finances, oversaw the bi-weekly cleaning woman and house upkeep, managed the progress of her five children, and organized a myriad of other household tasks. She could also discuss literature, music and every detail of the latest presidential election. Besides being president of the Women's Investment Club, the Wellesley College Alumnae, and active in the League of Women Voters, she participated in two bridge clubs and the women's Lafayette Club golf team. Her lack of chic was more than compensated for by her warmth and generosity toward everyone who came into the house. She soon attached herself to me. When I confided to her one day that I felt out of place at home, she told me she was an orphan of the Catholic Church, being left motherless at age four. I think she understood.

My mother and Mrs. Holt could not have been more different. My mother wore Tiffany jewelry and radiated charm and amiability, while Big Margo, as Margo's mother was called, was brilliant, intellectually informed, and efficient. Margo and I had similar differences. Margo was forceful and thick-skinned while I was scatter-brained and sensitive, traits that reflected our mothers enough to cause problems. In both our households the mother-daughter relations were charged. Margo went her own way, resisting her mother's every attempt to keep her in line. I did the same. We understood that our mothers would rather be anywhere than around us and that deep down we did not measure up.

Before long I was spending all my spare time at the Holt's.

Margo had the entire attic floor to herself, including a bathroom. "They put me up here to get rid of me," she said in her usual forthright way as we sat on the twin beds. "This is my oasis. No one ever comes up here but me." From the first Margo withheld nothing; she was full of details of her family and their intrigues and problems. I picked up a photo from the bureau of clean-cut Blake boys grinning into the camera. They stood tall in creased slacks and wool sweaters, gazing at the camera with handsome confidence. These were a different breed from the guys I was used to. They looked intimidating. Educated in a separate school, these snappy boys were out of reach and all I could do was admire them from a distance.

Sara, Margo's sister, often sat next to me at family dinners at the Holt house. A thin slip of a figure, frail and thin-boned, she was plagued with ongoing health problems, yet she entered the conversation cheerfully, responding to comments with an optimistic laugh.

Sara had contracted polio in seventh grade, the year polio hit Minnesota like a thunderbolt. That was 1947. Hundreds were crippled by the vicious disease and were clamped into in braces or crutches, special maneuvering devices, or the dreaded iron lung. For a year Sara underwent special treatment at hospitals in the Twin Cities and New York City.

A local physician described the crisis.

> *The first summer when I was home in Minnesota . . . we admitted 464 proven cases of polio just at the University Hospital. . . . And this was a very severe paralytic form. Maybe two or three hours after a lot of these kids would come in with a stiff neck or a fever, they'd be dead. It was unbelievable. It was just loads of people that came in, sometimes with only a fever but usually a headache and a little stiffness in the neck. And just absolutely terrified. At the height of the epidemic, the people in Minneapolis were so frightened that there was nobody in the restaurants. There was practically no traffic, the stores were empty. It was considered a feat of bravado almost to go out and mingle in public. A lot of people just took up and moved away, went to another city.*
>
> — Richard Aldrich, M.D, quoted in A *Paralyzing Fear*

The accident happened when Sara's parents were vacationing. With the consent of the baby-sitter, she had ridden her bike down Franklin Avenue to the grocery store and was returning with a newly purchased Pepsi-Cola in her basket. While passing a parked car, one of the bicycle's wheels slipped, tossing her and the Pepsi bottle to the pavement. Sara lay amidst shards of broken glass, one of which had pierced deep into her leg. When she showed up at the house, leg bleeding, the matronly sitter took one look, grabbed a dishtowel from the kitchen, wrapped it around the wet leg and ran off with Sara to the bus stop. At the Medical Arts Building downtown they located a physician and the wound was closed with twenty stitches. Two days later, when her grandparents arrived to drive her to the

Holt lake house as planned, Sara appeared to have a slight case of the sniffles. By the next morning her neck and head hurt, and she couldn't lift her head off the pillow.

Sara was devastated, as her craving to spend the next two weeks at Lyman Lodge lake camp in Excelsior had been crushed. Camp was out of the question.

And then the terrifying source of her illness was discovered.

At this time little was known about polio. The number of cases in the Twin Cities had increased so drastically over the previous two years that people were panicked. Friends were barred from Sara's presence, with parents fearing their child would be next. The main lake beaches were closed. Dr. Holt defied the skeptical medical community and persuaded Nurse Sister Kenny, fresh from working successfully with stricken children in Australia, to bring her methods to Minnesota. Following her recommendation, hot packs were duly applied to Sara's upper arms. The ravages of the disease were tamed, if not healed. Encumbered with a severely damaged lung and a fresh spinal fusion, Sara slimmed to eighty-three pounds. She eventually passed the danger point but was advised that she would remain too fragile for the rest of her days to have children. (Defying the odds, she eventually gave birth to three.)

Chapter Eight

❧ *Cross Fire* ❧

ꜰOR MY SIXTEENTH BIRTHDAY, Mother undertook what she knew best—throwing a party. I hadn't noticed any whispering or suspicious behavior at school, until one afternoon in the lavatory I heard a smattering of words—"up the hill" and "this Saturday"—that ceased abruptly as I exited the stall. A party for me—and the entire sophomore class invited!

I hated the idea. This would be sacrifice by fire. I would never emerge unburned. My entire being was geared to blending into the background, to not being noticed. Being the target of piercing eyes was terrifying. Now everyone would be at *my house*. How could I possibly act?

I never let on. I was resigned to pretending to be surprised, a role that would no doubt prove to be another failure. I didn't know which would be worse, actually being surprised, with all the emotional adjustment that required, or having to pretend to be surprised, calling for false responses and fake smiles.

When the big day arrived, I readied for a birthday dinner at Charlie's, dressed in a full black-and-white-checked skirt and white blouse with a Peter Pan collar, part of the new wardrobe Mother and I had purchased for the upcoming Northrop events, of which so far there had been none. Mother kept me busy in the back yard as the girls arrived, cars idling at the front of the house as they climbed the three flights of steep stairs leading to the front entrance. Finally I was called into the living room. The girls stood clustered in front of the windows, looking chic in their two-piece outfits, nylons, and heels. Luckily, my fake smile was accepted. A February fire crackled in the background, as Mother passed trays of punch and hors d'oeuvres and everyone admired the view of downtown from the picture window.

We filed down to the amusement room where the bar was spread with chicken salad sandwiches and potato chips. The girls sat sedately on the couch or at the bar, legs crossed. Mother was in her element, dressed in a soft ruffled blouse that peeped from her little blue jacket, chatting easily and winning the girls over with her Southern drawl and graciousness. After lunch Dad ran a Disney movie on his 8-mm projector. It was a silly thing about two boys lost on an island and a spotted cow they found abandoned in a cave. I had no idea how my classmates found this film, as they were all politeness, but I was certain it was too stupid for words. If Mother noticed my sour look, she said nothing. After the guests had left, I fled to my room. She had done another dumb thing. There was no accounting for her.

Mother couldn't understand my attitude. "Why are you always so *contrary?*" she would moan. I contradicted her at every opportunity, which drove her to heated silence. I'd walk into a room and see irritation sweep over her face, hear the frustration in her voice. "Your doctor's appointment was at 4:30. Where have you been, girl?"

More often, to avoid direct conflict, our skirmishes appeared in subtle disguise. No direct mention was made of her disapproval. Rather, she discharged double-edged remarks, offered a smiling compliment and then . . . zing . . . she'd finish off with a follow-up remark that cut to the quick. "Your hair looks nice. Your new hair-dresser does a good job," she would say. Then, after a few seconds, "It would, that is, if you got rid of those strings around your neck and wore a clean collar." I emerged from these skirmishes feeling deflated, a sharp knot in my stomach.

If she showed me directions on a map and I asked a question, she snapped a reply in an irritated tone. "*No, not U.S. 1. This one over here,*" running her finger along a black highway line.

"But this route looks shorter."

"*I told you*, that road is closed." The fire in her voice cut the air.

Just being together left us both feeling negative. I reacted unconsciously to her subtle jibes and *tsks tsks* of displeasure lobbed in my direction, slipped through the calm smiles and cheerfulness she turned to the world at large. She, in turn, no doubt reacted to my critical bluntness. I detested golf, which I considered namby-pamby, devoid of real exercise. Golf was just a highfalutin excuse to be outside with others of the same ilk and spend three hours pulling a long bag across manicured lawns dressed in yellow shorts and polo shirts. Skiing, tennis, now those were sports. I quit golf after two lessons at the Lafayette Club, vowing never to try again. Mother said I didn't seem to like anything new, which she thought was ironic, given that I didn't much care for what existed.

I was never without Chiclets or a stick of Black Jack. The habit of popping two sticks in my mouth and chomping vigorously rankled Mother continually. I perfected a loud, penetrating snap, of which I was rather proud, and could produce two or three in a row. For days, Mother said nothing, until her nerves were strained to the core and finally I heard a desperate "Pleeease!" At last she forbade me to chew gum except in my room, which I remembered some of the time.

Most of our interchanges went something like this:

"Judy, turn on the light. You can't see the book."

"I can see it just fine."

"Your hair needs a touch up."

"I just combed it."

"For heaven's sake, get into the elevator."

"For heaven's sake, it's full!"

I was decidedly not compliant and she was all nerves. We were like oil and water, doomed to co-exist and torture each other. She knew nothing of my private feelings, other than the negative ones I projected in abundance. In her house, feelings were kept under wraps, under the cloak of Pleasantness-At-All-Costs. The give-and-take skirmishes between children were anathema to her. And there was I, all contradiction, all skirmish. I, in turn, chaffed at her impenetrable pleasantness. While the outside world saw a charming, polished, Southern belle, I saw a creature who was superficial and shallow. There was no way out. We were incompatible and destined to inhabit the same house in mutual misery.

Mother was doomed to condemnation no matter what she did. I was convinced her efforts were disguised attempts to undermine whatever I did. She was out to get me. The truth is, I didn't know my mother at all. She was a caricature, a figure playing a role, shaped like a mother. Her reality was impenetrable. This cardboard cutout had to be handled like a formidable opponent.

I did this by proving I needed no one. Independence was my watchword, my banner, my ballast. I asked for nothing, except maybe a shooting star to spirit me away.

I rejected her world of light fun and momentary pleasure, her mellow southern speech, soft-edged demeanor, and sweet disposition, her musical and literary leanings. The truth is, I didn't see beyond her role, who she was.

❧ ◆ ❧

MOTHER AND MARGO also clashed. Margo backed Mother into corners. One Friday night during dinner, when we were seated around the breakfast room table, Mother started passing the meat loaf platter around. Dad helped himself, then handed it to Harold next to him. When it came to Margo, she lifted a large slice of meat loaf to her plate. She was lively as usual.

"This looks yummy, Mrs. Bradford."

"Have y'all been studying for your test Monday?" inquired Mother approvingly.

"Oh, yes," Margo replied, "Well, we got started anyway." Actually we had gotten no further than opening our books before getting into a discussion about Dr. Holt's attitude towards Negroes, which we were trying to evaluate. Monday was miles away.

Margo went on. "American history is not that hard. A lot of it is memorization. We have to learn the first ten presidents of the United

States, their dates of office, and major accomplishments. I already know that."

My brother looked up, skeptical. "Who was the third president of the United States?" he asked as he helped himself to the scalloped potatoes. "Mother, you know that. You're an American history buff."

Mother folded her napkin gently. "Well, yes, let me see." She looked out the window. "Well, first was Washington, then Adams, and then . . . let me think."

"Thomas Jefferson," supplied Margo. "It was Thomas Jefferson. Remember the feud between him and Adams?" Margo broke her roll in half. "And after him his son, John Quincy Adams, but there was someone in between—yes, it was James Madison."

With her sharp memory, Margo could pinpoint discrepancies and back up any fact with details. Mother said nothing more but I could see the muscle twitch in her jaw as she delicately punctured a slice of cucumber in her salad. Such intellectual contests were decidedly not to her taste, since she always seemed to be on the losing end.

Then there was the day Mother brought home a pair of inlaid bronze candelabras she discovered at a local antique store. Antique hunting was one of her hobbies, and she loved finding unusual pieces, especially English silver and relics from the American Civil War period. Nineteenth-century statues of Lady Hamilton and Lord Nelson sat on either side of the living room mantle, and brass fluted lanterns mounted on either side of our front door had once graced an English country house.

"I've never seen any bronze pieces like this. Aren't they lovely?" Mother commented.

"They're nice, Mom."

"Is this pure bronze, Mrs. Bradford?" Margo wanted to know, lifting a candelabrum to the light.

"Why, yes, it is."

"I can never tell if it's bronze or brass. How do those two differ?" Margo was always asking questions that Mother didn't know the answer to, at which Margo would dig out a reference book and look them up. Such digging was common practice at her house, but Mother was not impressed. Margo, however, was a stickler. Once when Mother didn't know the author of *Gone with the Wind*, Margo was incredulous. "You don't know who Margaret Mitchell is?"

Mother acquired a distinct dislike for Margo. She considered her a know-it-all. Little by little she found other things to disapprove of. "That girl doesn't know when to go home. She stays and stays. She doesn't take hints." Or if Margo phoned once too often, "That girl is so persistent. She never gives up. I told her you were not available until after dinner, but she calls back anyway. She's much too pushy."

Once, she and Margo clashed over bridge. In school we played the game at every turn: after lunch, during free periods, and while waiting for the bus. Margo was a natural. It so happened that bridge was one of Mother's passions. She took lessons, spent bridge weekends at friends' cabins, and played twice a week at the Lafayette Club, sometimes with Mrs. Holt among the players. On this occasion, Margo and I were watching a foursome seated at a card table in our living room. Mother won the bid and played out the hand, pulling in the tricks confidently. She went down one. The silence was broken as the women rehashed the play of the hands.

After the guests left, Mother walked into the den where Margo and I were playing gin rummy on the coffee table.

Margo looked up. "On that four spade bid, Mrs. Bradford. You could have opened clubs," she informed Mom innocently, "since you had all those points and no five-card suit." Mother stopped short.

"You don't bid a short club after another bid," she shot back. "I would have if Frances hadn't opened with a heart."

"But you could have bid two clubs to show a short suit," Margo went on.

"*Not* at the two level, that would show a club suit."

Mother had enough and disappeared into the kitchen to start dinner. Her coolness followed her through the swinging door, although Margo, slamming her cards down on the table with an exultant "Gin!" appeared oblivious.

❧♦❧

ALL WAS NOT CONFLICT. There were rare moments when Mother and I found ourselves pitted against the world. Mother, fresh from her afternoon nap, would settle on the couch and we'd munch popcorn from bright-colored bowls while watching *Your Hit Parade*. Mother loved perky Dorothy Collins bubbling up one of the seven top songs of the week, like "Harbor Lights" or "Shrimp Boat," and the fetching midget calling for *Phillip Morray!* She wiggled her toes when "Put Another Nickel In" came on, giggling, "Makes you want to kick up your heels." Behind Mother's observations, like a sentry guarding the Hall of No Errors, lurked a normalcy detector that was ever on the alert. We often found the personalities on the television screen wanting and pounced on every imperfection. Fat people were a particular target. Mother liked Jackie Gleason until he got fat.

"How can he let himself get that way?" she frowned. "Doesn't he have any self-respect?" When Arthur Godfrey sang, "I don't want her, you can have her, she's too fat for me," we laughed, along with everyone else. On one program the moderator with a pointed goatee and hairbrush eyebrows spoke with a cracked beer-barrel voice into the camera. "Honestly, this guy is terrible," she shook her head. "Who put him on the air?" She laughed over at me and I laughed back in agreement, feeling a warmth curl around my shoulders.

It wasn't just on television that we performed critical surgery. As we walked down a downtown sidewalk she spotted a man with a lumbering walk, wearing a beard shaped like a juniper bush and red suspenders.

"Look at that," she whispered, poking me with her elbow.

The worst offense was butchering the English language. Woe to the person who said, "It's me," instead of, "It's I." Once a waitress sauntered over and addressed us, "We don't have them rhubarb pies no more." Heavens above, a double negative! And the wrong pronoun! Worse, the waitress went on, "They're not so popular around here, doncha know. Anyways, the key lime is good."

As the girl walked off, Mother leaned over and whispered. "She was chewing *gum*, and did you see her dirty fingernails? What is the world coming to? I've lost my appetite." Although she went on to devour the pecan pie when it was set before her. "We're never coming back here."

At these times a coziness surrounded us. We were united in a mutual bond of superiority. I admired her sharpshooter skills and enjoyed our partnership and the hint of us against the world. It was a rare allegiance and I ate it up.

I developed critical skills of my own. I was able to pierce the normalcy of any scene and expose the fundamental faults veiled behind the surface. Flaws burst into light under my scrutiny, tiny as they may have been. I saw every uneven skirt, every crack in the cement. In this way I deflected much that came my way.

Decades later, after rounds of therapy, I made up my mind that these negative dissections were debilitating and had to go. One spring afternoon I visited the Aveda salon for my annual massage. Stretched out on the table, lulled by the scent of Jasmine and the purr of rippling piano notes, I was sinking into a libidinous submission when my mind began its familiar journey. *The room is a tad cold. I wish the masseuse would vary her strokes. The new age music is becoming monotonous. Why don't they soundproof the rooms?*

It struck me: here was my mother, speaking through me, and here was I, imbued with the very traits that had irritated me for so many years. By the end of the session I was as relaxed as an icicle, my mind having sabotaged the hour of anticipated bliss. And I couldn't even chastise myself on the way home, due to the vow I had just taken to mend my ways and forbear judging, even myself.

Chapter Nine

❧ Sailing for Boys ❧

*A*T THE BEGINNING of eleventh grade, a new girl named Bobby breezed in out of the blue from Chicago, a willowy brunette with windblown hair and an athletic, provocative stride, wearing deepred lipstick. Bobby moved into a house on the other side of Hennepin Avenue, a few blocks from me. Her mother had a painting studio in a sunroom at the top of the house and often answered the door in an oilstreaked smock. Brought up in the stifling hinterlands of Tennessee, Bobby's mother had escaped to New York City at the age of twenty-two and enrolled in art classes at a private studio in Brooklyn. There she met Bobby's father, a Brooklyn native who dabbled in art, philosophy, and economics before matriculating into the New School for Social Research degree program. Now a professor of Social Science at the graduate level, he and his artistic wife ran an intellectually liberal household. Bobby was something of a free spirit. Being new to the Northrop tradition didn't faze her in the least and she set about having the time of her life.

It wasn't long before Margo, Bobby, and I were spending weekends together, sharing family secrets and figuring out how to meet guys. Margo and I had already decided that to meet boys we would have to improvise. The lack of opportunities at an all-girl's school, for those who didn't attend the Blake dances and private parties, would have to be addressed. My older brother was no use, although he attracted a slew of girlfriends who were taken with this good-looking boy who retained a touch of Southern grace, with his red hair, slow manner, and gentle blue eyes, and who addressed our parents' friends as *ma'am* and *sir*. When he returned from an Alpha Tau Omega party or flew in with Don Levenius and several other boys in tow, my girlfriends, spying him pass, perked up. Who was *that*? My popularity was enhanced for a while, but Harold kept me and my companions at a distance, and the girlfriends went home empty handed.

Where to find boys? We had to use our ingenuity. One Saturday night Margo, Bobby, and I took off cruising in my mother's yellow Studebaker. We drove toward Lake Street through a throng of pedestrians completing their last-minute gift shopping. Christmas lights from the store windows reflected in the frosty car windows parked along the curbs, and the streetlamps glittered with garlands of green, yellow, and crimson. The marquee of the Uptown Theater flashed gold letters advertising *The Moon Is Blue* above the sidewalk.

"Oh, look," exclaimed Bobby, "there's the film starring Maggie McNamara everyone's talking about. It's caused a real scandal."

The reference to sex by the young heroine had nearly caused the film to be pulled from circulation. We decided we had to see it and impulsively pulled into the lot. In those days it wasn't necessary to see a movie from the beginning; we just walked in at our convenience and caught the beginning on the next round, which followed an interlude of newsreels and a short cartoon.

The film centered on the virtuous Maggie, who meets playboy architect William Holden on the top of the Empire State Building and accepts his invitation to join him for drinks and dinner in his apartment. There he pressures her to abandon her virginity, which Maggie successfully resists. The film violated the Motion Picture Association of America production code because it contained the words pregnant, virgin, and seduce. The idea of Maggie being soiled by using the word "virgin" and that the film was considered unsuitable because it dealt with a young girl's successful struggle for her purity seemed silly, but this mentality was common at the time and we didn't question it.

During the fifties, sex was not a big problem for girls. That is, we didn't have to worry when was the best time to give in and go all the way, whether we'd pay an emotional price, or how to pace the slow evolution to the inevitable. Sex was black and white, requiring no soul searching or advice. Intercourse was out of the question. Period.

Our formal sex education was skimpy. In ninth grade Mother left a few pamphlets on my bed. They contained diagrams charting the path of the egg down the fallopian tube and pictures of sperm: miniature particles capable of bursting out like atoms in search of a receptacle. When these two items met they sparked a fetus, from which babies grew. This happened when you were married. I'd seen the same diagrams at the Church of Youth at Hennepin Avenue Church, an automated film version that the boys and girls viewed in separate rooms. There was no discussion. Physical allusions were almost as taboo as the act itself. At Meadowbrook, Jean and I'd had to speculate how sex occurred by piecing together scrambled bits of information from older siblings of classmates. We got the general idea.

The limits were clear. Girls did not "go all the way." An absolute no-no, don't even think about it. Girls who transgressed were in the same category as single pregnant girls and the females in western brothels we saw in movies. A girl who did *IT* would see the news spread like wildfire. She would never be spoken of again in the same way. Other girls would be horrified and indignant, boys would titter and stare, and the bad girl would be bombarded with requests for dates and expected to "put out." She was then regarded as a lost woman.

Margo and I discussed this. Why was it the girl's job to maintain virginity and why did the boys feel it was okay to continually press them to renounce this responsibility? The only recourse was for the fallen girl to get married. Of course the boy was honor bound to marry her despite lack of any compatibility, and most did, begrudgingly, make the sacrifice. To save *her*.

After the movie we plotted our next move. I turned the Studebaker towards Lake Calhoun. High drifts of snow ran down to the shore and far off down the lake we saw the ice-colored dots skating around under a circle of strobe lights, like marbles swirling on a plate of glass. A mammoth spruce by the water's edge glittered with colored Christmas lights.

"Look!" Bobby pressed her nose to the car window. "Look over there!" We watched three figures emerge from behind a clump of oak trees, silhouetted in the shadow of drooping branches. As the figures crossed the sidewalk and entered the yellow circle of the street light, three boys came into focus. One boy was taller than the others. They were all wearing parkas with dangling hoods and had skates laced together hung over their shoulders. Walking easily in step they laughed and elbowed each other. The tall one with the athletic stride slid into the driver's seat of a black Chevrolet, the others piling in after him.

Here was a challenge that couldn't be passed up. As they drove off, I inched the Studebaker up behind them and managed to squeeze illegally through several lights to hold their tail. There was no sign that they had spotted us. Suddenly, before I knew it, their black car jerked into a filling station, curved past the gas pumps, careened out the other entrance and pulled up behind us. The sneaks! I coasted the Studebaker slowly down Hennepin, stopping at the next red light. The boys behind us were laughing and looking at us, sizing us up. We did the same.

Time for some crafty action.

Encouraged by Margo and Bobby, I continued slowly, made a quick turn onto Groveland Avenue and immediately pressed the accelerator, swerving into the Hennepin Church parking lot. Hidden behind a row of bushes we saw the black car slip by, and I hurriedly maneuvered behind them, leaving a car in between us. After a few blocks the black Chevy swept into a flagstone drive, passed under a porte cochère, and came to a stop next to a mammoth beige stone building.

"Turn, turn!" my pals cried. I twisted the wheel, and as the boys were opening their car doors we pulled up behind them.

We were parked between two three-story stone buildings set next to each other on a corner lot. The main building, large with heavy stone walls of pastel brown, was a mansion in the Italian Renaissance style. The boys had seen us and were standing on the steps grinning, unmindful of the light blotches of snow beginning to coil down on their heads like flakes from a pinwheel. Finally, they walked over to our car and stood tentatively, steam puffing from their mouths. Who were they and what were they doing in this stone bastion?

Bobby rolled down the front window. "Why are you stopping here?" she asked.

They boys stepped closer. "We live here."

"No kidding?"

"Where are you girls from?"

Bobby tilted her head to look up at them. "We live nearby, in Kenwood." She wasn't prepared to explain further. "We've been to the movies and had nothing to do."

"You might as well get out of the car," one of the boys said finally, "Unless you want us to stand out here in the snow. Come on, we'll show you around."

We followed them through a narrow side entrance and down several cavernous corridors lit by dim yellow wall lights. After climbing single file up a twisting staircase we found ourselves in a low-ceilinged apartment spread with Southwestern rugs and plump sink-in furniture.

"We've never had girls follow us home before," said the tall, handsome one named Bill, who walked with a svelte, nonchalant stride á la James Stewart . "We like being chased."

"You don't look very chaste to me," said Bobby.

"Ha, ha. You girls are tricky. We'll have to watch out." Once seated, we learned that Bill lived with his father, the building superintendent, in the bowels of the stone building they were in. Owned by the Minister's Life & Casualty Union, it was at one time a private mansion and carriage house. His best pal, Jim, seated himself on a low couch and spread his arms comfortably. With his stocky build, thick blond hair, and warm grin, Jim came across as everyone's favorite brother. The third boy, Riley, who spoke with a likeable intensity, was already attending the university. The boys told us they were long-time friends from the local DeMolay chapter.

"You know about DeMolay?" Jim asked.

Not about to admit I'd never heard of it, I extended my legs and leaned back. "Sure. It's a syrup used on barley pancakes in the Southern outback."

"It's a Masonic fraternal organization created to mentor troubled boys from the ages of twelve to twenty-one," the one named Riley explained, throwing an earnest look at me.

"I knew that. My answer's more interesting." *What's a white lie between strangers?* I thought, enjoying the turn of events.

Soon we were sitting with our feet up telling them all about ourselves. Maybe it was the other-world remoteness of the cavernous apartment hidden away in the depths of the building that put us at ease. Here in the reality of their home there was no choice but to speak the truth. We explained that we were fringe Northrop-ites who sang our own tune and operated outside the school structure. Bill, the tall, attractive one with a slow smile and blue eyes, didn't say much but threw droll comments into Jim's anecdotes, setting us all laughing. Riley talked about the competitive downhill ski program he belonged to.

Bobby sat cross-legged on a desk, head tilted, her quick laugh ringing as she and Bill eyed each other across the room. Bobby drew boys like sweet honey. Everywhere she went boys materialized, and she finagled endless ways to meet them. Now she zeroed in on Bill.

From that night on we saw the boys constantly, attending movies, football games, and backyard picnics, sometimes in the company of their West High friends. Bobby and Bill soon became an item, while Margo had fallen for Riley. At one of my basement parties, Jim met and was pursuing one of our Northrop classmates.

As for me, I met Dick.

THE PARKING AREA behind the stone gates in our driveway was packed with cars, and in our amusement room the party was in full swing. People squeezed into the kitchenette where the fridge was stocked with Miller Highlight, Coke, and Seven-Up. Bobby and Bill scrunched side by side on the couch, while a Northrop classmate, Caroline Hessen, reclined in a rocker with Jim leaning over her shoulder, talking into her ear. The pop and jangle of the slot machine mingled with the hum of voices and footsteps tapping down the stairs.

Margo at the bar, beer in hand, leaned towards Riley seated on the stool next to her. A university student, Riley was valued as one of the "older" boys. He followed Margo's words with an intent expression. Thin and sporty, cute, in a dark raffish sort of way, he was full of energy, with a passion for racing down ski slopes. Margo was not put off by his conservative, rather serious manner. She was entering into the whirling drama of first love and savoring every minute.

Margo began telling stories. How I complained that I'd been sideswiped by a streetcar a week after obtaining my drivers' license, which for some reason everyone found hilarious. How during school field trips to the symphony at Northrop Auditorium we snuck to the lavatory to smoke, strictly forbidden. How she had lugged her butterfly net up the wooded hill behind the Northrop grounds to collect butterflies for a school project in order to sneak a smoke. It was an assignment she detested, but she managed to collect, between cigarettes, a record number of butterflies. Subsequently, her butterfly display won a best-in-class award. This the group also found hilarious.

After practice for the school operetta, some of us snuck out to the same back hill for smoking orgies. But we didn't fool Miss Ingalls, the music teacher. When we returned from a break during *The Bartered Bride*, she remarked, "That's not Chanel No. 5 I smell." We started carrying vials of perfume in our uniform pockets.

It was time for a game of sardines. The lights were extinguished, except for a yellow streak that filtered through the window from the front entrance lamps. We hurried off to snoop out a hiding place. The girl who was It began to count.

I headed for the furnace room behind the bar, but heard whispers of "we're filled up," so I veered off past the half-bath, past the laundry tubs to the tool room on the other side of the back stair landing. Using my hands I felt my way towards the crawl hole hidden in the far corner, barely distinguishable in the shadows, nothing but useless space—until now. Only I knew its location; I would never be found here. The voice from the far room was chanting—*ninety-eight, ninety-nine, a hundred.* Better hurry.

Kneeling down I squeezed into the low space and crawled along the crumbly concrete toward the corner in total darkness.

My hand hit on something soft, alive. A foot? I inched forward until I was startled by a voice that was inches away. "Hello." A few seconds later the voice sounded again. "They'll never find us way back here."

I touched something warm with my knee. I considered the clues. Some strand in the whisper told me this was male. But which individual one I couldn't fathom.

Another whisper: "There's room here." Quickly I shifted towards the unknown body. Each person who was found joined the hunt, forming a more and more powerful body of offense. The two of us needed to stick together.

"Ouch!" A sharp piece of concrete jammed my thigh. I felt a searching hand against my arm.

"What happened?" came a thin whisper.

"It's okay," I whispered back. As I sank back against the wall, I felt the press of a shoulder and was aware of soft breathing a few inches from my face. "Sorry," I murmured lamely and then giggled. Some strange person was tilted against my side, and I felt a faint beating in his arm. This was cozy. *But who was it?* The only hints were the faint odor of musk and the feel of a corduroy jacket.

The voices grew louder as the searchers closed in. We could hear laughing as they groped in the dark, snatches of words, getting near, moving away. With each person discovered there were squeals and whispering. Then ominous quiet. I turned towards where my companion's face must have been, keeping my whisper low. "I'm afraid to move." Frozen, I listened to the voices moving closer. I felt the presence next to me like a warm mist.

He spoke softly against my cheek. "Do you know who I am?"

"I don't suppose you're somebody's boyfriend or you wouldn't be this close to me," I breathed, lowering my head. "I'll give you a clue about me . . . I'm not anyone's girlfriend." My arm received a squeeze and I heard a murmur as if he were about to speak. Suddenly the door squeaked open and a flicker of light shot through the opening, falling several inches into the hole. We froze.

"They must be in here," a familiar voice insisted. "There's nowhere else." I could sense someone crawling in, feeling their way along the wall. My companion and I squeezed closer, shrinking into the corner. "You're the only two left. Come out, come out." We felt the breeze of a hand sweep by—and disappear. The figure backed out and declared the space empty. The door then shut and the voices disappeared.

Slowly we crawled out. We had won!

It wasn't until we stepped into the laundry room under the glaring light that I saw my companion looking at me, sweeping grit from his sleeve and grinning. I recalled vaguely that he had arrived with Bill. We stood and blinked at each other..

"Ah . . ." I said.

He took up the slack. "I'm Dick Winston, a friend of Bill's. I saw you at the picnic Friday." Dick had a wide smile, square shoulders, and full, neatly combed blonde hair. His gray-blue eyes looked at me reassuringly. I didn't see how I could have missed him.

"I live four houses away from you, just up the hill," he said.

What? How could I not know who he was? "I live here," I replied idiotically.

He laughed. "I know that," he said. "That's one reason I came."

"There they are!" At that moment several partiers burst from the next room. "Where have you been?" they cried, "And what have you been up to? I can tell by your faces it was something!" The group pulled us into the other room, with admonitions that they were going to keep an eye on us. As for Dick, I was already keeping an eye on him myself.

Dick Winston began asking me out. On one date we attended a meeting of DeMolay, where his father was one of the officers. Dick stood at the podium and gave the presentation while I sat in the front row thinking he looked fetching in his dark slacks, white shirt, and tie.

This was the first time I had actually dated someone, and I thrived on the distinction of being a part of a couple. I guess you might say Dick was my boyfriend, as I saw him every weekend. Slightly taller than I was, with an air of sturdy reliability, Dick was on the quiet side, as I was, but it didn't matter for we were continually with other couples.

We enjoyed the soft summer evenings just beyond the blare of the campfire, sitting on a blanket eating hot dogs singing camp songs, and watching the smoke spiraling up into the darkening pearl sky. Finally, at the hour when conversation ceased, we ended up in each other's arms and that was enough.

I adored necking. As we sat watching a bonfire in the park or swaying to mood music in a party room, I grew excited at the thought that I would shortly be in the arms of the boy I was sitting next to, and every look into his face brought the moment nearer. Clinging together in the back seat of a car without having to worry about talking, enclosed in an intimacy where nothing else mattered, I enjoyed surrendering fully to the moment.

When I wasn't dating Dick I was a lake junkie. Margo would call me after breakfast. What was I doing? Why didn't I come on out? I'd throw some clothes into a bag and drive the thirty miles in Mother's Studebaker and out Highway 12 past Wayzata to Navarre. The white clapboard cottage, set on a slope overlooking Lake Minnetonka, had been expanded over the years with several additions, including three screened porches and a kitchen with its own side porch. It had arched ceilings, dark oak furnishings with wooden knobs, and boasted six bedrooms. Behind the main house a separate garage had been converted to a small guest cottage. A small two-room shack at the edge of the woods housed Elmer, the gardener. The house was reached by a long driveway lined with tall willow trees that wound past the remains of a clay tennis court.

Mrs. Holt and the children spent summers at the lake. Dr. Holt joined them on weekends. Now I was added to the list. I was practically a live-in. I'd stay a day or two, return home in proper order, and was back almost immediately. I raced up the stairs to the bedrooms gleefully, with the lake air swishing after me and the enticing warbles of a motor boat droning in the distance.

The warm, fuzzy days of lake breezes and gratuitous pastimes blended into weeks and months. Mornings, Margo and I lolled in twin beds under the eaves and read until Mrs. Holt called us to a lunch of sandwiches, Oreo cookies, and milk. At dinner time, I crowded around the dining room table with the rest of the family. Potatoes, green beans, and braised pork were passed while we discussed the new art center opening down the road, what the youngsters had been up to, the novel Sara was reading, and the local restrictions on motor boating at night.

Afterward, Margo cleared while I washed. She spent so much time in the dining room collecting plates that I had finished drying and putting the dishes away by the time she brought in the last bowl.

"What on earth were you doing out there?" I asked, but she didn't answer. Her mother praised my manners and competence. At my own house I would be playing Margo's role, I thought. Mrs. Holt's approving presence by my side, scraping leftovers into refrigerator containers as we chatted, kept me at the sink every night until the last lick of butter had been wiped from the white porcelain sink. I *liked* doing dishes in this house.

One night, Margo and I had crawled into twin beds upstairs and were sunk deep into our mystery stories. The musty scent from the lake and the muffled noises stirring in the house below lulled me into a soft reverie. I could hear Mrs. Holt puttering below in the kitchen, no doubt fetching fruit from the refrigerator to fill the bronze wicker fruit bowl on the kitchen table and stuffing freshly laundered tea towels into the drawer. Her voice, talking to someone in the next room, sent muted vibrations through the house. Once she called up to see if we wanted ice cream. A feeling of devotion swept through me. Even with all her children, Mrs. Holt had room for me in her affections. I would have done anything for her.

Sara lay in her room across the hall reading Mary Roberts Rinehart.

I heard fluttering near the ceiling over my bed.

"What is that?"

"Just bats. They're my buddies." And Margo went back to her book. I didn't say another word. I watched the bat, with its flighty webbed wings and mouse body, dart across the ceiling and disappear in a crack in the eave above me.

"I hope I don't get pooped on," I finally ventured, distracted from my book.

"It's never happened." Margo was lost in her reading. Evidently she had given up trying to drive off the bats. I decided to follow her lead. I sank into my pillow and turned the page in front of me. *You don't bother me, I don't bother you.* That would work.

Now that my parents were members of the Lafayette Club, Margo and I became regulars. We could spot the club across the lake. All we had to do was hop in the Chris-Craft, and after skimming for five minutes across the bay, we'd clamor onto the sandy beach and stretch out with novels and bronzing oil.

The lifeguard arrived regularly to take up his post, a routine we caught on to at once. His name was Craig. We pummeled him with questions, shared our fresh peaches, and set about to discover his life story and, ever so discreetly, if he was taken (he wasn't). When Craig's buddy, Hayes, showed up, our visits to the beach increased. We took up swimming and practiced the side-stroke and crawl assiduously.

One afternoon, after lunching at the lower-level snack bar on club sandwiches, potato chips, and Cokes, which we charged to our mothers' accounts, we wandered out to the beach and approached Craig, the club swimming instructor. Our strokes, we informed him, needed work, they were sloppy. He taught us the proper way to do the back stroke, the side stroke, the breast stroke, and the crawl, all of which we already knew.

When Craig informed Margo he had no more to teach her, she took up diving. I watched them standing at the end of the floating dock as she flew off and landed in the water flat on her face. Somehow, in the few seconds between the diving board and the water surface, Margo's perfectly formed dive, sculpted by Craig, fell apart. She improved, and before the summer was over Margo could perform a neat jack knife and we had invited the boys to go water skiing.

≈◆≪

DAD BUSIED HIMSELF with our lake activities. It was important to him that we enjoy ourselves. He loved providing activities for us that had been missing from his youth. He bought a twenty-two foot, second-hand Chris-Craft and docked it at the marina at Brown's Bay. It had a walnut hull, a paneled dashboard, and two front cockpit seats. Leather bench seats ran along both sides, and a white striped canopy cover was stored in a hull pocket. The boat looked like a poor relation lined up in its slip among the tall, gleaming two-deck yachts, but we liked the freedom of its old shoe look. It was the perfect party boat, and we immediately set about putting it into service.

Dad took her out on several trial runs. I think he could have spent hours tooling from bay to bay, for the boat proved to be surprisingly agile. With Margo and me in the back, Dad grasped the wheel and drove full speed over the water, his face blown clean by the wind. He looked relaxed as he turned a curve, swirling up a spray as the boat lurched ahead. I believe he would have liked to turn into a teenager and partake in our aimless forays over the lake, if he could have stepped out of the heavy restrictions of being an adult, at least temporarily.

≈◆≪

TO CROWN AFTERNOONS of swimming, water skiing and exploring the azure bays of Lake Minnetonka, Margo and I hosted evening parties at the Holt boat house. Blocked by a line of willow trees from the main house, the boat house was an ideal teenage hideaway where Margo and I could sink into long rambles about our lives or hold beer parties. Isolated at the end of a promontory that jutted arrow-like into the lake, the small, one-room boat house was surrounded on three sides by water. An outside stairway led to a flat roof deck with a white wooden railing.

≈ 146 ≪

One hot summer evening, Dick, Riley, Margo, and I drove to the nearby Navarre drive-in, where we gorged on burgers, French fries, and malts from a tray fastened to the car window. After a drive to Excelsior to pick up a few six-packs, we strolled the marina docks as the sailboats were dropping their riggings, then headed to the cottage for a moonlight swim.

We found Bobby and Bill waiting on the porch steps. Their flushed faces held a muted excitement. Those two were always up to something. They joined us as we headed for the boat house to change into our suits, stepping over shadowy patterns formed on the grass by tall willow branches. The water looked tame and sleepy, still warm from the afternoon sun, and the air held the scent of freshly mowed grass. Before long the stillness of the evening was invaded by our cries of anticipation and the wild sounds of splashing in shallow water as we roused the lake from its nighttime slumber.

The sound of a motor chugging softly along the far shore reached across the water, then drifted off, swallowed by the dark. Margo and Riley swam out into the darkness. Dick and I could see the bare outline of their heads gliding along the dark surface. Bill and Bobby were nowhere to be seen. I was used to their clandestine disappearances. They were, Margo hinted, in love. Bobby herself was not forthcoming, and I imagined that in their enamored state, they needed only each other. I was still contending with the niceties of dating and clung to the prevailing moral code.

After changing into shorts, we settled in the boathouse. Peggy Armstrong, a classmate, and her date, Les, soon came tromping up the grassy path, two six-packs under their arms. We stretched out on an air tube that extended over the entire floor, clutching cold cans of beer. Candlelight flickered from the corners and an errant breeze wafted in through the screen door, caressed our bare limbs, and passed out an open window.

"This is a neat place," remarked Les, leaning against the tubing next to Peggy. "You don't need electricity."

"You don't need civilized amenities to have fun," said Peggy. She laughed in her bell-like soprano voice.

Bobby, lying on her back with her head in Bill's lap and her legs angling up the wall, was investigating ways of getting beer out of the can and into her mouth. "I can't drink," she complained.

"Maybe you could quit for five minutes," chimed in Peggy, her long legs crossed and coddling a can of beer against her blouse, "but no more than ten." She tilted her head up to Les and gave one of her breezy laughs.

"You girls are underage," declared Les. He sank his good-looking, Scandinavian head back against the cushion. "Only Riley and I can drink legally."

Margo was indignant. "It's ridiculous to ban seventeen-year-olds from drinking beer. What's the harm in beer? Everyone we know consumes beer. How else can you have a party?" We all agreed, taking deep swigs from our cans. "If you ban drinking and smoking, kids will find a way. When will adults learn?"

"The adult world," I said, lighting a cigarette, "doesn't know anything about anything. The main goal of adults is to keep us reined in and obedient, doing what they program us to do." I spoke with some force.

"Parents can be a pain in the butt," agreed Margo.

"Oh, I don't know," said Riley, seated next to her under the window. He regarded her face in the dim light. "I've only got my mother, but I'm close to her. She's always been there for me and my brother. I trust her. Aren't any of you close to your parents?" Several no's drifted up from the air pillows.

"Parents have no clue," I said, tapping the ash from my cigarette into a tin can ashtray "They fuss over you, but everything they do is on their terms—it's their way or the highway."

Dick couldn't contain himself. He drew up his knees and leaned forward. "Parents devote themselves to making our lives successful. They provide opportunities and set the stage for us to follow their footsteps. Everything they do is for us. My parents are strict, but for my own good. They're always there, pointing me in the right direction. I think I'm pretty lucky."

Dick turned to look at me as he finished. He sounded sure of himself, although his tone was gentle. It struck me that he was from a different mold, inhabited a different zone than I, which didn't prevent me from secretly wanting him to move closer and put his arms around me.

"They support us—that is, the fathers do," Margo put in, "while the mothers keep busy enjoying themselves."

Riley's voice was firm. "Parents aren't perfect. I don't have both of mine. I'd be happy with two imperfect ones. Come on. You're fortunate."

"I'll say one really good thing about parents," exclaimed Peggy with enthusiasm, "they aren't here now." She let out a jingling laugh and looked up at Les, who turned his blond head to her and smiled.

"Well, that's enough of that," Margo commented as she slipped a Zippo from her pocket and lit up a cigarette.

Someone brought out fresh cans of Bud and fizzing noises circled as Bill punctured them with a church key. Then the songs began. "Put Your Arms Around Me Honey," "Beautiful Brown Eyes," and "Mocking Bird Hill." Dick taught us one he'd learned in DeMolay.

Young folks, old folks, everybody come
Join the darkies' Sunday school and have a lot of fun.
There's a place to check your chewing gum and razors at the door
And you'll hear some Bible stories that you never heard before.

Danny was a brave man, he sassed the king
The king said he wouldn't stand for any such a thing,
So he chucked him down a man hole with lions underneath,
But Danny was a dentist and he pulled the lion's teeth.

The verses were endless. We sang out, oblivious of the racial inferences. To us, it was just a silly song. Dick and I leaned on matching pillows listening to his baritone blending with my alto. One song triggered another. The favorite, known by every partier and repeated at every party, went like this:

Roll me over, in the clover, roll me over, lay me down and do it again.
Oh this is number one and the story's just begun,
Roll me over, lay me down and do it again.
Roll me over, in the clover, roll me over lay me down and do it again.
Oh, this is number two, and he's got up to my shoe," etc.

New verses were easily made up if someone was in the mood. *Oh this is number twenty and we all know you've had plenty.* We loved the raunchiness. The aim was to express as much daring as possible. This was followed by *Sipp'n Cider*:

> *The cutest girl, I ever saw*
> *Was sipp'n cider, through a straw,*
> *The cutest girl I ever Saaaaaaaaw,*
> *Was sipp'n cider through a straw.*
> *And not and then the straw would slip*
> *And I'd sip cider through her lip.*

Finally, when the candles had burned to molten stubs on the window sills and the smell of cherry wax and stale tobacco hovered in the air, we pulled ourselves up, gathered suits and towels, and headed for the house.

Dick and I stood on the bathhouse stoop. I looked at him.

"I'll walk you to your car," I offered.

"I think you should do that," he smiled, and taking my hand, led me towards the green Packard parked behind a cluster of bushes. The darkened yard reverberated with the chirping of crickets, and the lake slapped soft laps on the shore as we made our way along the point. Above us the outline of treetops stretched along the sky, backlit by the luminous blinking of stars. Walking beside Dick, anticipating a lingering good-bye, I felt light and airy and deliciously in tune with the summer darkness. We didn't say much as we climbed into the back seat of the car and Dick scooted along the upholstery after me, cornered me on my side and held me close.

I was thrilled to be dating a good-looking guy like Dick. I relished being a couple and the rewards of fitting into the social niche of the fun-lovers. On the one hand I could hardly believe my luck; on the other, my feelings towards Dick were ambiguous. There wasn't much to hang on to. Our conversations were strictly group oriented and I hadn't a clue how to approach him on a personal level. We knew nothing about each other. I had no idea what his feelings were towards me, or if he even had any. Best to have no expectations and to hold back. I assumed a blasé stance and coasted. Dick kept asking me out.

❧◆❧

IT WAS 2:00 A.M. when Margo, Peggy, and I entered the back porch. Bobby and Bill had disappeared. Mrs. Holt lay stretched on a chaise lounge watching an old movie on TV.

"We came in to say good-night," Margo told her.

"Oh, hello girls." Eyes brightening, Mrs. Holt turned her head, straightened the afghan over her lap, and reached for the highball glass at her side. "How was the lake? Refreshing?"

"You bet. The water was heavenly," Margo said. "What're you watching?"

"*The Bells of St. Mary's.* I do love Bing Crosby. I suppose its bed time."

"Yes, and I best get going," said Peggy. "Les has the car running. I just came in to say good night and thank you for having me." Like Margo and me, she looked a bit scroungy, but Mrs. Holt didn't seem to notice.

"You're welcome, dear. Come again." Mrs. Holt took another swallow of her drink. These night caps, as she called them, helped her sleep.

"Do sit down girls. Isn't Bobby coming in?" Margo, Peggy, and I exchanged glances. How were we to explain her absence? To have left without thanking Mrs. Holt would have been rude. To have vanished into the dark recesses of the grounds with a boy even worse.

"Uh, she and Bill had to go—I guess she had to get home," Margo mumbled lamely. We knew there was no excuse not to stop in and take her leave. Mrs. Holt only smiled and turned back to the TV.

"This is a good movie. Do you want to see the rest?" she offered. The TV screen flashed Bing Crosby standing in a white collar, upright and demure at an open window, looking out over a courtyard of student boys. "There'll be a new film on soon. I'm too tired to get up and go to bed," she chuckled. "Did the boat work all right? Tom was having trouble with it this morning. Maybe you should drive it over to Sinclair Marine tomorrow and have the engine checked. I think I'll have a top-off before bed. I'll sleep better." Mrs. Holt drew herself off the chaise with a burst of will and went over to a corner chest, where she replenished her glass with Bourbon and soda.

"No thanks, we're off to bed."

Just then the porch door flew open and Bobby and Bill breezed in, crumpled and out of breath, wearing limp smiles. "So sorry—we got lost. Bobby flashed a wide grin and moved forward a step. "Thank you so much Mrs. Holt for having us. I do love it out here."

"Of course, Bobby, any time."

"I'm very late—can't stay—great time. Goodbye." And she and Bill were gone.

Mrs. Holt peered into the misty liquid in her glass. "Such a polite girl," she said. "Always remembers."

As we left, I turned on impulse and looked at Mrs. Holt. All I saw was the gray back of her head that protruded above the chaise cushion and her soft chunky arms along the rests. Black-and-white images flickered on the television set across the room. Darkness pressed against the porch screens on all sides, boxing her into a space so small I wondered if she would ever be able to escape. I'd seen her sitting like that often, a lonely shadow in the circle of the TV light, and for some reason I didn't want to leave.

Settled a few minutes later in bed, Margo and I were still too invigorated to feel tired. We started a pressing conversation about the evening, especially the two boys with whom we had spent it, but before we got to the good part we fell asleep.

❧ ◆ ❧

LATER THAT SUMMER, Dick kissed me good-bye and went off to DeMolay camp for two weeks, leaving me his address and promising to write. To my surprise, I immediately received four letters, a new one every day. Chatty letters about canoe trips and cookouts that I read attentively, searching for clues to his feelings. I was being inundated with letters, but what did it mean? I calculated a decent interval and wrote him back in the same nonchalant tone as his, but it proved to be too late.

I never heard from him again.

I mulled this over. What had happened? What had I said in my letter or not said? I could not bombard him daily. On the contrary, I was careful not to be pushy or appear anxious. I was getting good at the art of distancing myself and maintaining an aloof air that kept me from unwise expectations. It prevented people from cringing at my eagerness, a skill that would serve me often in the future.

No more letters, no phone calls. No more envious glances from other girls. My mind reeled with possibilities: he was busy with scouting, his octopus family drained all his time, he had met another girl. As I gazed out the window of my bedroom at the dome of the Basilica, the rain eased its incessant patter and in the silence a note of truth sounded. It was me—plain, unappealing and boring. The idea burned a bitter taste in my mouth. Was this what I thought of myself? There were so many messages from different quarters, how to sort them out? Could I accept being mediocre and ignored?

I set about swallowing the loss. I was not going to let it bother me. But it was a spike in my self-esteem, a reminder of how much there was to lose if I ventured into a relationship with a male, where no true feelings were revealed and nothing was secure.

Chapter Ten

❧ Prancing with the Seniors ❧

S ENIOR YEAR PRESENTED a wealth of opportunities. In our small class of twenty-eight, every student was needed to fill a leadership slot or participate on a committee. My election as president of the drama club was aided by the fact that I was one of only two girls in the class remaining without an office. Miss Ingalls, the drama coach and music teacher, assigned me the job of keeping order during after-school rehearsals of *Sense and Sensibility*. I spent most of the time shushing people and telling them where to go, for which I received little appreciation. It was my first experience with official responsibility, very different from my usual passive role. I then joined the Athletics Committee. It took a while to overcome a tendency to daydream, but eventually reality sank in and I dutifully evaluated and recorded the proposal of the committee for the renovation of the school gym.

Often I stayed after school, caught up in meetings and practices, singing under Dr. Winslow in the Glee Club and pounding out the close barbershop harmonies of "How High the Moon," and "On the Sunny Side of the Street" with three classmates on the music room piano.

Special senior events included floor modeling at Dayton's where we strutted through the aisles in cocktail dresses and pumps; tea-leaf reading at the Tea House on Nicollet Avenue; and lunches at Dayton's Sky room and at Young Quinlan's Fountain Room. A canasta party Mother arranged was covered in the society section of the *Tribune* under the caption: JUDY BRADFORD ENTERTAINS CLASSMATES. Next to the

Northrop class of 1952 in senior room. I am in the first row, third from the right.

article ran a photo of Margo, Peggy Armstrong, Caroline Hessen, and me seated around a card table at the Minneapolis Woman's Club, spiffily dressed in wool tweed suits and pearls.

❧♦❧

MY FAVORITE TEACHER was Miss Bennett. Miss Bennett lectured our English class with a clipped British accent and orally drilled us on the works of Chaucer, Milton, Shakespeare, and Dickens. She was a tall, matronly woman with thick white hair tucked in a loose bun on the back of her neck, from which a thin strand sometimes strayed. Her white hose and thick-heeled black shoes contrasted with a crimson wool Jamawar shawl draped around her shoulders. Sometimes she showed up at school on a black bike and chained it against a tree in the back lot. The sight of Miss Bennett peddling along Kenwood Parkway, bent over her bike, was the source of curiosity and her strange manners were repeated in whispers as girls clustered by the lockers. I had to admit she was not like the rest of us, that she added a peculiar individuality to the school halls.

Miss Bennett soon won me over. Her classes were provocative. After a class discussion of *Hamlet*, during which I fiercely disagreed with every interpretation offered, I turned in a written analysis of the play, backing up my ideas, and was rewarded with an A-minus. This scrap of encouragement was all I needed. Sometimes I accompanied her to the teachers' lounge pelting her with questions.

One day Miss Bennett, aware of my sporadic writing attempts at home, suggested I submit a short story to the school literary contest. I hastily completed a draft and send it in and to my shock was awarded second place. When I opened up the *Tatler* yearbook and saw my name and story in print, I let out a whoop and flew down to Miss Bennett's desk. I couldn't believe it! Mrs. Bennett smiled her twisted smile, clapped her hands, and handed me the sprig of violets sitting in a blue Dalton cup on her desk.

In August, we piled in cars to spend the weekend at Mr. Reed's north woods cabin where we hiked, swam, water skied, sang around the barbeque pit, and played charades in front of a two-story stone fireplace. Afterwards, rolled up in sleeping bags, we whispered secrets in the dark, stories of Miss Nelson and Miss Silverson and how they had been seen by a student *kissing* in their car and other scandalous tales that shocked us down to our toes.

The senior slumber party was held at Cindy Appleton's Minnetonka Lake home. After patrolling the bays along the Navarre shoreline in the Appleton's pontoon boat under a golden sun, we played a game of croquet on the lawn and then lay and watched Mr. Appleton grill steaks in his blue-and-white checked chef's apron. Later, stomachs full, we divided into teams for a game of Mind-buster. A riddle was read off dilemma cards and the team that was up had to figure out the answer, a mind-twisting game that kept us up far into the night until we finally fell asleep on top of our nylon sleeping bags.

During senior year my class standing improved. Somehow I moved closer to the body of the class and became integrated, to some extent, into its ranks. Now that my class had moved to the top in our turn as rulers of the upstairs halls, everyone was more relaxed. New girls had joined the class and there was a burgeoning spirit of tolerance. It didn't hurt that I was dating Dick Winston, a feather in my cap, and had won a short story prize. Maybe the girls were getting used to me. Maybe some of the rough edges had been smoothed over as I learned the ropes. Some of the girls walked up the back hill and hung out at my house after school while waiting to be picked up by a parent, and we helped ourselves to chocolate-frosted cookies from the red-and-yellow clown cookie jar in the kitchen. I was invited to one of the Saturday overnights at Caroline Hessen's house.

I began to feel like a Northrop girl.

I enjoyed a stint as the class humorist. It was a big mistake. The class of 1952, as a senior privilege, had possession of the Senior Room facing Kenwood Parkway, with its second-story windows looking out over the Parade Grounds and the Dunwoody Institute beyond. It was Friday afternoon and girls were sprawled on low chairs reviewing weekend plans and applying lipstick in front of their locker mirrors. Margo, wearing her plaid senior jacket, was playing bridge on the rug in front of the windows. Behind her the wall next to the window was pasted with beer bottle labels collected from parties over the year, a class project we'd all been contributing to. I wandered in, and as I rifled through my locker I heard a question thrown out in a loud voice.

"Okay, answer this one. What is the purpose of the belly button?"

"To separate the upper half from the lower?" came one weak idea. I heard mumbling and a few quips but no more guesses.

What a coincidence! I had recently run across this very riddle in a magazine and remembered it clearly. There was a long pause as everyone thought for an answer. Finally, in the lull, I spoke up.

"It's for holding salt while you're eating carrots in bed."

The room exploded in laughter. From then on I could do no wrong. My response was passed around the school, increasing in weight.

I was willing to take on the role of class wit and never revealed that my brief stardom was undeserved. I liked the title of humorist and vowed to take my secret to the grave.

∾◆∾

NO WAY WAS I GOING to attend the senior prom. I didn't know anyone to ask. One afternoon, as we changed out of our gym clothes in the locker room, Peggy and Caroline informed me that a certain Blake boy had not been invited, and they knew for a fact he wanted to go. "Why don't you ask him?" Absolutely not! I'd never heard of Larry Stockard and didn't know how I could just call him out of the blue. Girls didn't phone boys—girls waited to be approached. At an all-girl's school, however, it was different; girls were required to seek out dates for Northrop-sponsored functions. I said I'd give it some thought. The dance was two weeks away, not much time to ponder.

The following Saturday I sat in my bed, legs drawn up, gazing out the window at the dome of the Saint Mary's Basilica in the distance. A sheet of paper for a short story lay on my lap, waiting for me to conquer its blank whiteness, to bring it alive. I waited for inspiration to sound the right note. What should I write about? What was really important in the revolving spin of days? The curves of the Basilica held me in their grip and I lost myself in the architectural image, a marble globe around which I could travel in circles and never go anywhere. Like my story.

The phone rang in the hall.

"It's for you," came my mother's voice. I went out to the desk where the receiver was lying on its side. It was Margo.

"Hi, what are you doing?" Without waiting for an answer, "Why don't you come over?"

"I'm writing. I'm working on a story." I'd spent the evening before with Margo and we'd walked to Becky's for pie.

"Oh, you can work on that tomorrow. Do you have anything planned this afternoon?"

"Nothing special. But I'm in the middle of writing this story." I had been sitting in my room for half an hour and hadn't written a word, but I counted it as preparation.

"Well then, finish up and come over after. There's chocolate cake left over from last night and we can watch Ed Sullivan." Margo had a way of countering any excuses with perpetual counter proposals, but this time I resisted, saying I absolutely couldn't make it.

An hour later I was on her doorstep. The writing had refused to budge. Almost immediately I heard Mrs. Holt's voice from the kitchen. "Is that you, Judy? You're just in time. Come on in and have some devil's food cake."

We munched on cake around the kitchen table as Mrs. Holt slipped a prime rib roast into the oven. After a discussion of the upcoming presidential election, all agreeing that Eisenhower would make the best candidate, I followed Margo downstairs to the laundry room. As she began ironing a sun dress I perched on an oak stool. I had to talk to someone! The senior prom was looming and I had to make a decision. Margo was taking Riley.

"There's this Blake boy," I began, "looking for a date to the prom. Peggy's after me to ask him. I'm not going to."

"What boy?"

"Larry Stockard."

"Really? He's cute!" Margo stopped ironing and tucked a lock of stray blonde hair behind her ear. "He's tall and dark and lots of girls want to go out with him." The iron resumed it's back and forth path over the ironing board.

"Tall and cute? Then why is he dateless?" This was formidable. Any inclination I might have had to consider him as a date evaporated. "How good looking is he?"

"Well, he has the dark hair you like so much, and is slender with dark-brown eyes, and is definitely one of the handsome ones. I can't imagine why he doesn't have a date already, except that he's not going with anyone. Our class is so small, with some of us asking boys outside of Blake. Maybe it's the numbers."

"I see." I would have preferred a normal loopy boy, one I could face up to. Maybe there weren't any boys like that at Blake. This guy was becoming more and more distant, like a star in a far constellation.

"Are you going to ask him?"

"Never." I tried to turn the conversation to the story I was struggling to write, but Margo would have none of it.

She went on. "Since he wants to go and you want to go—don't you—?"

"Well—yes . . ."

"Then you'd just better get on the ball and call him," she declared as she swept the iron over a print apron.

"I don't think so. No, I couldn't do that. Why doesn't he have a date already? Maybe he doesn't want to go. Maybe the girls at school just assumed. Maybe he wouldn't want to go with me? What if he doesn't like what he gets?"

"Don't be silly. What right has he to expect anything? He'll be lucky just to be at the dance."

"Right. He knows he's taking a chance. The worst that could happen is that we get to the dance and I never see him again because he's off dancing with the popular girls. Then what am I going to do? No, bad idea. Here, let me iron for a while." I jumped off the stool in what I hoped was a decisive move.

"You'll have your classmates there, you'll know people. You'll know me and Riley. Think of getting a new formal dress, Larry bringing you a corsage, the dinner Cat Morris is holding before the dance, the all-night afterglow at Cindy's afterwards. Think of all you'll miss. You should go for it."

Secretly, I was dying to go to my first prom. I watched the iron sweeping back and forth in Margo's hand, the nonchalant arc of her neck, the air of confidence in the tilt of her blonde head. Finally I caved.

"Okay, I'll call him. Who knows, he might say yes." I sat back down. "Next week," I promised.

"Now, call him *now!*"

Margo led the way upstairs to the den. I pulled Larry's phone number from my wallet and sitting at the desk, slip of paper in hand, I stared down at the black rotary phone.

"Well?" Margo waited, folding her arms and leaning against the doorway.

"You go downstairs. I'd rather call by myself."

"Okay, but I only have four more pieces to iron."

Finally I dialed. As the phone buzzed I resisted the urge to hang up. Why was this so hard? Of course he would refuse, he didn't know me. The girls may have *thought* he wanted a prom date, but they could be wrong. What will I say? I hope he doesn't answer! On second thought, he must, otherwise I'll have to do this all over again another time. I'm not up to it! Oh, my gosh.

At last I heard a click and a female voice said hello.

"Is Larry there? That is, does Larry live there? Larry Stockard?"

A pause. "I'll get him."

Another long pause that lasted about an hour.

"Hello?"

"Hello?" I plunged in. "Is this Larry?" Too late to think now.

"Yes."

"Larry Stockard?"

"Yes."

"This is . . . I'm Judy Bradford and I go to Northrop and I was wondering . . . a . . . well, I don't have a date, you see . . . you go to Blake, don't you?"

"Yes. Did you say Judy?"

"Yes."

"Do I know you?"

"No, but, well it's about the Senior Prom."

"Oh! Yes, my friends are going."

"Well, I thought you might—need a date. That is, uhh, would you like to go? That is, with me?"

A laugh on the other end. "How did you get my name?"

I told him of the tip received at school.

"Ah, I see. Yes, I would."

"What? Are you sure?"

"Certainly."

"You don't even know me."

"You don't know me either."

"Look, I don't know what I'm saying. I could barely bring myself to call you. I think I've asked you something but I don't know what it is. That is, I'm not sure what I just said."

Another laugh.

"How about if I ask *you?*" the sexy voice suggested. "Okay? Would you like to attend the Senior Prom with me?"

Now I had to laugh. "Don't mind if I do!"

I was downstairs in a flash. "He said yes!" I waved my arm in the air. "He drives! He has a car! He's got a voice like Gary Cooper!"

Margo nonchalantly replaced the iron in its iron rest and looked up. "That's great," she said.

చ•ళ

ON THE BIG NIGHT, the Woodhill Country Club ballroom was crowded with chiffon and satin formals swishing around the floor in time to the Jerry Landon band. The girls were perfumed and coiffed, the boys tall and confident in their tuxedoes, laughing easily. Larry was polite and attentive while I worried about protocol. Who was to be introduced to whom? On which wrist to wear my orchard corsage? Who would fill out my dance card, and how would I carry off an irresistible, winning chatter?

Larry swung me around the floor with casual nonchalance. I leaned into his arms and felt the rhythm pull me into a warm flow. Thank heavens for Arthur Murray! I danced with Riley, smoked five cigarettes on the porch, and gazed at the other girl's frosty formals and freshly curled hair-dos and the boys with their easy laughter. Later, Larry and I followed a line of cars to Cindy Appleton's house, where we curled up on pillowed chaise lounges and watched the other partiers dimly outlined on the lawn come and go. Above us the voices of Frank Sinatra and Margaret Whiting sifted through the shadows. Larry was the cutest, gentlest, most desirable boy I'd ever gone out with. I didn't mind that he was quiet; so was I. By the time dawn emerged from the horizon, bringing a silver lake into view, we had sunk to a state of inertia. The big night was over and so was school.

And so was my brief encounter with Larry Stockard.

To complete our academic education and prepare us for the full range of opportunity in the years to come, the seniors would go on to college. The honor girls struck out for Wellesley, Smith, and Stanford. Caroline was accepted at Mt. Holyoke. Margo would be flying out to the far reaches of Maine to Colby, propelled no doubt by the same craving for distance that drove me. The headmaster, Mr. Reed had advised me that Bradford Junior College out East would be a good fit, a small school that focused on the creative arts and social sciences. I selected a large university out west. I envisioned a rugged western countryside, with horses ridden full speed across the fields and a green campus spread out under the white-capped mountains of Colorado.

As usual I got my way. Luckily, after Dad appealed directly to the president of the school. I was admitted despite borderline grades. The next fall I would enter the University of Colorado.

Recently, as I leafed through the navy leather-bound yearbook labeled 1952, I came across notes scribbled by my fellow seniors at graduation those many decades ago. The entries, written in typical back-slanted script, were full of effusive declarations of friendship, pleas that I call, that we get together over the summer, keep in touch at college. Cat Morris, an Edina girl who would also be attending the University of Colorado, wrote a warm note hoping that we would be fast friends at UC and saying that she was looking forward to getting to know me better.

I didn't believe any of this.

The truth was that although I'd been happily caught up in the whirl of senior year, except for Margo I hadn't formed steady friendships with the other girls, didn't know their families or how they felt about anything, and hadn't caroused with them on weekends or over the summers. That last, lingering summer at the lake with Margo remains an empty blur. Our classmates had disappeared into the future. Maybe the distance between our neighborhoods was too great, or other lifelong friendships and family ties too insular, or Margo and I too insular. We were young and unaware, buried in our own lives, no one thought of such things, least of all me, who spent the days dreaming of enchanted ships and faraway lands.

One yearbook entry that caught my eye was from Audrey Noe:

> Dear Judy,
> Even though I was unfriendly in tenth grade, I hope I made up for it later. It's been wonderful knowing you and especially doubling with you. My advice to you for next New Year's Eve is to BE CAREFUL! unless I'm there to take care of you. I hope to take you riding some more in my limousine this summer so you can laugh at it. Good luck, Brad. Be good. Love, Audrey

Here was a real person reaching out! Maybe the last three years hadn't been such a misfire after all.

Part III

Making the Collegiate Run

Chapter Eleven

❧ *Mountains to Climb* ❧

𝕋HE COOL SEPTEMBER AIR nipped at my back as I walked along the sidewalk in a brown tweed suit tucked at the waist and alligator heels, carrying a russet leather purse. Around me I heard the *click-click* of high heels as a stream of girls dressed in suits and gloves perused their maps and peered at the house numbers for the first stop on their schedule. The novelty of the old three-story brick and stone houses lining the streets, the excitement of a new experience, and the conviction of being on my way to bigger and better things, propelled me briskly along.

I caught a glimpse of Mom waving from the Buick as it headed up the hill and back to Minnesota with Dad at the wheel. I gave a desultory wag of my hand. Mother held great hopes. We had shopped carefully for the sorority parties I would be attending during the week prior to the opening of the university year, and my room at Sewell Hall was full of new clothes in the 1952 style—saddle shoes, plaid wool skirts, pullover sweaters, and dress outfits with matching jackets. Other rushees, freshmen like me, following little maps from street to street, headed for the old three-story sorority houses scattered around the edge of the campus.

I felt a rising wariness as I climbed up the wide steps of the first big house where a bevy of girls gathered on the front porch. My curiousity was tinged with anxiety. There was something overwhelming in the clamor of smiling sorority girls who greeted us profusely and ushered us through the house—a spacious living room with picture windows and gilded mirrors, a long upstairs hall leading to white, sun-filled bedrooms—every girl's home away from home.

Each day I marched with a new flotilla of girls from house to house, reception to reception, where we were led to sunshine rooms and treated to cups of fruit punch and tea cakes. Once I caught sight of Cat Morris across the street, heading toward a different house. That evening she and I compared notes in a flurry of expectation. Our entire year, possibly our entire college experience, hinged on the course of these events. It was in these contained sorority house we would live, find our friends, and make our home for the next four years.

If I hadn't been so nervous, I might have enjoyed it. The air of extroverted confidence that surrounded me everywhere was difficult to match. Mine was the only uneasy face in a sea of beaming, self-assured optimists. With each introduction I stumbled, trying to discover what to say and how to say it.

At the end of the week I received several bids. The sororities wanted to take a second look. I picked the top-rated one on campus and tossed the rest out.

My return visit to the Kappa Gamma house included a formal sit-down lunch, where the sorority president enlightened us on the history, academic honors, and charity partnerships of the house. This was followed by coffee served buffet style from sterling coffee and tea sets. We carried on the usual conversations: What did you do this summer? *Not much.* I kept twisting my napkin into a spiral rope. This was not fun.

After a final screening the flood of applicants was narrowed to those who had been deemed acceptable. Girls flocked to the mail room, anxious to pick up their invitation bids. The day of truth had arrived. We had been appraised and now we would be found wanted or wanting.

I was found wanting. My mailbox was empty. No final bid. Everyone else seemed to be twirling and hugging and running out to notify relatives and friends. I stood glued to the floor.

Shuffling slowly back to the dorm room, leaving a cacophony of high voices circling in the distance, I threw myself on the bed. The scent of an apple on the desk a few feet away produced a wave of nausea. My head was buzzing. My hand as I rubbed it across my face felt like an icy appendage, as if it belonged to someone else. *Why had I been rejected?* I looked presentable, was polite, agreeable, privately schooled. What could possibly be lacking?

I picked up *Scaramouche* and started reading.

That evening, Cat Morris blew into my room full of excitement. She was pledging Kappa Gamma—the very one I had aimed for. She looked incredulous when I admitted, haltingly, that I was not pledging. She sympathized but couldn't find much to say. I rarely saw her after that. She was busy attending pledge dinners, meeting her new sorority sisters, dressing for parties, attending dances and exchanges at the frat houses, and generally settling into life at her second home at the Kappa house. Her room, down the hall from mine, was a mile away.

One day I wandered into Cat's room looking for someone to talk to. She was bent over, straightening the seams in her nylons.

"It's the big initiation dinner at the house tonight," she said over her shoulder, turning towards the mirror. Her uplifted face was excited, flushed as she fastened on pearl drop earrings. "I wish you were coming."

And she was gone. From the seclusion of my dorm room I heard the rush of fraternal activities, the joyful cries of decked out and breathless girls as they skipped down the dorm stairs, and later laughter and footsteps bounding down the halls as the new pledges returned. The girls I had chummed with during rush disappeared into the wave of sorority life, along with Cat Morris.

My position as outcast was assured. During the rash of celebrations that climaxed rush week, I stuck to my room. Plopped in bed I read stories, along with every magazine I could purloin from the dorm lobby. Other than Cat, I told no one.

Finally, I paid a visit to Sue Scott, who was staying in a dorm across campus. I knew her only because our two parents were good friends in Minneapolis. But I'd always admired her straightforward frankness, and when she told me she had pledged one of the top houses and asked me what I had joined, I told her everything. She didn't know what to say. Obviously she was too busy with the whirl of pledge activities and classes to involve herself in my plight. What could she possibly do? Come and see me any time, she offered sympathetically as she walked me to the door.

One night the following Christmas, while I was home on vacation, Sue's mother, Mrs. Scott, took me aside, gave me a hug, and whispered that the sororities had greatly misjudged and I shouldn't mind. I shook my head and gave her a grateful look. Then I shrugged. What could I do?

The hardest part was informing my parents. I imagined that their expectations were fulfilled: I had not made the grade. My letter to Mother explained that I had chosen only one house. That I was being invited places by my two roommates who lived near Boulder and had no interest in the fraternal life. That it was just as well, as I was not cut out for the formality and regimentation of sorority life. I preferred to concentrate on my studies. All of this was a lie. My roommates, saturated with friends, were too preoccupied with their boyfriends to attend to me. I was on my own.

Mother wrote back that she understood, and the subject was not mentioned again. The big question: what would she tell her friends?

On weekends I waited in my dorm room until the excited voices of pledges on their way to their new homes disappeared. Then I went down to the lounge and joined the few girls who sat conversing quietly or reading in an armchair. Even though the year hadn't started well, I was determined to keep going and hang on to whatever came my way. I joined the dorm Maintenance Committee and tried out for the school aqua dance team—unsuccessfully. Weekends I strolled to Talagi's for beers with some of the free girls. Once or twice I was invited to a fraternity party. One bash at the Phi Delta house centered on a western theme. Wearing a plaid shirt, neck scarf, and wide-brimmed cow-boy hat, I perched next to a boy at the dimly lit bar, drinking gin and tonics and smoking. I was aware of having no reciprocal sorority parties or anecdotes to offer.

"What did you pledge?"

"I didn't. I'm not in a sorority."

"What do you do?"

"Study. Go to bars. Not much."

❧ ◆ ❧

AND THEN I MET SYLVIA. Three of us stood on the steps of Sewell Hall with our suitcases, wearing parkas and knit scarves to break the gusts that blew in from the mountains and whistled up the front steps and through the stone pillars. John, Dan, Sylvia, and I had met several weeks before at a University Ski Club meeting while scanning Colorado ski brochures that advertised some of the best slopes in the country. We signed up for the trip to Aspen during semester break, and when John offered to drive, the four of us agreed to make the journey through the Rocky Mountains together.

Sylvia was poised on the top step looking out over the campus. She wore a short, red leather jacket and a white wool neck scarf, her uncovered hair blown back by the wind. Her eyes, when she turned them on us, were a deep-set, transparent violet. Don and I stood a few feet away, eyes peeled for John's dark-blue Oldsmobile.

Finally John drew up and we piled in. It would be a six-hour drive to the White Cap Lodge in Aspen, where we were scheduled to join the rest of the group. The Olds wound through Boulder and struck out along the highway past stretches of white countryside and rising slopes. John was tall and clean-cut with a get-things-done, no-nonsense manner, with even teeth that gleamed when he smiled. Dan was shorter, with straight brown hair and a cover of freckles over his cheeks. His face held a perpetual look of passive expectation. I knew these weren't frat boys, possibly because they showed up at the planning meeting unattached, without a slew of raucous buddies. These were just plain boys and that was fine with me. John and Dan were from North Dakota and Kentucky, respectively, and Sylvia had lived all her life California.

None of us had experienced mountain skiing. The sport was introduced in Minnesota in 1952. A new ski area in Bloomington had installed a single rope tow that pulled skiers up a three-minute run. I'd tried it a few times, scooting down the hill on my wooden skis, long thin planks that measured from the floor to my wrist raised above my head. Now I was about to taste the real thing.

A relentless snowfall whipped through the Rocky Mountains as we ascended, and soon we were barely able to see the tunnel of headlights in darkness. Thick flakes swirled and sputtered against the windshield as the wipers crunched slowly back and forth. We'd hoped to reach Aspen the same day, but it became too blistery to drive. The last motel we'd passed was miles behind us, and as the night grew late we peered anxiously out the windows for some sort of refuge. At last a blue sign appeared in the headlights and we quickly turned in. The landlady of the inn served up a light supper of hearty vegetable soup, Cornish bread, and roast beef slices. Afterwards we lounged in deep wicker chairs in the fireside room exchanging life histories. The fire warmed us. We smiled into the flames. Life was good.

BY THE NEXT AFTERNOON we were plunging down the slopes, invigorated, our muscles tingling. John and Dan raced off to a far chairlift and spent the day on a blue run. Sylvia and I signed up for morning lessons, and each afternoon we practiced pole planting and stem Christies until, tired of controlling every move, we'd give up and experience the thrill of racing down the mountain at full speed. You could start at the top and ski non-stop, getting to know the feel of the slope, falling instinctively into the rhythm of the turns and gaining more speed than you ever imagined you could handle, flying down steep runs no beginner with a rational mind would ever dream of attempting. By the end of the week Sylvia and I could last twenty minutes without stopping, flying under the chairlifts and sinking on our skis at the bottom, snow-bleached, out of breath, and exhilarated.

Evenings, after dinner at the lodge with the other students from the UC ski club, we stretched out on an American Indian rug in front of the two-story fireplace, surrounded by shelves of stuffed squirrels, raccoons, and mounted elk heads. Or we wandered out after dinner to one of the nearby bars lining the crowded streets of downtown Aspen.

One night, after a few beers at the Stilted Breast, John, Dan, Sylvia, and I returned to the lodge and collapsed around the fireplace in a circle of chairs. Soon a group of fraternity students from our group burst in, dusting off snow, and flung themselves down in front of the fire. They grabbed each other's arms, joked, and called out across the room. In contrast, our little clan of four was quiet. We were the only independents on the trip, an isolation that drew us together. This was fine with me. I was content. I liked small.

Sylvia immediately caught the attention of the group. The first evening, having changed into a blue velveteen top and mauve slacks, she appeared on the oak staircase. All male eyes turned her way. It struck me for the first time how beautiful she was. She floated down the stairs with the upright stance and grace of a ballet dancer, step by step, looking like a young Gene Tierney heading into Tyrone Power's arms at the bottom. Passersby gazed at her with admiration and a wary curiosity.

It was more than her beauty. Sylvia's manner of dress was unique, you might say foreign, compared to the matching slacks and sweaters the other girls wore. She dressed in Indian brocades, silk blouses, and flowing cotton skirts, with gold lamé earrings dangling from pierced ears, and thin turquoise bracelets circling each arm, looking more like a gypsy than a co-ed. The other students were not sure how to take her. She held ideas on every subject and introduced esoteric topics such as the superiority of leopard fur coats, the early poems of Ezra Pound, and the underground recordings of Ima Sumac. It appeared she knew about things of the world beyond us. The others, piqued by curiosity, found her irregularity suspicious. But it didn't bother me. I got used to her as we sat on the twin beds talking, or rode up Snowmass on the chairlift. She was friendly and seemed to like my company.

I wondered how this would work. Sylvia was an artist. Next to this girl with her sophisticated ideas and alluring style, I was plain and conventional. Clearly we had nothing in common, yet I couldn't help but like her. She was full of ideas. She talked willingly about herself and listened patiently to my abundant thoughts. While the others sat around pitchers of beer, we cruised the shops and thumbed through art books. We fell in love with Cezanne's Fastnacht paintings of Harlequin and the strutting Pierrot and set about finding ways to obtain prints.

One night, Sylvia stood up from her chair by the fire and announced she was going outside to look at the stars. I remained sitting with John and Dan, holding a half-full cup of hot cider and staring into the yellow flames. After a while I drew on my down jacket and followed her out onto the deck. She was leaning on the railing, gazing up at the pearl sky where a million tiny stars flashed patterns of light. I leaned next to her.

"The mysteries are there," she said in low voice. "We just have to divine them."

I looked upwards without replying.

"Look! Look there's a falling star!" she gasped.

I squinted.

"Do you know the constellations?" she asked, turning her head towards me for a brief moment.

"No," I replied. "Not at all."

For me the stars had never been anything other than sparkling cover lights to snuggle under. Sylvia described how the ancients saw their feats outlined in the sky in star-rimmed clusters.

"Oh, I think I see Auriga!" she cried. "See those little balls of light? Those are the wheels of her chariot racing through the sky!" She stood on her toes, face lifted.

"Well, yes, I see," I said. I didn't see anything except a mass of brilliant sparkles exploding in the night sky. It was breathtaking, but I wasn't going to show my ignorance of celestial pictorials and ancient myths.

"I guess I'll turn in," I said, but we stared into the darkness without moving, each in our own thoughts.

"I always wear this," Sylvia said after a while, fingering a turquoise necklace around her neck. I turned and caught a glimpse of a smooth stone outlined on her throat. "It's been blessed by an ancient visionary of the Plains tribe, handed down to an old Indian woman from my mother's grandmother's tribe." She was proud of her remote Indian ancestry. I considered my own take on the subject and didn't seem to have one. I guess it was preferable to be unique—I could buy that.

The air was quiet above the mounds of snow. The distant sounds of night music trailed across the treetops, curving along the horizon where titanic mountain shapes burrowed into the sky. The night was too captivating to question anything.

EASTER WEEK OVER, the Oldsmobile sped over the curving road towards Boulder, Dan at the wheel. I sat in the front looking out into the white cover of snow engulfing the landscape, stark and blinding. Not a sign of movement or life. The white brilliance was so powerful I became lost in its icy vastness. Leaning my forehead against the pane, I gazed at the solitary mountain in the distance, conscious of its staggering beauty, yet the poetry eluded me. Instead, I felt a vast emptiness. A chill had displaced the warmth under my Norwegian sweater and an ache pulsed under my ribs. I wanted something so badly it hurt, but I didn't know what it was.

I stared at the unending road ahead of us, which disappeared at every turn into white nothingness.

My attention was drawn by Sylvia's voice from the back seat. The boys were quiet and Sylvia was in the mood to talk.

"As I said, when I get back to Los Angeles I intend to resume studying with my former art teacher, Ada Gar. She was trained in New York. But my parents insist that I complete a college education before I throw myself full time into art. They want me to pursue art classes on the side. I guess I must appease them."

I informed her I was a writer, which wasn't exactly true. Thoughts of writing had been skimming through my mind for years, and I had filled several legal pads. Partially finished stories languished in my desk, stuffed in a black manila folder. I had nothing to show.

"I've been writing since I was eight," I told her. I determined to prop up my feeble claims of being a writer. I had plans. "I've been thinking of writing a script for *Inner Sanctum*, something macabre, weird and unbelievable." I hadn't actually worked out a plot. Now I revived the idea, hoping to meet this exceptional girl's expectations.

"There's nothing wrong with horror shows. Money can be made there," Sylvia noted.

"I also write poetry." Here too my ambitions suddenly soared.

Sylvia was devoted to poetry. She described long writing sessions, isolated in her bedroom loft at home in Los Angeles. It appeared her talents were endless.

"My goal is to be a novelist," I added.

During our week at Aspen, Sylvia and I had discovered a strong commonality—we both suffered under parental domination. As an only child, her every move was tracked. She wasn't allowed to make her own decisions, and her creative dreams were overruled in favor of sense and practicality. As for me, I felt smothered by overprotection. When I kicked and protested enough, my parents let me have my way. The choice of college had been mine. I'd pretty much picked UC out of a hat. What did I know? It was far away in the opposite direction of where I had been pointed. That was enough.

Sylvia laughed. She understood.

The boys remained silent through our conversation.

"They don't know from anything," Sylvia said later. She considered John and Dan quite ordinary and boring. For her, boys had to be *interesting*. I had to agree with that.

☙ ♦ ❧

CAT MORRIS ASKED ME to room with her second semester. She needed a roommate until next year when she would live in the Kappa house. Why not? Secretly, I was thrilled. Her roommate, Mabel, a chubby girl with wide, demanding eyes and a way of repeating what had just been said as if it were something new, spent most weekends with her family in Denver, far from the bustle of sorority row. Her slipshod ways were getting Cat down.

One afternoon after class, Sylvia took me to see her paintings that would be showin in the class art show scheduled to open the following weekend. We entered a large gallery on the third floor of the student union. Sylvia's two canvases hung side by side. One depicted a skeleton and pagan Gaelic symbols hovering behind willowy human shapes. In the other, a clown in a tight argyle suit of sunken black, plum, and purple colors raised one arm against a smoky background, a woeful expression on his face. The effect was mystical. Sylvia held a vision that was all her own, different from the daisies and sky blue mountain scenes hanging nearby. I was sure her canvases were the best in the room.

Sylvia was unlike anyone I had ever known. During the winter months, she traipsed from class to class in a long damson neck scarf and a mohair coat. As the weather warmed into spring, she wore full skirts with Navaho trim and clipped braided belts around her seventeen-inch waist. Her hair flowed freely around her face or was pulled back in a bun, emphasizing her violet eyes. Curious, interested, and captivated, I absorbed her artistic creations and ideas. Here was someone who scorned the ordinary, who created her own vision.

And I was a writer, self-proclaimed. My plans gained momentum. Plans that dovetailed with Sylvia's.

The other students didn't know what to make of Sylvia. She appeared oblivious of their coolness. Within our self-defined orbit, the conventional, epitomized by the sororities, was not to be taken seriously. We eschewed the cookie-cutter dress styles, the Levittown houses, the plebeian tastes that ran to hamburgers, French fries, and Velveeta cheese and the roughneck sports and slam-blast drinking in bars that were devoid of all taste. Society pressured everyone to fit in, to follow mass standards, to dress, speak, and act alike. We would rise above all that, bring out fresh ideas, strike out for individuality, create our own codes.

Saturdays we walked to the nearby main street of Boulder for coffee, poured over our journals, read poetry, and visited book and art shops. Although I didn't know a Pollock from a Picasso, this would change. I was the appreciative learner, although I claimed more experience in the realm of literature. Sylvia started reading the classics, and I browsed through bookstores selecting prints and buying books on the French Barbizon School and the Impressionists.

Sylvia was, I discovered, rarely without a boyfriend. She was seeing Gerhard, a handsome foreign student from Holland. I was taken to meet Gerhard and Leif, his Norwegian friend. The four of us attended foreign films, art exhibits, and concerts. Leif cooked us dinner in his off-campus apartment, where we discussed the superiority of European culture and the greats of Scandinavian literature.

Leif was my height with strong shoulders and straight blonde hair, on the quiet side, very agreeable. We got along, but the sparks weren't flying. Maybe a kiss would have broken the ice, but Leif left me at the door with a slow smile.

Since Sylvia and Gerhard often left us and disappeared into the night, I assumed they were going to bed together. Sylvia was guarded on the subject, aside from remarking that Gerhard was a good lover. But she kept him at bay and fit him carelessly into her schedule. I couldn't figure how she could be so cavalier. I could never be that sophisticated. Sylvia was curious about Leif. Were we sleeping together? No? She had a hard time accepting my virginal status—Minnesota was so *conventional.*

When the exhibit was over, I helped Sylvia collect her paintings from the gallery. We were lugging canvasses down the staircase and discussing Sylvia's next project. I carried a painting neatly wrapped in a poplin cloth with one arm and two empty frames with the other, trying not to let the protruding hooks brush against my pleated skirt.

"You'll meet my parents," Sylvia was saying, adjusting a canvas more tightly under her arm. "And you have to meet Paul, my best friend from high school. He's a dancer. Won't they be surprised? I've never before had a friend like you."

"What do you mean—like me?" The frames were slipping and I paused to tighten my grip.

"Well, I mean, someone who is, who is so . . . well . . . common."

We had reached the landing and I whirled around to face her.

"What do you mean?" I wasn't sure I had heard right. For the first time I saw her blush.

"Oh, just that you—don't have—oh, never mind. It's nothing."

I stared at her incredulous. "What did you mean by that?"

"Nothing at all."

When we arrived at her dorm, I placed my bundles on the entry floor and gave her a brief glance. "I have to go," I said, and stalked out the front door. I felt she had dashed our artistic alliance, that I had been tossed coldly to the other side among the unenlightened. Anger soared through my veins and I didn't look back.

For the next few days I avoided her, ignored the note she left in my mailbox, and slipped out of the history class we shared without looking in her direction. I hadn't yet figured out the word *common*. I had thought we were on the same unique path, crossing the same Elysian field. But finally I had to admit I knew what she meant. Our backgrounds were very different. She grew up in liberal Los Angeles, attended Hollywood High School, a school filled with the children of film stars, and cultivated a serious art talent under the guidance of a high-level art teacher. Her mother worked part time in an antique store and attended local museum acquisition meetings. All I knew about was clothes and parties. I hadn't even had a real boyfriend. I had done nothing. I *was* a Minnesota outback, by her standards. Why had she taken me as a friend?

But I knew the answer. We shared a dream of striking out and creating our future. No other friendship in Boulder could match that.

Two weeks after our estrangement, I entered our usual coffeehouse on Main Street and found her sitting in a window booth, bent over a notebook. I slipped in across from her, and we resumed talking as if nothing had happened. The waitress served a warm caramel roll with my cocoa. We didn't discuss the episode. She understood that I had forgiven her, that the issue was too petty to carry. I did not admit that her words stirred a deep fear that my quietness translated into dullness, and that basically, despite the outfits and privileges, I was boring.

After that we became inseparable. She respected me, and for my part she was my muse. I asked no more.

Sylvia and I talked endlessly about our next move. Clearly, returning to the University of Colorado was out. We would not spend one more year in this rigid enclave dominated by the fraternity system, the heart of the very conformity we resisted. To marry, raise children, and follow the usual route of domesticity was not for us. It was paramount to pull out from under the control of our parents. Sylvia's drive to form her life in the artistic mold was matched by my determination, at any cost, to break from my past and the smothering direction of my parents and all that was keeping me from following my true bent.

One evening, a few days before the end of school, I lay on the hill beside Sewall Hall arms tucked under my head, watching the low clouds drift by in slow motion as if floating in a blue sea. I felt warmth spread along my skin. I was imbibed with new confidence and no longer felt adrift. It was as if a hardening agent had entered my bloodstream. There were oceans to cross and it was good to be young! There was nothing lacking. I had a place, I was viable.

❧◆❧

I SPENT THE NEXT YEAR in limbo. Our plans to share an apartment in Manhattan did not materialize. That summer Sylvia swept off on a road trip through New Mexico with her parents. I toured New England with Mom and Dad in our new Buick. Our rooms were redecorated: Sylvia's was transformed into a studio with a standing fireplace, and my twin bedroom set was replaced by a studio couch, coffee table, and two ebony pole lamps, with prints by Rufino Tamayo and Edvard Munch above a low chest. None of this dampened our resolve.

By fall it was clear Sylvia's parents wouldn't allow her to quit school. I also had to continue my studies. I applied to and was accepted by New York University but my parents refused to allow me to attend—they considered NYU a hotbed of communism. I couldn't break away. At the last minute I enrolled at the University of Minnesota for fall quarter. Sylvia scoffed at my vacillations. She was ready to make it on her own and said I was a wuss, and I guess I was. I couldn't accept the idea of giving up college and striking out penniless with nothing to offer.

Sylvia mailed me a copy of Henry James' *Washington Square*. I sent her Santayana's *The Last Puritan*.

Back home I took up with no one.

My parents were eager that I sign up winter quarter for sorority rush—a small informal open house without the splash of fall pledging. Yes, I would be compromising my principles, but the truth was, I was lonely, listless, and I also harbored—as I look back—an urge to blot out the lingering curse of failure and achieve what had been denied at UC.

Sylvia was incredulous.

"I suppose you have to do something to keep your sanity," she said finally.

It was a mistake. I went through the rituals of pledging Delta Gamma like a robot, unable to muster enthusiasm for the parties and communal activities expected of new pledges: the making of party decorations and float banners, the meetings about household maintenance, and the alumnae teas. My heart wasn't in it. I had vowed that I would avoid living an ordinary life at any cost. My track led elsewhere and I was determined to follow it to the end.

The drive to be somewhere else—anywhere—was consuming. Nothing could compensate for the lack I felt of an environment that supported my ambitions and a friend to share it with.

Me—1954 or 1955.

Between classes I hung out in the student lounge at the Student Union and watched the senate hearings to ferret out communism, watched senator Joseph McCarthy pound the table and grind one American citizen after another into submission with his wild accusations. Students crowded around the television screen, and we stared in outrage at the businessmen, film stars, artists, and officials co-coerced into the spotlight to be driven to their ruin. McCarthy was obviously possessed. And I was becoming a radical.

MEANWHILE, SYLVIA CASHED some bonds, collected her easel and suitcase, and moved to New York City to enroll in the Art Students League. Her small roll of money didn't carry her very far, and soon her letters were detailing her various scruffy jobs, mostly modeling in clothing manufacturing showrooms, combined with girl-Friday tasks. None of them lasted. The score of itinerant men she took up with didn't last much longer.

Where she met these men I don't recall, but she wrote of being wined and dined at the 21 Club by a Hormel heir and pursued with silk Persian scarves by a count from Romania. These men were rich or knew celebrities—one had ushered at Marlon Brando's wedding. She seemed to expect that through the adoration of a "man of the world" she would be whisked off to some fascinating foreign villa and her troubles would be over. When one of her freaky men stood her up and then appeared at her door at three in the morning, we exchanged harsh words. I wrote asking what she thought she was doing hanging out with such a jerk. She shot back for me to just shut up about him and she meant it. "You don't know him and have no right to judge!"

Her letters turned morose. "So I learn once again that loneliness is life's eternal shadow. I do not seem to find anything to be one with. I seem always on the outside." Echoes of my own voice. A soul mate on the planet and I had found her! With renewed strength, I doubled my efforts to get to her and enter the life I knew I was destined for.

Tingling with anticipation, I landed in New York that very November to spend a long weekend with Sylvia in a city that pulsed with endless novelty. She booked a room for me next to hers at the Y. I tagged along to her painting classes at the Art Students' League, and we visited out-of-the-way art museums and basement art shops in the Village and stopped for tea at the squalid apartment of a young, male Japanese friend.

I decided to check out the creative arts program at Sarah Lawrence in nearby Bronxville. The college offered just the kind of individualism I was looking for. A small, dark-haired woman at the admissions desk looked me up and down. In my best brown tweed suit and gloves I thought I looked presentable enough, but the woman was immoveable.

"The dean doesn't see prospective students without an appointment."

"But I've come all the way from Minnesota. I just got off the train. Surely five minutes—"

"I'm afraid you'll have to make an appointment."

The woman bent over her typewriter and wiped a tiny brush of white-out over the sheet. Evidently it had to be done by the book, no exceptions. I sat down. The family story of how Dad had broken through the iron gates of Harvard rung in my ears, but I could come up with no clever idea. The secretary was a linebacker and I was a rookie. Maybe I didn't really believe in dreams, for I stood up and left without another word.

For the next few days we scoured the city, snooping out funky dives and art shops and sitting in Washington Square on white marble benches, dreaming and sharpening our philosophies. We parted with a promise to see one another again soon.

❧ ◆ ❦

A LETTER ARRIVED SOME MONTHS later alerting me that Sylvia had scraped up the money and was coming to Minneapolis. New York was depressing and she badly needed a respite. At last! I could hardly sleep and plotted out all the museums we would visit and the site-seeing trips

I would take her on. Sylvia arrived in high spirits—she'd met a new man on the plane and they'd arranged to meet back in Manhattan.

My friend admired our spacious house at 57 Groveland, which took on new energy with her in it. We spent hours in my studio bedroom reading poetry, savoring the perfect sync of our minds, and rehashing our options. Dad treated us to lunch at the Minneapolis Club and Mother to a fashion show at the Women's Club on Oak Grove Street. Gerhard, Sylvia's handsome Dutch boyfriend from U.S.C. in town on a long business assignment, was invited to dinner. Sylva had declared she found Gerhard too devoted and boring. Her indifference lasted until he gave up and stopped writing. She would then bombard me with worried questions—could he be losing interest?

When earlier she learned that Gerhard and I had met a few times and that he'd been to the house for dinner, she wrote and suggested I go to bed with him, which neither of us were inclined to do. There was a wide gulf between Sylvia's sexual standards and my own. She made comments like, "I'm late this month, I'm getting nervous," and "I'm in

Sylvia, Gerhard, me, Mother, Harold, Susan.

the mood for making love." I didn't know what to make of this voice of experience with all her sexual partners. It was part of being a free spirit, I supposed, and after all she *did* hail from Los Angeles.

On the appointed evening, Gerhard showed up looking fresh, trim, and smiling, resembling a tall Edward VIII. I glanced with pride at Sylvia and Gerhard sitting beside me at the dining room table, talking of foreign parts and far-off interests. Here I was sharing a prime-rib dinner with my two best friends in the world and my family. Finally I had something to offer.

My parents were not sure what to make of Sylvia. She was not the norm, by Midwest standards, but they extended a warm welcome. They might even have appreciated her wide range of interests—if they could be sure they approved.

Sylvia's air of sophistication didn't impress my brother Harold in the least. This set Sylvia in motion, convinced that her beauty and imaginative artistic flights would turn the head of any healthy male, especially the sheltered ones of Minnesota who hunted and worked hard, and had never met anyone so freewheeling. Harold had an instinctive aversion to what he considered phony. Down to earth, that was his style. He had no use for females who spun fantasies. Sylvia left without this conquest, which she could not comprehend. I thought he was a prig.

As the weeks passed, Sylvia's letters from New York became more plaintive. She was frazzled and exhausted. She could no longer endure it. She hated the working world, women were mean to her, and no one understood her. The condescending treatment she received at the hands of her supervisor, plus late night dates, were destroying her nerves. The supervisor nagged her unmercifully about trivia. "These accounts aren't registered properly," the supervisor chastised. But the tasks were too menial; Sylvia couldn't keep her mind on them.

"How can I be expected to do math while I'm philosophizing?" she complained. She was at her wit's end; she couldn't even paint. Then a new man would materialize and she would revive—temporarily.

That spring a letter arrived from Los Angeles. Sylvia had returned home. And I was on my way to a European fandango.

Chapter Twelve

❧ Europe Young American Style ❧

𝒫ARIS!
The photo of the Paris streets on my desk I'd stared at longingly at for so many months had come to life. The square St. Suplice below our hotel window was filled with students drifting to and from the Sorbonne. All day I had thrilled to the sight of the ancient buildings, the dark-framed shops lined along the narrow streets, the heady aroma of French tobacco, and the guttural French of the staff and drivers.

Hotel Select, Place de la Sorbonne, Paris, 1954.

It was July 14, 1954, Bastille Day. French flags hung from every roof in the Latin Quarter. Shopkeepers were busy arranging chairs along the streets for music and dancing and strains of various bands drifted around corners. Margo and I watched from the hotel window as lines of gray Deux Chevaux inched through the intersection, nose to nose, and pedestrians scurried along the sidewalks. The air was alive with expectation, and every nerve in my body was tingling with excitement.

Little did I suspect that I would, within the next two months, meet the boy of my dreams, sneak into enemy territory in the dead of night, and part with my burdensome virginity.

Our group tromped down the stairs of the Hotel Select for an evening on the town, the strains of *La Marseilles*—"*le jour de gloire est arrivé*" echoing from the streets. Ian, our English tour guide, herded the twenty-three Golden Bears, mostly students drawn from California and the Twin Cities, to a Latin Quarter restaurant. After a leisurely dinner of *coq au vin*, green beans in almandine sauce, Camembert and crusty French bread, the group members were free to go their separate ways. Margo and I wandered down a crooked alley accompanied by the beeping of traffic, strains of string and horn ensembles, and excited voices issuing from open windows.

Rounding a corner we came to a tavern from which party sounds blared into the street. As we pressed our faces to the glass, a few male hands flew up on the inside, beckoning us. We looked at each other. Such an invitation could hardly be ignored.

Inside, a throng of young German boys were laughing and talking over each other in rapid German. They looked blond and clean-cut, despite their state of late-night disarray. One had tuffs of hair sticking up from a Nordic hat. Another was balancing a foamy mug of beer perilously on the edge of a long table. They greeted us enthusiastically, and several boys slid their chairs over to make room for us. Margo and I exchanged glances.

"Come on, have a beer on us," the boys insisted. Finally we walked over.

"Can we join your party?" asked Margo.

"YEEESSSS!" came a chorus from the table. "YAAAAAA!"

"Where are your girlfriends?" I asked.

My question was greeted by wild laughter. "Back home in Germany!" the reply echoed down the table.

The German boys were, it turned out, on vacation. When we told them it was our first time in Paris there was another uproar and two steins appeared in front of us. We joined in the singing that rang through the bar, lifting our steins with the rest to toast France. They set out to teach us their favorite beer songs:

"*En Müchen steht ein Hofbräuhaus, eins, zwei, g'suffa.*" (In Hofbrau House in Munich, one, two, bottom's up.)

We soon knew the entire first verse by heart. Suddenly one of the German boys leapt onto the table and started jigging in time to the music, prompting more laughter and clapping all around. Finally, after a last stomp, the boy jumped down from the table and managed to squeeze into the chair next to Margo. He sat grinning at her as he caught his breath and before I knew it another boy with a long yellow scarf had seated himself on the other side next to me. The two boys introduced themselves as Werner and Heinz. They told us they'd been sent to Paris on an apprenticeship program to study the French metro system as part of a massive rebuilding of the subways in West Berlin destroyed during the war. Werner, an engineer student, lived in West Berlin, and his buddy, Heinz, had moved from East Berlin to Paris to room with him and find work since there were no jobs in his sector. Now Heinz was also in the apprenticeship program.

"We don't have girlfriends," they claimed, laughing. Talking loudly over the din they asked about our trip. "You not go to Berlin?" Heinz asked. "Too bad. You must see it. Only nine years after the war and it is being rebuilt. There are many changes."

When we left the bar at 3:00 a.m. beer was still flowing. Heinz and Werner walked us back to the Hotel Select where lingering Bastille Day festivities still enlivened the streets. Clusters of partiers were traipsing through the square, and a few lone instruments streamed low jazz notes over the sparsely filled chairs on the sidewalk. We sipped wine at a café next to the hotel. By the time Heinz and Werner got up to leave at 4:00

a.m. they had briefed us on the plight of Germany and obtained our address.

The next evening I sat nursing a Coke with Margo and Mary, a young teacher from the tour, at an outdoor café near the hotel. The street had fallen into a humming quiet as if spent after the recent all-night festivities. Tonight we would turn in early. As I fingered the glass in my hand, a young Frenchman moved up to our table. He was a tall boy dressed in a brown corduroy jacket with a pixie smile on his face, hands burrowed deep in his pockets. Would we like to join him and his two friends for a beer? We looked over at the next table. Two young boys in crew-necked shirts and slacks were smiling at us.

Instead we invited them to our table. The tall one sat down next to me and with a wide smile introduced himself as Jean Paul. He was full of inquiries: our home towns, our travel plans, our ambitions. His halting English was filled in by his two companions, Jacques and André, who spoke with heavy French accents.

Margo and Mary soon left for the hotel and welcome sleep, but I stayed on despite the fact I could hardly keep my eyes open. I wanted to listen to Jean Paul. I was transfixed by the sound of his words, a combination of broken English and French, by the rhythm and inflections of the French language. Clearly the garrulous one of the trio, Jean Paul shared his battery of ideas on French people, American culture, and the French political scene. His brown eyes glittered with intelligence, his manner was respectful, and a playful hint of impudence accompanied his smile.

"*Quelle heure est-il?* (What time is it?)" I stammered in my meager French, anxious to communicate with him directly. Besides, I needed to practice.

Jean Paul looked amused. After a few exchanges he learned over and said, "You must learn French."

I assured him—making up my mind on the spot—that learning French was one of my top priorities. "And you learn English. You live here on the continent. You have no excuse," I teased. Jean Paul gave me a lopsided smile and we agreed to meet the next day after the tour returned from the Louvre.

The next afternoon I was in the lobby of the Hotel Select on the dot. Jean Paul and I walked along the narrow sidewalks of Boulevard Saint Germain-des-Près to the Deux Magots and scooted around a small round table. Next to us people were talking softly and reading newspapers. Soon his friend Jacques joined us, ordered a *café-au-lait* and offered us a Galois cigarette. Jean Paul told me he worked at a carpet shop and lived with his parents in the 16th *arrondissement*. The talk led to Jean Paul Sartre's latest book, De Gaulle's triumphal resistance during the war, and the fierce French sense of individualism. I was amazed that a non-college boy knew as much as he did. Decidedly, the French were the most interesting people on earth, and, I was beginning to believe, the most beguiling.

Jean Paul insisted on walking me back to the hotel. At the door he turned to face me, said he was sorry I was leaving the next moring, and asked for my address. Please would I write to him? I expressed a desire to return to Paris.

"You are—*plein de curiosité*," he said in his hesitant French. "You learn."

Jean Paul said he would wait for my letter. I would write in English, he in French. Paris had captured my imagination and I knew I would return. And if Jean Paul were there, so much the better.

৵ ♦ ৵

WHEN THE GOLDEN BEARS arrived in Hamburg, Margo and I found an invitation waiting for us. It was a letter from Heinz. Please come and see the real Germany. He and Werner would meet us and show us around. Wow! A once-in-a-lifetime opportunity. I was ready to go in a second. Margo, after discussing the pros and cons with Ian, our English tour director, finally agreed, and before we knew it we had landed at the airport in Allied-occupied Berlin and caught a taxi to a nearby hotel, where we were booked for the next three days.

Later that afternoon a bus dropped us off in a rather dingy neighborhood where the apartment buildings looked alike: tall slabs standing side by side, one after another. One of them displayed the number we were looking for. Once inside we scanned the list of apartment numbers. Werner's number wasn't on it. That was strange. We felt suddenly dependent, lost in a foreign country, surrounded by a language we couldn't speak. The only tactic was to keep knocking on doors, floor after floor, until we came to his apartment. We had to hope and pray that it was the right building and that he was home. We were dubious—a needle in a haystack. But what choice did we have?

We decided to start at the top, the fourteenth floor, and make inquiries. Would they even talk to us, foreigners who had floated in from nowhere and knew no German? The first door we knocked on at the end of a dark corridor was silent for several long minutes—no rustling, no footsteps, no gleam of light under the door. Finally, the door cracked open a bit, stopped, then it opened wider and—amazingly— there stood Werner. He was delighted to see us and set about serving coffee while we waited for Heinz to return from his work at the U-Bahn.

When Heinz showed up he was equally pleased. He could not believe we were there. Over dinner at a nearby restaurant, our two new friends plotted sites and marked bus schedules for us to follow the next day while they were at work. I stashed the directions in my purse, along with a miniature German-English dictionary, a guide book, and a coin-purse full of Deutschmarks.

The next day Margo and I set out to see West Berlin. We found ourselves in a singular landscape. This grim scene of black-and-white destruction contrasted with the carefree colors of the other European cities we'd seen. Rows of crumbled buildings stretched block after block, pitched archways were attached to nothing, and remnants of walls stood here and there on blocks of dry flat land. All that remained of a former shopping center was one wing of a building protruding into the middle of an empty lot.

The people in the streets looked solemn, dutiful, going about their business. We saw an old woman with an armful of mauve flowers and a bundle slung over her shoulder walk into the remains of an apartment building. It was still inhabited, even though only one corner remained standing. The skeleton structure stood like an abandoned obelisk in the center of the flattened block, piles of concrete crumbled on the ground beside it. Shirts and sheets hung on lines between the windows of the apartment walls that remained. Occasionally we saw workmen digging into the rubble, attempting to resurrect the city that had been brought to its knees by relentless bombing. We walked on, conscious of being carefree foreigners in a laboring city.

Later that afternoon the bus let us off near the Brandenburg Gate, our destination. The gate loomed, still intact, proud and dominating despite its blackened façade and the splintered columns. Not far from the gate we passed an obscure concrete structure fronted with circular steps and decided to investigate. There wasn't a soul in sight. The round-walled interior contained murals of battle scenes and plaques engraved in a foreign alphabet. The building appeared to be deserted. Curious, we approached a narrow flight of stairs at the end of a hallway and started up, looking for someone or some sign. It was dead quiet.

Suddenly we heard muffled noises coming from the top of the stairs. Carefully, we inched up to an iron trap door above our heads. I gave it one push and the door flew open. The voices immediately ceased, and a dead, suspenseful quiet filled the air. Margo and I gingerly stuck our heads out the opening and observed a scattering of guards in uniform sitting on pipes and standing by the roof railing. They swirled around at once, uttering shouts in a foreign language as we climbed onto the deck and stood looking at them, astounded. Several grabbed guns that had been lying next to them and pointed them directly at us, locked into assault position. I heard Margo gasp and I couldn't move, too shocked to think or even register the knot of fear that grabbed my stomach. *What in the world?* It seemed we had surprised the men on a break—several held beer cans and were smoking cigarettes in the open air. We took them to be not more than twenty years old. They stared at us, as shocked as we were to have their off-limits territory invaded.

There was a ponderous silence as we all took in the situation. They looked youthful in their casual disarray; not at all like the helmeted guards we had seen standing at attention elsewhere at the perimeters of the war zone.

"*Touristes!*" we repeated several times.

They stared.

"Spreken English?"

Not a sound from them.

"*Americanes*," I blurted and pointed to Margo and me and held up my guide book with the word *FODOR* in big green letters.

Finally, one smiled and called out, "Russkiy," pointing to the hammer and sickle on the sleeve of his jacket. *Russian!* He then rattled off something in Russian, to which there was answering laughter. Margo and I looked at each other. I pulled my jacket pockets inside out and splayed my hands palms up, trying to indicate we were harmless.

"*Verboten!*" one said sternly, not budging. But the others sat back down, took up their beer cans and evidently discussing the situation, exchanged a few indistinguishable words.

In a minute they were talking rapidly and smiling. Finally, one of them lifted a beer can in our direction and I reciprocated with a miming arm raise in return. This was greeted with laughter and the atmosphere relaxed considerably. Just as I thought we were going to be invited to their party, footsteps sounded on the stairs and two older guards appeared. On seeing us they began barking loudly. Margo and I grasped their meaning at once: we were to get *out*. As the two guards directed us down the stairs, I glanced over at the boys who had resumed their serious expressions and did not look in our direction.

Heinz and Werner were reproachful when they heard about our experience at the Russian War Memorial, shaking their heads at our pleas of innocence. I realized we had acted like naive, careless Americans, but I was too hungry for adventure and novelty to care. No harm done! Nor did they sympathize when we told them about wandering inadvertently into East Berlin territory, where we were turned back by the strident cries of "*Verboten!*" thrown at us by the border guards.

"You must be more careful!" the boys told us.

After dinner, they led us to a local pub where we squeezed into a wooden table in the back. The sparsely lit room was crowded with people, mostly students, who piled in with much exchanging of chairs and squeezing between tables. Conversations were intense and I thrilled to the sound of crisp German words on all sides, the sight of tall ceramic mugs swinging past on trays, and the presence of two comely boys seated friendly and serious across from us. I was in a state nearing euphoria. Margo must have felt something of the same for she was quizzing our new friends excitedly. They had heard a great deal of our history and now they were eager to tell their story.

"Werner and I have known each other since childhood," Heinz explained. "Werner's uncle owns an engraving business and set Werner up with an apprenticeship in his shop."

"I was too young to join the German army," Werner put in.

"Were you a member of the fascist party during the war?" Margo asked.

"I was a member of the German Youth Camp. It was required of all fifteen-year-olds," replied Heinz. "I obediently recited the Nazi chants and marched to the party tunes, but I wasn't political or especially nationalistic."

In the nine years since Germany's surrender and its division into Allied and Russian zones, Heinz told us, the Germans were slowly recovering but the split was causing dissension between the two sides, democratic and communist, with their different economic structures. After the war, faced with high unemployment in the East, Heinz had moved to the Western Zone where he found work and moved in with Werner.

"I am now cut off from my family in East Berlin. It is a great hardship." Heinz passionately wanted Margo and me to understand the uncertainty of Germany's economic future and its vital need for reunification.

As we parted that evening, Heinz offered to take us to East Berlin before we returned to Hamburg. I jumped at the chance. To be able to explore a closeted city with the intelligent Heinz appealed to me. Margo objected. It wasn't legal. Americans weren't allowed into the Russian zone. It was madness.

I wasn't going to let such an opportunity pass. The next afternoon while Margo relaxed at the hotel with her *Fodor*, Heinz and I set out for

East Berlin. We had dressed in dark clothes and I wore a scarf tied around my head, trying to look inconspicuous. It was 5:00 p.m. but the subway was only half-full. People sat silently, their bland faces looking straight ahead as the car chugged towards the Eastern sector. I pulled close to Heinz. Three men seated across wore drab, indistinct clothes. Something about them was strikingly impersonal. Before the Berlin Wall was erected, people were able to pass cautiously between the two sectors. Usually, only those with approved business made the trip. Everyone was afraid of being questioned. We were careful not to speak or make an unusual gesture as Heinz handed the passing conductor our tickets.

When the train arrived in East Berlin it was getting dark. People on the streets of East Berlin, dressed in shades of black or brown, passed by wordlessly. There were no young people about. Most of the men carried a bag or briefcase and looked solemn. We found an exchange post and changed our western marks into eastern money, which was worth a lot less—for one western mark we received five eastern marks. Along Frankfurt Allee—now called Stalin Allee—tall rectangular apartment buildings lined each side of the street; identical blocks repeated as far as the eye could follow into the distance. Here, Heinz explained, deserving communist party members lived. It was one of their privileges.

There were no buses running or passing taxis as we walked far out into what used to be the outskirts of the city, which was now bombed into a dry desert full of crumbled buildings and debris. Block after block showed the same destruction as parts of the West sector, but here rebuilding was more urgent. Many of the ruins had been cleaned up. Old buildings and foundations had, for the most part, been cleared away and chain fences surrounded neat plots of empty ground. The sidewalks lay flat and empty like a ghost town. There was not a single tree.

I mailed a card with a photo of Stalin Allee on it to Minnesota. On it I wrote:

Dear Mom and Pop, Am having a wonderful time, wish you were here. We leave East Berlin in several hours and then back to Hamburg. Love.

Bombed buildings in East Berlin, 1954.

I slipped the card into the post box with satisfaction. I felt a need to brag, as if we had broken a record or pulled off a coup. The impulse to shock was irresistible—I wanted to knock my parents over with my unique run of luck.

We walked the streets for hours. As night deepened, the sidewalks emptied and the ruins of buildings disappeared into darkness. Glad to sit down, we stopped at a small café for supper. By the time we were back on the street it was late. Several drunken men staggered around corners, illuminated by street lamps that shone a harsh glare into the dusty air. A Russian factory blazed in the darkness, lights popping and machines humming.

It was nearing midnight when we boarded the subway to return to West Berlin. I pulled the scarf around my cheeks and refrained from speaking. We remained wary, although we expected no interference if we minded our own business. It was far tougher to get out of the eastern sector than to get in. In 1954, people were technically allowed to cross in and out of the two sectors freely, but cars were checked for prohibited goods, particularly those headed to the west. Phone calls were not allowed in either direction. I sat silently next to Heinz, feeling the train drawing us back to the West Zone, to the Golden Bears, back to openness where one could breathe freely, back to frivolity.

Once the train was under way, Heinz began speaking with a quiet intensity. "You must know," he said in a low voice, looking at me steadily, "two Germanys are impossible. With separate Germanys brothers are separated, families are split, and the economies go in different directions. Each side solidifies its system as the years pass and the rift becomes irreparable. We are one people. Reunification is imperative."

Heinz wanted me to understand. He wanted America to understand. America, with its freedom, high standard of living, influence around the world, and its vast resources. Americans lived on another continent. How could we possibly understand?

But he thought I might. I squeezed his hand and believed every word he said.

࠾ ♦ ᔋ

THE TOUR GROUP MEMBERS had broken into pairs and groupings as kindred spirits formed alliances. By the time our bus ascended the mountain and deposited twenty-three weary tourists at the chalet in Wiesen, Switzerland, Ian, Margo, Don, and I had become something of a foursome. We walked the streets of each new town together exploring, sampling the pubs, sometimes accompanied by fellow tour members.

The tour leader, Ian Wright, a graduate student at Cambridge, charmed us with his English accent and erudite manner of speaking, his clear white complexion, brown tweed jacket, and red tie. In his proper and efficient way he managed the tour smoothly, joining up with local guides in each country, who were mostly young fellows like himself. Margo was taken with him and followed his lectures on local history with rapt attention.

Ian seemed to enjoy Margo's lively chatter. Since he and Don gravitated together as the only two single males in the group, and since Margo and I were best friends, the four of us found ourselves branching off to out-of-the-way spots together. Often Don and I found ourselves sitting side by side in a booth sharing a menu. It happened so gradually that I barely noticed, until one of the girls moved over to make room for Don next to me when he came up to the dinner table. In the eyes of the others it seemed we had become something of a couple.

Don Maurier, a junior at Stanford in Oakland, California, was quiet with dark hair, keen brown eyes, and the unpretentious demeanor and assurance appropriate for one on the edge of being handsome. His good looks were marred by thin pockmarks dotting his face, which I soon became used to and decided they added a rugged aspect to his clean-cut fraternity appearance. Don was not the forward type. I believe we kissed a few times, but we were rarely alone. The four of us enjoyed each other's company: Ian with his educated take on world history and everything else in sight, Don with his sweet smile and easy accommodation, Margo with her vivacious sense of fun, and me with my jarring curiosity.

I didn't know why Don, who was eyed by the other girls, was spending so much time with me. I wasn't sure what attracted the opposite sex. It seemed that a lure of some sort was necessary, some flare to draw the attention of the scanning male eye. There were many sources: striking beauty, skillful wiles, a flair for flirting, verbal enticements, a warm enveloping personality, a vivacious charm, or maybe even just a devastating smile. I possessed none of these. Or it could have been the night Don caught me flying back to my room from Mary's room next door in a sheer yellow nightgown. I had been counting on the late hour and empty corridor for cover. Maybe the embarrassment of that incident sparked a new awareness between us. Although Don was the upright collegiate boy, not the artistic renegade I felt I could relate to, we drew together more and more.

One warm evening in Switzerland, the four of us strolled down to a mountain lake that lay glistening in front of the chalet. Only a few lights remained in the scattered houses set high in the foothills. The

European tour: Ian, Margo, me, and Don, 1954.

moon was low and creature sounds crackled into the air from the across the water. Far down the beach we discovered an abandoned rowboat, and we set out with a container of beer across the lake, letting the smooth surface of the water glide under our fingertips as Ian rowed steadily over the glass surface.

We found the far shore deserted. Don and I meandered off along the waterfront listening to the pebbles crunch under our feet, then turned to follow a narrow footpath leading into the woods. After walking some time we were about to turn back when suddenly Don pressed my arm and pointed to a streak of flickering light. Through a breach in a tapestry of spruce, pine and fir trees, we spied a lone cabin with a broken shutter hanging ajar from one of its windows. A shotgun leaned against the log siding. Curious, we moved up gingerly. As we stood in front of the window, the curtains were swept aside and the shadow of a face appeared, inscrutable. We waved sheepishly and gave our best smiles. The window scratched open.

"Hi. We seem to be lost," Don said hurriedly.

A pause. "Come around to the front," a voice from the cabin said.

We were met by a young lad with a raft of brown hair and wearing khaki hiking pants. He looked us over with some curiosity, as if we'd landed from the sky. Then, seeing our confusion, he collected himself, smiled and motioned us inside. The cabin, a single room, was plentifully furnished with homemade bookcases, brass table lamps, beat-up club chairs, and a bulky wooden desk strewn with books and papers. Our new friend motioned for us to seat ourselves.

His name was Marten. He was spending the summer in his uncle's cabin and would be returning to the university in the fall. It was his habit to settle there during vacation to write.

"I'm currently working on a novel about my uncle's experiences as an undercover agent for Swiss intelligence. In 1943, my uncle was captured by plain-clothed SS men on the train route between Switzerland and Compiègne. He managed to break away by leaping from the car and broke both his legs. Through all this he continued to guard a secret code embedded in his wrist watch."

We were gripped by his stories and his life as a writer. How did he like living deep in the woods on his own?

"I don't mind. I prefer to be alone. I seek it. Alone with my work, that's a happiness. I need nothing else."

Despite this statement, he appeared to be glad of our company and served us a hearty wine. Occasionally he tossed another log in the free-standing wood stove. The warmth from the fire and the sense of being secluded in the wilderness drew an intimacy around the small room. Time slipped away as we talked and smoked Swedish cigarettes.

It was after eleven when we returned to the lake and found Ian and Margo slouched against a tree. At the sight of us they jumped up.

"Where the devil . . . ?" Ian lashed out impatiently, sweeping sand from his trouser legs with his hand. "We have to get the boat back!"

"Wait until you hear—"

"Get in. I'll row." Ian was untying the lead rope and had no time to listen. We piled into the bow.

"We only *borrowed* the boat," I suggested hopefully. "We've even cleaned the seats and tossed out the empty Rivella bottles."

Ian harrumphed.

Don and I whispered together in the darkness, rehashing our meeting with Marten and plotting how we would enrich the story for Margo and Ian. At the end of the evening, outside my door, Don gave me a long kiss, and he seemed to mean it.

કે♦ક

DURING A TWO-DAY layover in Oslo, Margo and I set out on a hitchhiking jaunt to see the countryside. Eyebrows were raised. At the last minute Ian decided to join us, either to make sure we were safe, because he wanted to be with Margo, or because he was finally loosening up. Don didn't go along, probably concurring with the rest of the group that such a venture was foolhardy. One didn't just start out in a strange country and beg along the road for a free ride.

The three of us walked briskly along a two-lane road that wound out into the hills. The day was sunny with a pure solid blue sky overhead. We felt bright and carefree. Margo and I sported leather shoulder bags, along with Peck and Peck skirts, polished cotton blouses, and nylons. I wore a three-strand beaded necklace around my neck. All part of the formal travel wardrobe our mothers had fashioned for us in preparation for the big trip. Ian sported his usual jacket, shirt, and tie. We had no overnight bags, no destination, and no intention except to go far enough to see the fjords and return the next day.

We hadn't gone two miles when a car stopped and offered to take us as far as the driver's farm, twenty miles down the road. After that rides were plentiful, but as the day progressed traffic thinned. We walked for over an hour. It was exhilarating to be on foot in southern Norway along rich green pastureland veined with swift-flowing streams and peaceful lakes. The forest-laden hills, stretched out in the distance in vast magnificence, didn't appear to move as we crawled along at their feet.

Finally, a pick-up truck pulled to a stop and a hefty woman motioned us into the open back. Through an open window we caught a glimpse of a wide gruff face and blonde hair pulled back in a knot on her neck. Before we were completely seated she took off without inquiring where we were headed. As the truck moved deeper into the country we spied farm buildings lodged among the rolling hills, separated by patchworks of flowing green trees.

At last the truck pulled to a halt and the woman motioned for us to descend. Margo, Ian, and I jumped out and looked around doubtfully. The road had come to a dead end, cut off by the string of fjords looming ahead beyond a far-off wall of cliffs. We were in the middle of nowhere. No houses, stations, or road signs. Nothing in the vicinity but the endless countryside. The sun was already starting to sink behind the distant hills.

Ian ventured up to the cab window.

"End of road," clipped the stout woman from the truck.

"Excuse me," said Ian, looking up at her and adjusting his glasses, "We're new around here. Could you direct us to the nearest hotel?"

Margo and I exchanged glances. The last thing we wanted to do was stay in another hotel.

"Hey, we're hitchhiking!" I cried.

The truck driver started to laugh, throwing back her head and letting the full force of her baritone voice blast out through the window. "You see a hotel hidden behind those trees? Ha, ha, ha! These foreigners! You're in the country, now, my boy. No hotels, no room service, no taxis. We live in that farm house down yonder. Can't even see our nearest neighbor from here. There's just us. Ha, ha, ha."

I saw what she meant. There were no visible buildings from there to the mountains. The woman was still laughing loudly as she motioned us back into the truck and drove us to her farm which was a mile off the main road up a dirt drive. We would be allowed to sleep in the barn. When we reached the house the woman jumped down from the cab and led us into a barn. In one corner was a wooden trough filled with straw and a few straggly blankets, wide enough to hold the three of us easily.

"Here your bed," she said in broken English before departing.

Ian removed his gold-rimmed glasses and wiped them thoughtfully, looking as if he weren't sure what he'd gotten himself into. As we sat leaning against the side of the trough our hostess called us in for bowls of hot barley soup and thick bread slices punctured with olives.

The farmhouse was plain but warm, and after our meal we moved to the next room where a long couch covered with two striped blankets and several wooden chairs faced an open-hearth fireplace that crackled with dry wood. Energized by the food, the comfort of the four walls, and the ruddy faces of the farm woman and her husband, even Ian loosened up and we conversed until evening deepened into night. The couple firmly refused, as we were leaving for the barn, to accept any money for their hospitality.

The barn was dark except for a few strips of moonlight along the wooden floor. The musty odor of manure, fresh straw, and fermenting oats hovered between the walls. After some maneuvering we arranged our three bodies in the straw bed. Ian suggested that to conserve space we stagger heads and feet, lying down alternately in opposite directions, but no one wanted someone's feet by their face. Being the only male Margo and I thought it would be more balanced if Ian was in the middle, but he claimed he needed more space than that would allow.

Finally Margo fell into the middle and pulled up a blanket. "I don't care where you guys sleep," she said. "I'm hitting the hay, ha, ha."

"Ha, ha," Ian and I replied, giving up.

"There's a remote possibility we can get some sleep in this hog bin," I said from my slip of a spot next to Margo. "Just don't make any noise. No snoring or snorting, and no flinging arms. Make sure nobody hogs the blankets. Try not to wiggle. And most of all—*no* going to the bathroom within hearing distance!"

"Shut up!" the two of them snarled as Ian turned out the lantern.

Summoning our by now well-developed capacity to accommodate awkward sleep positions, we fell into a fitful, restless slumber, shrugging off the sharp pricks of straw and movements of tiny bugs until the cow bells ushered in the first rays of the morning sun.

Our arrival back at Oslo was greeted by the other tour members with great curiosity. Ian had slivers of straw stuck in his hair, Margo's Peck and Peck skirt was torn, and we all displayed scratches and bites along both arms. They heard our accounting with skeptical interest and had to admit that it was a good story and must be all right if Ian liked it. Several days later two of the girls decided to try a one-day hitchhiking trip themselves, which they thoroughly enjoyed, although I saw some disapproving frowns hovering in the background.

OUR EUROPEAN TREK was drawing to a close. After two months our group was getting weary of climbing on and off buses and tromping past church naves. Everyone claimed they never wanted to set eyes on another cathedral. We had whipped through hotels, inns, pensions, hostels, and dorms and spent nights in train cars stretched out on bench seats or slung in an overhead luggage hammock. Often we bumped along country roads, heads tilted against black bus windows. We put up with continual inconveniences and mishaps: the communal bathroom was down the hall; we had to drop coins in a slot to obtain hot water; the bus didn't show up; our suitcases grew bulkier and heavier by the week. There were compensations, however: the unexpected adventures we met around every corner and the open-arm receptions that greeted us due to the immense popularity of Americans in Europe in the post-war fifties.

Margo and I had drifted apart since my relationship with Sylvia blossomed, but now that we were continually thrown together our old camaraderie had revived. Hanging out with Ian and Don, we became almost as tight as before.

I liked being paired up with Don. His preference for me raised my status in the group, although in my mind we were hardly an item. As I gazed out the train window at the jagged mountains in the distance, it struck me that I no longer needed approval from my companions. I felt grounded and self-sufficient. Since connecting with Sylvia I carried a sense of her presence and the binding power of our relationship. I now had an ally, a collaborator, a soulmate. Our mutual quest filled me and I needed nothing and no one else. It felt great to be alive. I was soaring.

But—it was time to conceive a plan.

≈◆≪

AN URGE HAD BEEN lurking in the shadows, dodging my steps. Before long I would be back in the United States. During the summer in Europe I'd encountered cultures that opened new avenues, unique approaches, broader understandings, and more experiences than I ever dreamed of. Everything except the experience I wanted most of all—I was not yet a real woman. Don was sweet. I liked him. In fact, he was adorable. He would come to my rescue.

The plan was simple. At first I wasn't sure I could go through with it. The event would take place on the last evening after our farewell dinner.

The dinner was an elaborate affair, served at a long table covered with a lace-trimmed linen cloth and lavishly spread with yellow-red and blue wooden vases in the center and blue-bordered china serving dishes. Several rose-colored kerosene lamps flashed ruby beams above the miniature dance floor. The eminent return to the States enlivened everyone's spirits. We sat around the table and listened to a lively trio of yodelers, followed by a local *dansband*. People constantly jumped up to dance or threw their arms around someone's shoulders for last-night photos. We rehashed trip stories, laughed and drank wine to what was conceded to be the trip of a lifetime that none of us could stand one more minute of. Hooray for the Golden Bears!

I could hardly wait for the festivities to end. After dinner I took Don aside. Could he meet me in an hour by the boathouse? It was important.

When we met at the appointed time, the only shapes visible in the moonless night were the pointed tree tops etched like patterned Christmas stars against a charcoal sky. This part of the grounds extended beyond the reach of the hotel lights, and the lawn and bordering woods were hidden under a canopy of darkness. A delicious sense of daring that had been with me all evening had been replaced by a fluttery excitement. I hardly knew what to expect.

I would soon find out.

Don and I started down a narrow path listening to the pat-pat of our feet against the soft dirt and the low rustling as we moved out over the grass. Neither of us had as yet said anything. I could tell Don was waiting.

We stopped near an arch of trees and I asked him to kiss me, which he did, grasping me slowly and firmly. There, in the dark curve of his shoulder, I told him what I wanted and asked if he would he be willing. Taking me by the hand, he led me into the Alpine forest, the darkness closing in on us as we penetrated deeper into the woods. We lay down on a blanket of jackets and leaves and he took me in his arms. I breathed in the spicy odor of his skin and the nutty smell of earth under us. His touch felt warm. Our kisses were soft at first, then we let ourselves go and I felt his hands on my bare body and pressed him closer. The rest was lost in darkness and the novelty of our two bodies finding each other.

Don held my hand as we walked silently back to the chalet, both of us lost in a haze of bewilderment at what had just happened. He didn't appear to know what to make of this new development, coming on the eve of our permanent separation, while I was flooded with a tingling sense of relief and accomplishment.

At the door to my room Don took me in his arms for a last kiss and I searched his face, but his eyes were shadowed in darkness and I couldn't read him. I slipped into my room and sat on the bed as Margo dozed, puzzled at the sense of satisfaction I felt and the delicious warmth that was coursing through my body like waves seeking new ground. The experience was riveted in my mind, not the sensuality of it, which was lost in expectation, but the fact of it. I wanted to immediately wire Sylvia in Los Angeles and bowl her over with this latest exploit and the fact that I was no longer a child. Now I had the assurance of one who knows. I had arrived!

Margo emerged from the shower the next morning and poked me to get up, but I remained silent under the sheets. It seems strange that I didn't confide in her, but I wasn't in the habit of sharing my sexual experiences with anyone, even a best friend. Not that she would have condemned me or raised objections, but I wanted to guard my most intimate feelings. I wanted to hold my life of dreams, fantasies, and expectations within, safe and nurtured, where they couldn't be punctured. With girlfriends there was a line regarding males that we didn't cross. Besides, Margo and I played it pretty cool. She assured me that she found Ian fun but could take or leave him. I told her that Don and I would not meet again, as our territories were too distant. I kept my true feelings guarded, which was not hard since I didn't know what they were anyway.

The next day the tour left for the airport and I caught the Paris train for one last meeting with Jean Paul and the decks of the Liberté. I kept my word and wrote to Jean Paul, beginning a trans-Atlantic correspondence that trailed me faithfully during the next bumpy years to come.

Chapter Thirteen

❧ *Los Angeles at Last* ❧

ERCHED ON THE RADIATOR in my room, I stared dreamily out the window at the brick house across the street with its curved driveway and the familiar white dome of the Basilica in the distance. I was torn with indecision. Enrollment for the fall quarter at the University of Minnesota was about to start. I had to come up with something! My one aim was to reunite with Sylvia and pursue an independent life together. Nothing else was real. Sylvia was losing patience with my lack of action, and I had to take a stand. Her constant letters urged me to "get out here!"

"I have just the man for you," she wrote. "His name is Perry." She had nearly knocked this Perry fellow down as her new MG-TD careened into the University of Southern California parking lot. Alighting from the car, she went up to apologize and learned that Perry Manheim was an associate professor in the psychology department, recently divorced. He invited her to stop in at his office in Founder's Hall after her Western Civilization class, which she immediately did. The professor seemed to find Sylvia's youth and non-conformist spirit a refreshing novelty. But she declared him a bit stuffy for her taste. She was grooming him for me.

My friend's ideas didn't end there. She couldn't wait for me to meet Paul Sanchez (later Paul Sand, star of the 1970s TV series *Friends and Lovers*), her longtime friend from Hollywood High. "He likes your picture." Paul, an American with Mexican/Russian parents, had studied with Marcel Marceau in Paris and was now dancing in small clubs in

Los Angeles and San Francisco. "He is tall and beautiful," Sylvia wrote. "You two will get along like twins. We'll have a grand time."

The next afternoon after returning from the university, I carried a newspaper clipping to the hall phone, cradled the black receiver under my chin, located an underlined phone number, and dialed. A male voice answered.

"Is this Jeff?" I asked. "I saw your ad in the *Minnesota Daily*. Are you still looking for someone to share expenses? He was. As soon as finals were over he would be driving a new Plymouth from a Minnesota dealership to the owner in Los Angeles. The cost was minimal; expenses would be covered by the dealer. It couldn't have been easier.

I signed up.

My parents were incredulous. Traveling across country with a complete stranger! They did not approve. Who was this Jeff person and had I even met him? Yes, we'd had coffee in Dinky Town to arrange the details. Sylvia's mother had invited me to L.A. for Christmas and I announced firmly that I planned to go. I also assured them I intended to finish college and reminded them that Dad had promised to back any reputable school of my choice. He pondered a while and finally wavered. My restless despondency at home had long been only too apparent. With a heavy heart he purchased a ticket for me on the Great Northern Empire Builder.

FINALLY I WAS ON MY WAY! It was December 1954. The train sped through the Badlands, across Nevada and into the Rocky Mountain ranges of California heading for Los Angeles. The scenes of dramatic rock formations, rich farmland, and mountain peaks rising one after another in waves of lavender blue, passed outside the window in a blur. I was wheeling with expectation, unable to focus. The whistle let out a long blast, as if to blow away the clouds and part every shadow barring the way west. The train flew through the mountains and across the desert, glued to the tracks, unstoppable, heading for distant shores and unimagined encounters. And a reunion with Sylvia.

I was still flying when I arrived in the City of Angels. The figure dashing towards me lit up the platform with her youthful stride and bright expectant air. I watched as Sylvia threaded through the crowd, fetching in a Prussian-blue jacket and charcoal skirt, her auburn hair pulled back by a tortoise shell head band.

"Hey, old bean!" Sylvia stood before me and her eyes took in my pressed wool suit, freshly washed hair, and the satchel of books and private journals I carried over one shoulder. "At last you're here!"

"Did you ever doubt?"

There was so much to tell, but I could hardly get a word in edgewise.

"Wait until you see my room!" Sylvia exclaimed. "Mother's cooked a special lamb roast for you! Paul's coming over and we're going to China-town! I already have your Christmas present and you're going to love it!"

I could only get in a smile before she continued. "Was the train a big bore? Glad you brought a jacket, it can get chilly in December. Don't you love the Spanish architecture? Very *passionnant*. I have so many places to show you! My new car's in the lot, a two-seater, a dream to drive. Wasn't Daddy a sport to get it for me?"

We sped along the Golden State Freeway in Sylvia's yellow MG with the wind sweeping our hair and a full gold sun pouring over the passing landscape of sprawling houses. A faint whiff of ambrosia blew into the window and along my cheek. The little MG careened by cars with a roar, and occasionally we received a wave from a grinning fellow MG driver. I'd never felt more alive—I was being transported on a wave of intoxication I'd not experienced before.

Leaving the freeway, we climbed up into the Los Feliz hills, curving around spacious lots with Spanish style houses set back at various angles among the plantings. Palm trees arched like peaceful sentinels on front lawns. The MG swerved into a driveway and stopped before a white stucco house. It was a diverse structure with a variety of walls and gables facing different directions. A path edged by bulging red fuchsias wound up to the front door. A staircase wound behind the porch and disappeared into the upper reaches of the house through a dark wooden door, which turned out to be the outside entrance to Sylvia's attic room. The scent of lavender and gardenia sifted through a wrought iron railing as we walked up the sloping path.

Besides two single beds, Sylvia's room held a low wooden shelf lined with ruby candles in wrought iron holders, and in one corner three fringed hassocks encircling a low marble table. Oil canvases of various sizes covered the walls and I breathed in the intoxicating odor of oil paint.

Here at last! I couldn't believe it. Mrs. Newton rushed up to greet me. She was stunning, with brushed-back auburn hair, a gold mesh necklace, and a sparkling black sweater. In her presence the house breathed a simmering fragrance of warm wax and rosebud. In a few days it would be Christmas and the rooms buzzed with preparations. Sylvia and I accompanied Mr. Newton to a specialty store to select an East Indian brocade vest for Mrs. Newton. Evenings, we decorated the fresh spruce tree with silver tinsel and bulbs while Mr. Newman read the paper in front of the fireplace.

On Christmas day, Sylvia and I helped Mrs. Newton serve honeyed ham and sweet potato soufflé in the lofty dining room. We were joined by a couple, long-standing friends, and a girl named Bonnie, a friendly girl with short buff hair and rather thick arms and legs whose parents were in Europe for the holiday. We made a warm party by the living room fire, sipping tea, opening gifts, and listening to choral music of St. Martin-in-the-Fields. Sylvia presented me with one of her charcoal drawings and a book of Emily Dickenson poems. I gave her a marble statue of Athena and a long silk scarf embossed with violet and vermillion swirls.

Afterward, as we lay in bed, I stared sleepily at the ceiling. Soon I heard Bonnie's breathing deepen to a soft purr. Suddenly, in the darkness, I felt a hand squeeze mine and heard Sylvia whisper, "Good night," a gesture made more intimate by Bonnie's presence. I was moved with a swell of emotion to reach over and squeeze her hand in return,

The Newton family: Silvia and her parents, 1954.

a gesture that I had never made before in my life. I fell asleep in a state of contented fullness.

❧ ◆ ☙

THE NEXT NIGHT Paul Sanchez arrived. Tall and slender, his gentle face was surrounded by locks of magnificent black hair, and he projected a youthful amiability that I liked immediately. He and Sylvia wanted to show me the Mexican market, so we drove across town to Olvera Street, strolled along the stalls, sipped wine at one of the open bars, and listened to guitar music drifting from the bead-curtained doorways.

Back in Sylvia's room, I watched Paul's tall form ease gracefully onto one of the hassocks. He looked simple and artless, even rather tender as he turned his soft hazel eyes from Sylvia to me. As we sat talking around the low marble table sipping hot tea, I was aware of Paul's physical presence. We discussed the conventionality of the University of Colorado, Sylvia's New York exploits, Paul's latest dance engagements, and my tour of Europe the previous summer.

"You like it here?" Paul asked me.

"Yes, indeed I do. I like Sylvia's parents, the Spanish houses, the rolling hills, even Tito, the Japanese houseboy."

"You've met Tito?" he asked.

I nodded. "Very friendly," I said.

"He writes poetry," Sylvia put in.

"Tito surprised me one night," Paul said in a low, confiding voice. "As I was passing through the shadows on my way to the car, Tito made a pass at me. You know," he turned his eyes on me, "Tito lives in the apartment above the garage. He has been with the Newtons for years and no one has known." Paul put him off. As a dancer, Paul was used to being taken as homosexual, a misunderstanding which, he complained, restrained girls from veering his way.

Imagine! Homosexual! I had much to learn.

As I lay in bed that night it occurred to me there was nowhere else in the world I would rather be than right here, right now.

❧ ◆ ❧

THE BIG QUESTION: what to do next? In the month since my arrival we'd driven with Sylvia's parents to Santa Barbara to visit friends, spent afternoons at the antique shop where Mrs. Newton worked part time, frequented Paul's favorite musical clubs, written poetry in the park, discussed Zen philosophy with Tito the houseboy, and spent hours holed in the attic room plotting how to achieve our artistic and educational pursuits in an enlivening environment.

Finally, we registered for spring semester at the University of Southern California where Sylvia was already a student. My classes looked intriguing: Theory of Modern Criticism, Semantics, Philosophy, Introduction to Concert Music, and Ceramics. For now we would forgo exploring Guatemala, sharing a studio in Manhattan, or finding a bungalow in Taos. We would return to college and lose ourselves in U.S.C.'s park-like campus with its grey and pink Romanesque buildings and long paths curving through clouds of oak, palm, and bay fig trees. I would work towards my goal of earning a degree, Sylvia would major in art, and the two sets of parents, who were pressing for us to settle safely in college, would be satisfied. On the side we would indulge our creative talents.

We located the perfect apartment within walking distance of campus. Part of an old clapboard four-plex, it was dingy and bare, and best of all, cheap. This fit Sylvia's pocketbook, as she had to pay a portion of school expenses from her part-time clerical job. It fit my idea of living where things were happening, where things were *different*.

We furnished the apartment with donations from Sylvia's mother and purchases scrounged in Japantown and flea markets. For the living room we procured a faded couch spread with a fringed red Chinese throw, a desk fashioned from a long block of Formica supported by pumice blocks, an antique chair with curved wooden legs, and a side table of unfinished wood draped with a long Persian coverlet. A brown-and-maroon Navajo rug dominated the floor and the walls were covered with Sylvia's paintings, drawings, and photographs taken when she'd modeled in New York.

Apartment at the University of Sourthern California, 1955

We wanted the apartment to convey our mottos: Art Before Function—Expect the Unexpected—Individuality Beats Conventionality.

I took a job at the Union bookstore selling school supplies. I loved it. Holding a job gave me the feeling of being on my own. They dubbed me the most cheerful clerk they'd ever had. The thing was, even though Dad was footing my college expenses and seeing to my every financial need, I *wanted* to work. I had always wanted to work. Being denied the chance because of Dad's prohibition—he thought attending to my studies and having fun while I could were top priorities for fleeting youth—had only increased the desire. No longer was I going to be kept from the adult world of responsibility and the satisfaction of earning my own way. I was on the road to self-reliance. So while Sylvia drove off in the MG to clerk at the music shop, I hiked to the bookstore; we were now included in the ranks of the employed, the dependable, and the producers of the world.

Four months later, bored out of my mind, I quit.

⁂

ONE RAINY MORNING I was peering out the back window, a window so blistered it was almost impossible to distinguish what was on the other side. Abruptly, a shadow landed on the pane, a shape emerging from the distance. As the shape approached, it slowly transformed into the outline of a face. I stared as the form swept by at eye level and made out a pair of smoky dark eyes that leveled on mine for a quick instant before disappearing.

"I think there's a man living next door," I said to Sylvia, walking into the kitchen.

There were two. Several days later, we ran into them on the front walk as we were returning from campus. We learned they lived in the rear flat next to ours. One of them spoke up anxiously.

"It must have been one of you!" the one with the full mouth said, looking from Sylvia to me. "I've been dying to know who you are ever since I saw a pair of saucer-like eyes at the back window, staring out at me through the glass. I thought I was being spied on by Audrey Hepburn."

"That was me," I exclaimed, glad to have the mystery cleared. "The glass was deceptive."

"I've been haunted," he went on with a smile that stretched across his freckled face. "Now at last we meet. This is Buddy and I'm Max."

After traipsing through what they called our funky pad, the two invited us over for tea. There was a unique quality about their apartment. Several nude male statues rested on the tables, and blue candles etched with Greek floral designs lined the top of a tall ebony cabinet. I spied a large print of two scantily-clad men lounging on a sauna bench beyond the open door of the bedroom. As Max hustled out to the kitchen to steep the tea. Buddy told us that Max was employed as an orderly at a nearby hospital, and he himself worked on a commercial construction crew. Buddy was surprisingly frank as he described their early lives and how they'd come to the big city to find work and create a lifestyle unavailable in a small town. As we relaxed into the mounds of oversized pillows and sipped a second cup of tea, they began to confide in us.

"Yes, to answer your question, we've been together a long time—six years, right Buddy?" Max leaned back in his chair, his knees pressed together and arms loose in his lap. "We're a couple, you know," he said with a direct look. "We're gay." Max then nodded toward the statue next to me. "How do you like our Greek Adonis?"

I regarded the naked figure, an alabaster rendition of strong, sensual male youth. These boys' lives obviously centered on their sexual orientation, but I wasn't sure if the sensuality or the identity issue preoccupied them.

Did Max and Buddy minded people knowing? I wanted to know.

"Not our friends, but at work it's a different story. We're careful to play it straight there." Max, the outgoing one, known as Maxine, had an expressive full mouth and blue eyes that never left your face. Buddy, or Bette, resembled a baseball player with a gruff face and reticent grin. He moved about with a shy shuffle. Before we left we had agreed to drive together the following Sunday to Japantown for brunch.

One Saturday evening our two new friends escorted us to one of their parties. The apartment was crowded with males dolled up as gorgeous female stars and melodramatic queens. It was startling to hear a deep male voice emanate from a glamorous face dominated by scarlet red lips and blackened lashes. Nude male reproductions were everywhere. While the drinks flowed and exotic music played on the stereo system, figures spread out over the couches and floor or danced seductively under orange lights. A crowd gathered around Sylvia and me, the only girls present. Through the din they flooded us with questions and then opened up about their lifestyle, which seemed to be focused on sexual encounters and relationships. Experimentation and exotic methods of sexual expression flourished. Max and Buddy described how they cruised Venice Beach on weekends, hitting the gay bars and splitting off with separate partners for the evening. Didn't they get jealous? Yes, sometimes, but these flings were strictly recreational, restricted to one night stands involving no entanglement.

I couldn't figure out why anyone would choose a lifestyle that was so prohibitive and limiting and required a constant shield of secrecy. Why would Buddy, a nice, kind man with no noticeable feminine attributes, make such a gender switch, isolating himself from the rest of society? It was apparent they didn't fit into the conventional mold. Max was high strung and became overexcited at the slightest stimulation. Buddy kept a calm exterior, but if challenged or reprimanded tears would form and run slowly down his cheeks. They only ceased when he received a comforting squeeze, and he would turn his damp face up in gratitude.

Both were highly sensitive, a male trait strongly rejected by society. Only with friends could they be themselves. In the business arena they were constrained to blend in with the heterosexual norm. Max was delighted when I agreed to attend a Christmas party at the hospital as his date, which would bolster his image of normalcy. He primed me ahead of time. No compliments on his tie or how handsome he looked. Rather, I was to behave in a friendly fashion with a hint of admiration thrown in whenever possible. There wasn't a trace of fey or swoosh in his manner as, handsome in his navy business suit, he conversed with his coworkers over dinner. We both put on what we hoped was a convincing front. Everyone in the gay community did this, including, I was informed, Rock Hudson and Caesar Romero, whose proclivities were well-known in Hollywood circles.

This was in the days when the term "gay" had just come into wide use and homosexuality was denounced as unnatural and sinful by the traditional mainstream. I couldn't say how much of its sordid aspect was caused by forced concealment, implying evil and fostering feelings of ostracism and shame. But exposure to the offbeat and subterranean was just what Sylvia and I sought in our urge to experience everything possible beyond our restricted upbringing. I wanted to be available to anything that came my way, to seek out and accept the foreign. That Max and Buddy took to us with such openness was flattering, a privilege not open to most. I prized their friendship.

The day after the Christmas party Max brought me six red roses and a card signed "The Gay Blades."

❧ ◆ ❧

SYLVIA'S VOICE ON THE PHONE was trembling. She was devastated and had to talk to me! Drop everything. She would be home in twenty minutes and could I go for a drive? When I heard the rev of the MG I ran outside and we tore off towards the beach. It was a bright Saturday afternoon without a cloud in the sky. A long rain during the night had diluted the gauze of smog that usually hung over the mountains and the sky was unusually clear. I could see Sylvia's eyes were red and her cheeks streaked with tears.

"Oh, Judy, it's Mother." She bit her lower lip. "We've just had the most dreadful row. She accuses me of—of all sorts of things."

"Tell me everything. We'll work this out."

That morning her mother called Sylvia into the den and proceeded to tear down her life. She was concerned about the direction Sylvia was taking.

"She accused me of not taking my studies serious," Sylvia moaned, "of playing at being an artist, of being a dilettante, fluttering here and there and accomplishing nothing. 'Your dates come and go, with no stability. They don't last,' were her words. She says I dally with unseemly types and lack real friends. She wonders why I don't associate with the other students at school. She says I'm neglecting my education."

One of her mother's complaints was that Sylvia's friends revolved around her. People latched on to her, followed her lead, let her run the show. They were leeches. Without being named I knew this included me. I suspected it included Paul. Who else was there? Her mother had been firm. Sylvia needed to look closely at her life, and above all, at how her present situation contributed to her goals. Mrs. Newton admonished her to examine exactly what those goals were. Half shamed and half angry, Sylvia protested, denying everything.

"I've been completely demolished." She held the wheel tightly and a strand of auburn hair fell over her cheek. "Mother has not an ounce of appreciation for what I'm trying to do or how far I've progressed." Anger flushed into her face. "I had a job. I've been contributing to my own schooling. *I'm responsible!* Maybe I'm not employed at this particular moment, but I have three good prospects, and I'm sure one will come through. It is really too much! I'm putting so much effort into everything. *How could she not trust me?*"

While Sylvia continued to agonize, I pondered. During my month as a house guest at the Newton's I had gravitated into her world: I lived with Sylvia's family, adopted her chosen college as my own, kept pace as she procured the apartment and everything else, tagged along at outings with her family and friends. Of course, this was her city, her turf, and being an outsider I followed her lead. But there was no denying it, I revolved in her orbit. Was it possible Sylvia was losing something in this dynamic? Would she, in retrospect, consider that that role of diva was not such a favorable one, that she didn't want to have to pull all the weight, and that she was lacking balance and input from me that would enhance her own efforts?

It occurred to me I paid a price as well. As a satellite, I was subjugating parts of myself in order to adapt and reap the benefits of a life I'd always craved but might never have realized on my own. Was I so dependent on her? The answer had to be yes. Sylvia had created our artistic enclave, the social milieu in which we lived. I guess I owed everything to her. All I could do was get good grades and continue to write. What alternative did I have, now that I had committed to the same lifestyle she wanted, which was what I wanted as well?

Still, maybe I was dead weight. Maybe I had relinquished my ability to shape a singular identity of my own.

Maybe I'd never possessed it.

As Sylvia continued to vent, the heat of her protest suggested that she didn't buy into this categorization. I didn't feel accused by *her*. She had turned to me, as her closest intimate, and we would share this together. The best, the only thing I could do was listen sympathetically. Her mother didn't appreciate the transformation Sylvia was going through: trying to balance the Hollywood superficiality she grew up with, the dual demands of higher education and her artistic calling. I was convinced Sylvia possessed rare talent. She was original, ingenious, and compelling. Her haunting beauty was an asset that opened doors, but it also interfered with the hard grind of accomplishment.

➤

SYLVIA AND I DIDN'T FIT IN with the co-eds sporting plaid skirts, saddle shoes, and bobby socks and the football fans who populated U.S.C.— Sylvia, with her black cinch belts, billowy skirts, and exotic beauty, and me with my black tights, massive silver rings, and cropped Shirley MacLaine hair. We kept to ourselves.

When I wasn't holed up at the school library and Sylvia wasn't out on some jaunt, we worked on individual projects. Occasionally I wrote poetry propped up against oversized pillows in bed, and Sylvia attended painting classes two evenings a week with her longtime teacher, Ada Gar. A few U.S.C. students stopped by to investigate our little studio, as we called it, and I imagined I was leading the life of a writer, which was proving to be almost as absorbing as actually being one.

Sylvia could also write. I treasure...
How did she do it? Her talent was boundl... imsical poems. Drat!

Sylvia

Cracked clock hands spun still
withered gloved fingers of fright
flattened faces against my dreams
boxed in laughter without light

Me

To poets long and sprawlèd out
I dedicate this song;
To those who plop the phrases out
While lounging unstrung on
The heedless couch of grass strewn plump
Presuming only will
Their humming sound so soft today,
Their breeze-lit limbs so still.

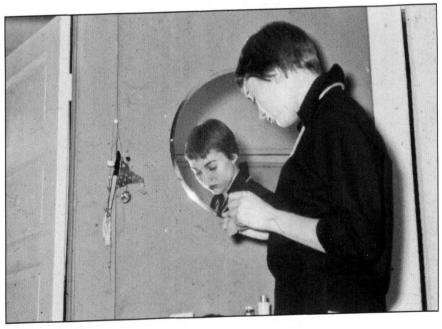

Me at the apartment.

Perry Manheim, a young professor Sylvia was grooming for my advancement, was a liberal outlook and a conservative manner. His brown hair neatly combed to one side and he wore a tan jacket over a turtleneck jersey. As a recent widower he lacked female company, and Sylvia thought I could fill the gap. She promoted our attributes and suitability to each other and arranged for the three of us to dine at our favorite Chinese restaurant.

The plan fizzled when Sylvia started seeing him herself. She often ran into him on campus or dropped into his office. They sat on a bench near the library and she read her poetry to him. As a psychologist, Perry understood and accepted our youthful yearnings. He possessed an intelligence and maturity lacking in the other men in Sylvia's orbit. She liked his professorial good looks. In the beginning I readied myself to accept his advances. There were no advances. He was clearly enamored of Sylvia, and although his feelings were muted—still grieving his wife—his eyes followed her everywhere. He began sliding in next to her in the booth or pulled her onto his lap when three of us piled into the back of Paul's roadster.

One morning, Sylvia showed up after an intimate dinner at Perry's apartment bearing a Polaroid photo of her wearing his pajama top. She commented on his lovemaking. I accepted this. After all, he had shown me no more than sincere friendliness. Sylvia kept her options open. Perry was well aware that she kept up dalliances with other men. He hung around but maintained his cool. By now he knew her only too well and held hopes that some time, some day, she might become disenchanted with her capricious lovers. But Sylvia was being drawn in new directions and saw both of us less as the weeks passed.

The following year I received an invitation to Perry's marriage to a woman I had not heard of. I did not attend.

ॐ ♦ ॐ

PAUL HUNG AROUND constantly. As he sat on the couch drinking cream soda, I drank in the sight of his soft green sweater and striking black hair. I was intrigued by his tall suppleness, sensuous lips, and the sweet expression he had when he looked at me. But he showed me no preference. I continued to enjoy our silly antics as the three of us drove along the road to Carmel harmonizing "Side by Side" or improvised swirling dances on the sands of Santa Monica beach under a spotlit moon. Paul presented me with an amber necklace nestled in a black enameled box for my birthday, and I gazed into the reddish depths of the stones, fascinated by their ruby hues and the hint of his soft eyes in their depths.

Sylvia was fixed on the idea that Paul and I should sleep together. One night she invited Paul over, tucked clean sheets into the bed, and served up an abalone and squid dinner she prepared herself in the tiny kitchen. The three of us sat cross-legged on pillows around the black marble table, plucking morsels of meat and rice from our plates with chopsticks. The squid was tough and tasted like motor oil, but I gamely swallowed every bite without chewing, hoping my stomach would cooperate—experiencing new things was now my watchword. A long swish of wine after every bite helped.

While I did the dishes, Sylvia disappeared into the bedroom and Paul put on an Amália Rodrigues *Fados* record she had collected from her job at the music store. Just as I sat down at the Formica desk and switched on the swivel-necked pole lamp Sylvia emerged, overnight case in hand, informed us she wouldn't return until the next day and quickly slipped out of the apartment.

I moved with my wine to the couch, the only comfortable seat in the living room, where Paul was leaning back with eyes closed, his head against the Chinese throw. We listened to records and spoke in a desultory fashion about this and that over the throaty tones of Amália Rodrigues. He told me about his Mexican grandparents and their move to California when his father was an infant. When Paul was a youth his father was killed in a machine accident. His mother, determined that her children would make it in the land of opportunity, scraped to give them private lessons and pushed them to exert themselves. At the age of eleven Paul took up acting at a local children's theater.

When I tried to find out about his personal feelings, he was less forthcoming. Finally I ran out of things to say. We sat listening to "Boeuf sur le Toit," "Bachianas Brasileiras No. 1," and "Carmina Burana." The low haunting strains combined with the warmth of the wine, the scents of oil paint and clovery perfume lingering in the room lulled me into an agreeable inertness.

But in the midst of the soothing quiet, I felt sparks of nervousness. Implications of the evening were clear to both of us, but we said nothing. I hadn't the slightest clue as to Paul's feelings, whether he was interested in me or how he found the idea of our making love. He didn't seem to be objecting. Maybe it appealed to him, as it did to me, despite the obvious setup. We liked each other and, besides, the idea of embarking on a sexual experience had its own enticement. His slender form stretched out beside me looked more and more appealing as I absorbed the impact of his nearness.

After finishing our third glass of wine he leaned over close to me. "I'd like to kiss you," he said softly.

I looked at him, feeling suddenly shaky, wondering what demeanor to assume.

"I would like that." I kept my tone noncommittal.

He appeared gratified and stretched an arm around me. I inched closer. He then bent his head, looked at me with a soft gaze, and slowly, without withdrawing his eyes from my face, placed his mouth on mine. The kisses were sweet and gradually grew more intense. I floated into a dream world of ruby wine and soft green pillows.

The next morning, in the bedroom, we lay quietly side by side, observing each other's nude bodies in the pale light from the window. I liked the feel of Paul's arm against my shoulder as I lay stretched on my side and the way he ran his fingers along my body, breathing words of admiration for the female form. I guessed he hadn't had much experience with lovemaking, maybe no more than I had. We smiled at each other, both quite pleased with the stepped-up activity in our sex lives.

After Paul left I lay on the couch listening to a Kabuki record, mulling over my womanly status. As of last summer I was no longer a virgin—first Don, now Paul. I beamed at the ceiling in satisfaction. After a while it dawned on me that something was not right. The demise of my virginity had been a philosophical choice, and I carried this latest intimacy like a prize. But the act itself I found lacking. Where was the pulse and passion of former high school embraces in the back seat of a Valiant? Now that I was over the threshold something was missing. It was puzzling.

I regarded the raft of drawings and oils papering the walls of the living room—Sylvia's work, streaked by shafts of morning light that filtered through the bamboo curtains. My mind reeled with indecision. *Shouldn't there be more bonding? More emotion?* All I knew was that the old thrill wasn't there. Somehow this did not seem, in one sense, like progress.

I didn't discuss this with Sylvia, aside from mentioning I had liked intimacy with Paul and wasn't sure what would be next. Sylvia and I didn't discuss sex, bound by the strict code of female privacy prevalent in the fifties.

Paul continued his drop-in visits. He felt at home in the apartment, draping his legs over the cushions gracefully, listening to Sylvia relate the story of her latest escapade. He didn't attempt another encounter between us. The probable reason for this hadn't escaped my notice. During the drive the three of us took to San Francisco to celebrate the Chinese New Year, it became obvious Paul was devoted to our mutual friend. He hung on Sylvia's words. He beamed at the commanding way she addressed him and complied with her every wish without complaint.

Journal Entry

Paul is impossible. He follows Sylvia around like a dog. He will do anything. She bosses him and he jumps. Can't he see that she takes him for granted? How can he let himself be walked on, how can he be so

Paul and Sylvia dramatizing at the apartment.

easygoing, without backbone? He is too boyish and unsophisticated for her. Too easy. She has so many irons in the fire, even though up until now most of them have been pure chaos.

I let go of any expectations that might have emerged from our night together. Paul was too pliant. He revolved around Sylvia like a limp puppy. Maybe—did the thought enter my head?—we were too much alike. Both of us hovered about Sylvia, caught up in the web of mystic fantasy and unbridled experimentation she created.

Sylvia was her own most successful creation. The impression she made was primary. Her favorite expression was, "It's not what you are that counts, it's what people think you are." In my total endorsement of Sylvia and everything she stood for, I slipped this concept into my pool of ignorance. If this was how she was so be it; my admiration for her talent, her assertiveness and knack for uncovering the unexpected outweighed all else. I wanted to be more like her. I knew she admired and stood by me, and that was all I needed to know.

As the months passed, the tone in the apartment began to subtly change. I first noticed it one evening as I was preparing to go out and Sylvia lay stretched on the bed following me with her eyes.

"That skirt doesn't go with your top at all," she remarked as I entered from the bathroom, "And those shoes are too mealy. They won't do."

I felt a rush of irritation. I'd heard these critiques before.

"I'm only trying things on to see if they work. Wait until I'm done before commenting," I snapped. I pulled on a different blouse, a shade lighter than the skirt I was wearing.

"No, no, all wrong," she exclaimed. "That bracelet is too shiny; it looks cheap. Try something bronze."

I shot into the bathroom and slammed the door. Sylvia had determined I had no taste. Usually I surrendered to her objections, but this time I pushed back. I had to admit that my discernment did need a bit of refining. I knew little of exotic foods, the various types of Italian fabrics, or the difference between Afshar and Saraband Persian rugs. Once I purchased a decorated plate that was too corny ("A smiling girl with a daisy in her hair—really!"). Except for *White Shoulders*, which had wafted for years from the folds of my mother's dresses, I knew nothing about perfumes.

"It pays to become identified with one scent, it adds to your mystique. The only perfume worth wearing is French," Sylvia said more than once. By then I was using *Replique* and *Ma Griffe* exclusively. The perfume bottles were tucked in the bureau alongside my jar of Germaine Monteil moisturizing cream and the Pierre Cardin neck scarf.

Sylvia commented on more than my attire.

"Really, those nasturtiums don't show up well in that vase. You need to *arrange* them." There was a bite in her voice that took me back. Before I could say anything she snatched her packing case and was gone.

Sylvia was absent most of the time now. Doing what I wasn't sure. Sometimes a low sports car pulled up to the curb and she was off for a cruise to Catalina Island. The people in white jackets and sunglasses I saw ushering her into the back seat were strangers to me.

Weekends I was often on my own. One evening as I was having dinner at a Mexican restaurant packed with students, Randall, a tall boy with a sweep of brown hair across his forehead and horn-rimmed glasses, approached and asked if he could share my table. After we'd discussed the novel assigned in our French lit class over plates of enchiladas, he walked me back to the apartment. I led him up the front walk and around the side to our recessed entrance.

"This place has a lot of character," he remarked, studying the marble dining table and the four Asian floor pillows. "Quite original. Like a Left Bank *atelier*." He regarded the oil canvases hung along the walls. "That's interesting work."

"Sylvia painted those."

Randall inspected the paintings closely. "Very unusual. Dark, mysterious, fanciful. All of these were done by your roommate? And who is the woman in these photographs?" He pointed to the opposite wall. "Your roommate?"

"Yes. She's done some modeling. She also writes poetry. Here's a hand-made book of her poems." I lifted a burgundy and ochre booklet from the desk.

Randall sat down on the couch and before long I'd told him the story of my friendship with Sylvia, my Midwestern roots, and my writing efforts. I even touched on Sylvia's frequent absences.

Randall shook his head. "I get the idea. This whole place," he swept his arm over the room, "Is inundated with Sylvia. Her work covers the walls, her photograph is everywhere, her furnishings, her taste, even—" he held up a peacock colored umbrella, "I'll bet this umbrella belongs to her. Where are you in all this? Why don't you put *your* picture up? Where are *your* books?"

"I'm really not inclined to do that. I have no interest in displaying myself."

What had I to display? Now he was regarding me closely.

"Look, I understand what you're saying," I added, "but I'm not a painter and posing for beauty shots doesn't tempt me in the slightest."

Randall looked unconvinced.

"You're too modest and you'd better look to yourself," was all he said.

At this point Sylvia breezed through the door, and seeing us sitting cozily on the couch set about fixing a pot of tea. As she did so she chatted blithely about her afternoon at Malibu Beach and impending date for the evening.

Randall stood up. "Thanks for lending me the novel," he said. "I'll return it." I followed him to the front stoop and he turned to look at me. "Sylvia is so obvious. Why do you put up with her?"

But I would have none of it. My best friend, my muse, my one intimate was not to be faulted. Sylvia could brag as much as she liked. What was that to me? I didn't want to change anything. But change seeped into our bohemian life without me making a move. It wasn't until weeks later that Randall's words came back to me, this time with a piercing significance.

❧◆❧

I HEARD THE FRONT DOOR BANG and saw the living room flush with light. Putting my book down, I slipped off the bed, trod bare-footed into the living room, and stood in the yellow circle of light from the overhead bulb. Sylvia rushed past me with blazing cheeks and a set of keys clinking between her fingers.

"I'm in a terrible hurry," she said breathlessly, flinging a gold velvet tote on the couch and swishing into the kitchen, "I'm to meet the Schisgal's in half hour and I'm not at all ready. A group of us are tooling up to Monterey. Oh, my, so much to do, so little time. I don't know how I can stand it."

She swished past me again.

"Judy, will you get me my bathing stuff from the top shelf if in the closet: suit, mauve terry jacket, white cap, and my towel, the lime and purple one? They put in a new pool where the arboretum used to be. Oh, where's my chiffon scarf? I'm dying for a ginger ale!"

Since I had a test to study for and a novel to read and underline I couldn't have accompanied the party, but I felt a sting of disappointment at being excluded. Sylvia had acquired new artist friends from her painting job at the Santa Monica hotel, while my studies and part-time work at the campus recruiting office consumed most of my time.

"Hurry, Judy, I'm late," sounded Sylvia's voice from the kitchen. I could hear the refrigerator door open and ice cracking into the sink.

"Are your arms broken?"

"Don't be stupid. I'm in a bind. Please." I went to the closet and fetched the articles she'd requested. "Put them in the alligator overnight case under the bed. Thanks."

Irritated by her commanding manner, I drew a breath and went over to the kitchen door.

"Sylvia, the way you tear about—how can you do justice to your work, your studies, or your art? Shouldn't you be thinking about priorities?"

"You are judging *me*? I can handle my life just fine, thank you."

"Who are these people you spend so much time with? The ones I've met seem pretty questionable."

Once, at a party with Sylvia in West Hollywood, I eyed the guests gliding around the punch bowl. The women were shrill and caked with glitter and paint and I thought of people I'd heard referred to as the Hollywood glams. Their continual bragging about movie roles and being noticed by big shots and Hollywood insiders exposed them as wanna-bes and hangers-on. I'd noticed a similar superficiality in the people Sylvia brought to the house.

"How dare you criticize my friends?" Sylvia's voice whipped through the apartment like a released tentacle. "You don't know them. You're a fine one to talk. You *have* no friends. You're all the time at the library or moping about the house waiting to see what arrangements I make so you can tag along. You're no one to judge!" She brushed by me holding a tall glass of ginger ale and strode into the bedroom

This was our first full-out argument. The anger in my chest threatened to erupt as she continued her tirade, but when I reached overload a safety valve snapped inside me, the tart retort I'd contrived fizzled, and the irritation faded.

"Just asking a question," I said in a subdued tone. "Will you be back in time for the Ahamid Jamal concert on Friday? We have tickets, remember?"

"I don't know. The Schisgals are driving." Sylvia reentered the room carrying the overnight case. "I can't deal with that now. You'll have to wait."

With a wave of impatience she set the case on the couch, tucked in an organdy scarf, and snapped the silver latch shut. I was about to ask if I could use the MG to pick up some lacquer pots in Japantown, but backed off. With the air in the room crackling like broken ice it was not the time to ask for favors. I changed the subject.

"Sylvia, your mother called this morning."

"I'm not speaking to her."

"What's going on?"

She gave me a quick look. "I don't want to talk about it." And slipping her brocade handbag over her shoulder and snatching the overnight bag, she was gone.

A few days later as I sat at the desk twirling a pencil between my fingers, Syliva entered the living room, towel twisted around her wet hair. The footsteps stopped. I glanced up. She stood by the desk, her eyes fixed on a letter lying beside my pile of spiral notebooks.

"What is this?" she asked, holding up the letter. I shook my head. "It's Paul's letter. Have you been reading it?"

I put down the pencil and looked at her in astonishment.

"I have not! Sylvia, why would you think that?" We stared at each other, then without replying she opened the front closet door and pulled out a long silver jacket.

"Sylvia, what's with you? You've been in a strange mood lately. I don't know what you're doing or when you'll be around. And now you accuse me . . . tell me what's bothering you."

"You really want to know?" She'd been heading for the kitchen, but swirled around and planted two feet on the floor, eyes blazing. My heart gave a start, but I felt a simultaneous relief that at last the tension of the last weeks would be broken. "I don't like your passiveness, the way you take and take. You have no ideas; everything is left to me to arrange, initiate, and you just go along."

I turned on the chair to face her.

"I have to do everything," she went on. "When will you start to pull your own weight?" This was delivered in a vitriolic tone I'd never heard from her before.

My cheeks grew hot and I stood up and grabbed the doorknob behind me, as if feeling for an escape route. But I wanted even more to have it out, to puncture the melancholy that had been suffocating me recently. I felt a stubborn anger surge into my throat.

"I admit I'm a learner," I told her heatedly, "but I have other things to do than dash about from one Hollywood bash to another, full of silly young girls who are convinced their attractiveness will someday, somehow, land them a part in pictures if they can just latch on to one of the powerful men who rule Hollywood."

"My friends are not all Hollywood types! And you don't have to go!" She paused. "Have you got anything better?"

"No. Why do I have to have something better?"

"Sometimes you're hopeless. You lean on me too much. I've had to teach you everything—I even had to show you how to sew those skirts you're always hemming. You stayed too long in that dullsville Midwest. You're so—so *provincial*. Maybe you should go back to the life of sunshine suburbia."

"That's the last thing I'd do, as you know very well." The onslaught caught me up short. I felt a familiar bolt of shame weighing in my stomach, making it hard to speak. "I just—I'm not sure what to replace it with just yet. I thought I was replacing it by living here with you."

I moved into the bedroom, looked out the smeared window pane at the line of bulging garbage cans lined up against a cement wall. Then I walked back to the doorway. "Sylvia, I thought you and I were *simpatica*. I thought we were both bent on pursuing our art, creating a life for ourselves."

"I *am* making a life for myself. I don't know what *you're* doing."

"I'm working towards a degree. What is it exactly you expect? You want me to lead a revolt against conformity? Join the Black Panthers? Produce a novel? I know I should be working harder on my poems and I don't study nearly enough, but I'm in new territory here. Don't expect grandiose accomplishments in four months."

"It's not that at all. You've lost your . . . your center, your drive to create your own circle. You're satisfied with cruising along in mine. *What do I get out of it?*"

"How about a roommate who shares your beliefs and keeps you company?"

"Ha! Now that I'm studying with Ada Gar and painting a mural in the lobby of the Santa Monica Hotel, I feel like I'm making a statement. Old acquaintances have started to resurface and people are all of a sudden interested in me. I'm getting what I want. What do you have?"

The first word that came to mind was *you*, which struck me as pathetic. The truth of her words sent icy curls to my spine and I cringed.

"Nothing," I replied with what I hoped was an ironic ring. I turned and sat down at the desk, too disturbed to say more.

Five minutes later, tossing the silver jacket over her arm, Sylvia charged out the door without a backward glance. Leaning my chin in my hands I remained immobile on the desk chair feeling the warm tears inch down my cheeks one by one. All I could see, through a blur, was the white wall in front of me stiff and unyielding.

᷂•◆•᷂

ONE WEEKEND AS I was leaving the campus library, I ran into Perry. He hadn't been around for a while, and I perked up at the sight of his tweed jacket and old leather briefcase. At his friendly inquiry I blurted out that things weren't going well. He looked at me hard. Before I knew it we were sitting in his nearby apartment.

"You look depressed," he remarked, handing me a cup of coffee and settling into an easy chair.

"Sylvia and I are not getting along. She's out most of the time, and when she's not off painting a mural at the Santa Monica Hotel with a group of fellow artists she has other irons in the fire. We don't have any of the same classes. I rarely see her." I had Perry's total attention. "She's become so *critical*. Finds fault every time I turn around. And I can't respond because part of me thinks she's probably right."

There! It was out.

Under Perry's sympathetic gaze I felt a jarring pain that had been submerged until now. He was leaning forward, taking in my every word. He knew Sylvia; he could understand. Perry pressed my hand.

"It's time for you to develop your own life, undertake projects, set goals, and meet people with mutual interests. Develop your writing. Find what interests and nourishes you. You and Sylvia are cut from different cloths." Perry leaned back and set his cup on the end table. "Focus on *you*."

But though I understood the need to get out from under Sylvia's influence, I couldn't bring myself to let go of the life we had forged, a life larger than either one of us experienced on our own. I had finally found an independent home base and that included Sylvia. I espoused our new life—*and all those dreams . . .*

I sat upright on the couch looking straight at Perry. I felt strangely alert and overcome with a luminous relief. I knew what to do.

When the branches outside the window faded into the blackness, Perry walked me home under a star-streaked night sky.

"Don't confide in Sylvia," Perry warned as we walked past a pole lamp that spread a circle of light on the sidewalk. "Leave her out of it. This is about you."

But I couldn't do it. As soon as Sylvia returned I blurted out everything. I told her how despondent I'd been and of my talk with Perry. I relayed my fears, my insecurities. I sought her understanding. The two of us could work it out together.

Sylvia listened until I was finished and said she was sorry, but she didn't really know what I expected of her. If she were critical she couldn't help it. I should look to myself, do my own thing. She really didn't have time for this now. She had to be somewhere. Before I could say anything, she left.

My admission of insecurity only served to increase Sylvia's confidence, and she now assumed an imperious air. I thought over what Perry had said—Sylvia was removed from mundane realities; she floated nymph-like in a web of her own making, never touching the solid earth. Even now she had no real friends she could count on who stood the reliable test of time. Her primary creation was herself and what she represented—the bohemian free spirit. The image was more important than the reality. How did this fit with me? Hadn't I always considered myself down to earth, no frills, say-it-like-it-is? Had I been thwarting my own nature by falling into her fantasy world of Medusa and the Faerie Queen?

Finally, the whole affair came crashing down in one big explosion. One afternoon, while cruising in the MG through the streets of West Los Angeles, distracted and alone with my musings, I swiped the back end of a pickup truck while turning into a parking lot. The truck was parked rear-out and didn't show a mark, but the MG sustained a dent on the front fender. When I returned home I inspected it carefully and saw that it didn't appear too serious. I figured I would deal with it later as Sylvia was out of town. By the time she returned I'd managed to put it out of my mind, buried, along with thoughts of the impending crash of our relationship. I said nothing.

Of course the damage to the car would be discovered eventually, so my silence was irrational. I just couldn't bring myself to confess. Any moron could have figured out what devastating results this subterfuge would lead to, but I was blocked. I procrastinated. When at last Sylvia discovered that her beloved MG had been damaged, she flew into a fury. It was inexcusable! How could I wreck the car and say nothing?

I had no defense.

Soon my mother received a letter from Mrs. Newton explaining that I owed $250 for her daughter's car repair and could they please cover it? Mother shot off a note to me suggesting without reproach that I really need to take care of this. I sent the Newtons a check.

It was all over. I could only withdraw in shame, wondering if enfolded in Sylvia's territory and directed by her code I had truly become the satellite her mother predicted.

I found a single room twelve blocks away and packed my suitcases. Bags at my feet, I stood in the doorway of our living room where Sylvia's painting of a strutting Pantalone leered down at me. Unable to find words, scarcely believing our parting was real, I said lamely, "I'll come for my trunks tomorrow. Well—good-bye."

"I won't be here," Sylvia said, pulling a chiffon scarf from her neck and moving into the kitchen. A moment later I heard a cabinet door click shut. "This makes up for your brother!" she shot out from the other room. She had not forgotten Harold's distain for what he considered her affectations. "And be sure" she added as she reappeared at the kitchen door, "to let me know when you're gone."

The next day I returned to find a note on the table: "Leave the keys here."

So my muse vaporized out of my life. I was on my own.

❧◆❧

LOOKING AT THIS PERIOD over the crest of the years, I've tried to figure how I could have been so passive, given my habit of determined resistance. But throughout Sylvia's conceits and recriminations, anger never ignited in me. How could this have been? Usually I was the non-accepting one, slicing a critical sword through every false or threatening gesture that came my way. But in this case I raised not a syllable of protest. Why didn't I yell out "I don't need your teachings or your ideas. If you don't like how I do things, look elsewhere." I can only guess. I had shifted from the accuser, in the security of home territory, to the accused, unanchored in space.

Maybe the leap to complete independence was further than I imagined. Or maybe I knew nothing about relationships and negotiation and compromise. One thing was clear: I had sunk to a level of total dependency. I was adrift in the middle of an ocean in a vessel piloted by Sylvia, existing in her environment, ruled by her network, unable to alter course. To confront her or to strike out under my own sail was not yet within my power.

I allowed it. It was a lesson well learned. Little did I know how many others awaited me as I coasted to the next port.

Chapter Fourteen

❧ Roommates ❧

$\mathcal{I}$ WAS ON MY OWN. Each day I walked to class, down Jefferson Boulevard, along Trousdale Parkway, past Founders Hall, and Bovard Auditorium. Winding around pink and white stone buildings spaced with lush green grass and thick-leaved oak, palm, and bay fig trees, I beat a familiar path down a tree-lined walkway to the Boheny Library. The sidewalks stretched dry and dull, blanched by the eternal sunshine. *If only it would rain*—but it never rained, never let up the bland sameness. I shriveled in the relentless firing of the sun. Occasionally Sylvia's voice would filter through my mind from some faraway place: "The beadwork in that tapestry is fantastic. Come on, maybe we can find some remnants," and "Oh, let's do go to the beach. I know a guy who lives in Venice."

I seemed to be made up of empty space, and a feeling of deficiency weighed my every step. *Something must be wrong with me.* I stopped at the bakery for donuts and without thinking consumed the entire dozen.

One of my routes crossed the university's Exposition Park, along a profusion of yellow hibiscus, red and yellow roses, and pink sweet ladies blooming in the sun. But after a while I took to avoiding the rose garden. I could no longer bear the pungent scents, the sweet tang of fresh grass, or the stream of bright colors. They were a reminder of how split I was from all that earthy abundance.

It was time to get a grip. I could do this, finish what I had started, make it work. After this semester, only my senior year remained. I liked the invigorating class discussions, the challenging assignments. The coveted degree was within reach.

In June I set off for Mexico.

༂ ♦ ༂

ACCOMPANIED BY BENJAMIN and Ed, two boys from my German lit class, I took a bumpy train to Mexico City, where the boys settled into a large apartment while I rented a room with a Mexican family for forty-eight dollars per month, including meals. My next move was to enroll in classes at the University of Mexico City—drawing, beginning Spanish, and the newly deciphered Mayan language. Living in a foreign culture and attempting Spanish with the aid of a purse-sized dictionary, gradually I came to life. I traveled to Acapulco on a third-class Mexican bus with chickens squawking from the luggage rack, explored the mysteries of the ancient Mayan ruins, and learned to do a snappy cha-cha.

Every time I turned around I met a new friend. One of them named Lorena introduced me to her Mexican family and took me to parties swarming with young people and loud Latin music. An architect who frequented the Archeological Museum gave me several clay artifacts unearthed on his recent dig in Guatemala. I was continually thrilled by the vibrant colors of the markets and horrified by the bloody brutality of the bull fights and cock fights.

My parents, despite my raving reports, were not so sure about the whole thing. They frowned on a single girl alone in a foreign country, especially an ancient one lacking the restraints fostered in the northern climes. Mother urged me not to go out at night by myself and to be wary of foreign men. She told her friends I had gone to Mexico with two girlfriends as she couldn't bring herself to admit they were boys. I was to be sure and write every week, even a postcard, so she could sleep at night.

By the end of two months Benjamin and Ed had returned to Los Angeles, and I had dyed my hair black and was wearing three malachite rings and a flared turquoise-and-black Mexican dress. In my suitcase was an obsidian Chac Mool statue for Mother and linen Mexican shirts with embroidered collars and trim for Dad and Harold that they wore once with sheepish expressions.

≈•≈

It was the beginning of the 1955 school year. I needed a nucleus, a place, a foundation, some structure to delineate my place in life. Since the split with Sylvia, the bohemian life on Park Grove Avenue had vanished off the face of the earth. I was no longer approached and asked if I were one of the girls in the Park Grove apartment. My tendency to remain detached and allow others to discover my potential was no longer enough. What had I to offer now?

One lazy California afternoon when the only place to be was outdoors, I took a stroll near the U.S.C. campus. Passing a row of small bungalows, I came upon a Spanish courtyard surrounded by one-story stucco villas, each fronted by a low stoop. The central courtyard blazed with blue and purple flower beds, and two palm trees dozed in the September sun. Seeing a For Rent sign tacked on the front trellis, I turned in. Each villa consisted of two separate apartments with bedroom and full kitchen, along with its own entrance front and back. A small plot of yard in the rear was big enough to hold a few chairs and my dark oak wooden table. Captivated, I signed a six-month lease on the spot.

Several weeks later, I walked to the gym and spent half an hour doing laps in the university pool. Lingering at the pool's edge afterward, I stirred the water with my feet, musing that a plate of enchiladas would taste really good about then. I barely noticed when a young girl dove in and came to rest close by, one hand on the drain. She sent me a friendly smile and I soon learned that she'd been a member of the synchronized swim team in high school, had just entered U.S.C. as a freshman, spent several evenings a week at the pool, and didn't really know anyone. We ended up eating enchiladas together and the next day I showed her my new apartment.

Before the month was over April Patterson had moved in.

April was nice, but I was dubious. The courtyard apartment would be tight for two people and we were very different. I spent hours with my nose in a book, stretched out on the bed in black leotards, black Capezios, and an Italian tunic. Based on what I considered my idiosyncratic beliefs, I proclaimed myself a member of the opposition. In contrast, April adhered to a conservative tradition with her breezy rose blouses, gray skirts, and sweater sets. But since April visited her parents in southern California weekends and we sustained full class schedules during the week, I thought we could manage. It would be a relief to share the bills and hear someone in the kitchen stirring pungent dishes on the stove. April's youthful freshness made for easy company. I could get used to living with a pretty girl with a bouncy pageboy cascading around her face, like one of those platinum blondes in the Lifebuoy soap ads.

I commandeered the desk and portable typewriter, while April took over the armchair and table in the corner of the living room and set a picture of herself on the bureau—a close-up showing her flowing blonde hair and sweet, retiring smile. Once, as we sat in the little yard in the evening twilight, she confessed to harboring thoughts of becoming a singer.

Before a month was out reality began to seep in. April had never lived away from home before. Used to being pampered by a doting mother and indulgent brother, she hadn't followed through on our household arrangement, and the work she had agreed to didn't get done. It was up to me to see to the dusting, sweeping, cleaning, and small needs like buying bulbs for the stove. A written work schedule didn't produce any improvement. Nor did she follow through on the bills. Because she imagined I was flush and made it clear that she was poor, she felt I should contribute the most while she contributed the least. The bills went mostly ignored and I had to practically poke her nose in the red ink to get her to pay up.

Sometimes we fell into an easy camaraderie, exchanging stories of April's costume falling apart during an aqua show, and the interesting boy from New York I'd run into at the Cinema Department that morning. April loved to giggle and if I happened to be in a silly mood she joined in and went around singing, happy as a lark.

The pressure to carry on a running stream of small talk and be pleasant at all times became wearing. She chattered in sweet tones, bidding me good-bye with a sprightly, "Have a good day." I didn't see how she could be constantly saccharine and upbeat. It was too phony. On top of this April never said anything remotely interesting. She waited for me to initiate the conversation, making enough idle comments to uphold an atmosphere of pleasant harmony. Then when I started something she would chime in and be off and running, flying into a topic that never went anywhere.

I couldn't keep it up.

❧ ◆ ❧

I WAS TAKING EIGHTEEN CREDITS. It was my senior year, and I spent most of my time closeted at Doheny Library. Between classes I joined a cadre of students in the lounge of Founder's Hall, where we hung out on couches and contested the state of American society, the ramifications of the cold war, and the oppressive nature of tradition. Drinking Tabs and filling pewter ashtrays with cigarette stubs, we probed existential philosophy on the meaning of man and existence investigated by Knut Hamsun, Miguel de Unamuno, Samuel Beckett, and the Beat Generation.

Occasionally, a few of us drove to the Santa Monica beach and baked in the sand, sprawled in our bathing suits. One of the boys, Cretin, carried a copy of *Nausea* in his pocket and argued hotly that the supreme power of the individual to create his or her own destiny overrode the life of despair life dished out by life. We analyzed the French philosophers and the existentialism of Sartre and de Beauvoir until the sun dropped into the ocean. The sporty Trojan types accused us of living in an ivory tower, above the petty sand and gravel of life. I joined in when I was able. I found the sessions intoxicating.

One evening after a dinner of fried egg sandwiches smeared with ketchup, I reclined in a canvas swayback chair reading an article in the *Los Angeles Times*. The piece featured the arrest of Rosa Parks in Alabama for refusing to relinquish her bus seat to a white man. Massive Southern vigilante groups were forming to keep blacks in their place. I had just finished the article when April entered the room. She sat on a chair, hands griped in her lap, and informed me that she was unhappy.

"You don't seem to like anything," she said. "I feel criticized, nothing I do seems to be right." Her tone became more confident as she warmed up. "The atmosphere is—well, cold. You never have time, I'm swept aside . . ." She wanted to be appreciated and respected.

I looked at her in astonishment. But I couldn't disagree.

"I know my mind's elsewhere," I said. "I guess I'm not very good company."

The oppressing thought hit me that there was nothing I could do to change things. April said she understood I had a full schedule. I promised not to read the paper while she was talking. She agreed to take charge of paying the electrical bills. By the time we'd hashed out our differences it was ten o'clock. It felt clean to get things out in the open. Surely improvement was bound to follow such frankness. We were filled with relief as we slipped into our twin beds savoring the feeling of good will that flowed between us.

Three weeks later April moved out. This came as something of a shock. There was no way around it—here was another failure. I sat by the window and took stock, filling several pages of my journal with probing rationales, trying to revive my self-esteem. Was this a huge loss? Well, no, we didn't have much in common. But I had tried to revise my attitude towards her and believed our intentions had fallen into alignment.

The fact was I had ignored April, seeking no more than the comfort of having her around. It hit me that I had been treating her in much the same manner as Sylvia had me: welding a critical superiority and erecting exact standards for her to live up to. No allowance made for petty traits and weaknesses. I held an image of the ideal existence and April had not lived up to it.

A new word showed up on the page in front of me: *acceptance*. The word didn't seem to be in my repertoire. But how could I accept traits I detested? There was a blockage somewhere, and I couldn't see it in the bright stucco walls beyond the window where the brilliance blocked out all distinction.

Journal Entry

I am living alone in earnest. I acquire a Siamese cat and name it Zigane. I exchange long letters with Jean Paul and Heinz. I sit on the front step and chat now and then with my neighbor Joan Aquino, a painter. I put on cha-cha, mambo, and calypso records and dance around the apartment until exhausted. I soak in a hot tub until I am a noodle. I see few people socially and no one often. I think about changing my first name.

Maybe I am too much alone. But I am too sad to be good company. Besides, being with others has presented some difficulty. When someone comes close to me, I begin swallowing. This makes me nervous. I am afraid the other person will notice and I become even more uncomfortable. I have taken to sitting apart from others so the reflex doesn't kick in.

There is nothing I can do, no one I can tell; it is too horrible. There is no remedy.

My soul mate is Franz Kafka. I read him over and over and understand him like no one ever has.

It was about this time that I discovered the Cinema Department. Chester claimed he'd first been drawn to me by my funky outfits. During geology class he would squeeze his slight form into the chair next to me and stayed by my side during a class field trip to Solana Beach to witness mansions along the California coastal bluffs sliding into the ocean. Extremely verbal, Chester would grasp a topic on the fly and run with it until all possibilities were exhausted. There was no subject in which he didn't possess a store of knowledge. He'd transferred from Cornell to U.S.C. to learn filmmaking. With his small intelligent blue eyes, generous mouth, groomed goatee, and tweed jacket, Chester did not resemble the run-of-the-mill undergraduate. His earnest eyes held me as he talked, and his air of friendly chivalry soon won me over and we became good friends.

One afternoon he led me across Figueroa Street to a one-story building with a sign above the stone-framed doorway: Cinema Department. This was Chester's hangout, where he took in one film after another and crafted his scripts.

"You must see it," he urged. "It is the best film school this side of the Statue of Liberty. People come here from all over the country because of its reputation."

The low plain structure stood in stark contrast to the stately Romanesque buildings that dominated the U.S.C. campus. At one time a stable, the building retained a rural, scrappy look. Beyond the entrance a bare-floored courtyard was filled with rickety picnic tables, the kind with an attached bench on each side, and a few miniature trees grew right up out of the hard-packed earth. Encircling the courtyard a raised platform stretched along the walls, and from it a ring of doors opened to various classrooms and offices. Attached to the wall in one corner I spied a thick iron ring that Chester said had once been used to tether horses.

The courtyard was scattered with students in jeans and loafers sipping from paper cups at the tables, or heading for one of the production rooms in the back of the building. Some were transplants from out-state, some Korean War vets, and some grad students with vocational backgrounds drawn by the department's focus on the emerging field of educational and documentary filmmaking.

Perhaps because of the lack of females—I was the only one visible at the time—the department gave off an air of casual, almost careless informality. I doubted if such laxity could result in any serious work, but later I was to find that, on the contrary, productivity was the main focus around which a continual hodgepodge of activities revolved. The production process of making films outranked any concern of dress, decorum or other non-essentials. This was an engine of creativity.

I decided to enroll in Mr. Sloane's camera class, where I ran up against the technicalities of lens structure and focal lengths, that required heavy study. Editing and cinematography I found fascinating and actually managed to shoot a short film with an 8mm Bell and Howell camera, trying to copy the social-oriented documentary style being ground out by the advanced students. Many film students hung out in the dusty rooms at all hours of the day or night looking for a film to view—there were constant new arrivals—or pitching in on someone's production project. There was always a chance Frank Baxter

Me at a U.S.C. Cimema Department party, 1956.

was lecturing on his televised series about Shakespeare, or James Ivory was polishing his film *Venice: Theme and Variations* for his master's thesis. Anyone looking for company could wander in and find strobe lights flashing, a Motorola running, or at least someone lurking about.

I became a regular. As a female I was something of a novelty, which suited me just fine. The boys invited me to their parties where discussions on films, Hollywood, and politics lasted into the wee hours. Chester carted us around town in his prized black 1929 Packard limousine, huddled behind the tinted windows, to see film after film. Phil, a recent graduate from the University of Wisconsin, set up a campus-wide showing of the French New Wave films—Jean Renoir, Claude Chabrol, Francois Truffaut, and the rest. We attended them all. Then there was Joel, a precocious seventeen-year-old from Manhattan, outgoing and curious, with thick dark hair and a disarming smile. He was the goofball, friendly and funny, the one most likely to drop spit-balls on the professor's head. A loner like me, Joel was always looking for someone to talk to and often I was the willing target.

I didn't date these guys, mostly searching souls pouring their passion into the world of film. For some reason I felt a bond I hadn't experienced elsewhere—like we were in the same boat. I loved that they were all film crazy. We discussed every new release, the direction of Jean Renoir, the scripts of Ben Hecht, the cinematography of Orson Welles, and the morbid humor of Alfred Hitchcock. When Joel purchased a 1938 six-cylinder Chrysler for fifty dollars, we took off to see Resnais' *Hiroshima Mon Amour*, *Rashomon* by Akira Kurosawa, *The Seventh Seal* by Ingmar Bergman, and anything by John Ford.

❧ ♦ ❧

ONE DAY, ELLIOT, a tall, quiet fellow with brown hair curling over his temples, and small cockleshell ears, showed up on my doorstep. I'd seen him whiz in late to my film-editing class and slip into a back seat. Did I want to go riding on his motorcycle? I had rarely spoken to him, but it was a warm day sweetened by fresh air from the coast and without a car I was landlocked. I agreed.

I clung to his waist as we swept past the campus and out to a distant park where a meandering stream flowed between massive chestnut trees. Elliot sat across from me on the grass, leaning against his knees and rubbing blades of grass between his fingers as he talked. The soft gurgle of water droned in the background. He told me he was putting himself through school by working three menial jobs, and that he was thinking of dropping cinema in favor of developmental biology. He was more than cute and I found myself enjoying the company of a boy who was gazing at me with light in his eyes. What if he took a liking to me? The though struck my mind and shattered like broken glass. I had enough to deal with, like pulling myself erect and creating a successful university life.

After several forays into the surrounding hills, we stood late one afternoon at my front door. Elliot stepped closer and told me he was looking for a girlfriend and wanted to know if I were interested. Taken back, I was at a loss for words, wondering exactly what he had in mind. I told him I was sorry, but I wasn't ready to be involved with anyone right then. My studies and writing were foremost. The words spoke themselves, driven by some unconscious resistance. His low-key manner and the way his mass of brown hair hung around his ears were likeable. But such a step? I wasn't sure.

Elliot stopped calling. One afternoon a few months later, I spied him across the street on his motorcycle talking earnestly to a blonde girl in a plaid skirt. She stood close to him, turned her face up to his for a long moment, and then slid onto the seat behind him and they sped off. Not long after that, while hustling across campus with Joel, I saw them walking down the sidewalk in front of Bovard Auditorium holding hands. I stared after them. Elliot looked taller than I remembered, and the blonde girl walked briskly beside him with smooth, graceful strides. They were chattering and exchanging glances, lost to the world.

The sight of Elliot and his new girlfriend stirred an inexplicable wave of envy. Maybe I was missing something! Decidedly this guy had become more enticing. Why was it I was only interested in boys from a distance? Since the days of worshiping Harold from afar, never catching up or seeing him turn around, had I desired the unattainable? Looking back it did seem that as soon as a boy became interested in me, my own interest diminished. There was something about direct, unequivocal attention that was uncomfortable, made me want to back off into the safety of indifference. I felt invaded if the person closed in, and if the closeness evolved to anything like intimacy I felt smothered. The feeling of having no air to breathe, nowhere to move, was intolerable.

Any boy who liked me too much was suspect. He must be a fool if he couldn't perceive what an insecure, bungling person I was, if he didn't understand that far down, buried under the visible shell, was nothing at all. He must be an idiot. Besides, what did I know about guys or relationships? Resistance was my expertise.

❧◆❧

THE DAY I MOVED into my apartment I noticed a small, dark-haired, bronzed girl perched on a wobbly stool in front of an easel. She had on a flowered print dress, orange sandals, and a smock. A painter! I was immediately intrigued. She looked up and we exchanged smiles. After that when I returned from class she might be sitting in the front courtyard next to the fanned-out palm tree, or I would see her breeze by and into an apartment two villas down from mine. One day she emerged from her front door and crossed the courtyard as I sat reading in a yellow striped lawn chair.

"Hi," she began, looking at me evenly. "I've seen you so often and I've wanted to meet you. I'm Joan." She approached with an unaffected smile and expression of frankness impossible to resist.

I eased the book onto my lap. Joan sat on the stoop next to me and tucked her skirt around her knees.

"So you thought I was a painter?" she asked after we'd exchanged introductory remarks. She laughed, smoothing her print dress with her palms. "No, it's just a hobby. It keeps me busy." Joan swept her arm out in front of her. "Don't you love this patio? It was a find. There was only one apartment left so I grabbed it. I've been here three months. The manager doesn't mind if I bring my things out on the grass and paint. It's just paint-by numbers, you know. I'm not a real artist. You're a student, aren't you?"

Joan talked on cheerfully in a candid, little-girl way, words flying from her mouth slight and warm like fireflies on a summer night. No, she didn't go to school, she worked in a telephone office near Vermont Avenue. Her mother was dead, her father lived in New York City; both were Filipino. Joan had been born in the Philippines but the family had moved to Los Angeles when she was two months old. She had an aunt living in the valley who sewed uniforms for monastic soccer teams.

I didn't mind Joan's windy chatter. Her enthusiasm enlightened the balmy day. I relaxed as she talked about her elusive boyfriend and the boss at work who watched her like a hawk. Sitting back in the lawn chair, legs stretched out, I felt pleasantly at ease. Our talk turned to the future. Joan was eying New York where her father had moved when she was a teenager, but she didn't want to leave her sometimes boyfriend.

Her eyes grew wide when I told her I was not in the least interested in settling down or getting married, and that it was far better to follow your dream and immerse yourself in unknown experiences waiting out there and find out whatever it is that holds you true. Joan rested her chin in her hands with a compliant expression.

One Sunday, Joan persuaded me to attend a self-realization service. She believed that spiritual peace was the only lasting attainment and that all else was unsubstantial. Ideas were not fulfilling, people were not all-knowing. The spiritual path was the true response to life. Faith was required in something superior to oneself, something to fill the universal lack.

It was a clear afternoon when we boarded a bus traveling to a part of town I'd never seen before. Entering one of the temple-like buildings that bordered a central courtyard, I found myself in a high-ceilinged sanctuary filled with rows of chairs circling a front dais. We bumped past a line of knees and slipped into two empty seats in the middle of the row. Almost immediately chanting began, the congregation repeating the lines in unison. I joined in. The man seated next to me was braying loudly. I threw him a furtive glance. He was in his fifties, wearing khaki pants and a polo shirt. He echoed the preacher's words loudly, exaggerating the intonations with throaty abandon. "We *will* become the sp*i*rit," emphasizing the "ir" of spirit. He seemed to be regurgitating the words, and his exultations filled the air. I could concentrate on nothing but his booming voice.

A lady in front of us kept looking around. When we reached the phrase "I'm a bubble, make me the sea," I hoped she didn't notice my grimace as I tried to form the word "bubble." I repeated "noble spirit, now" with the others, listening for the euphony of voices in full unity, but I could hear only the warbles of the man next to me spinning towards the rafters.

After the service I made my way to the rest room. Silence filled the space between the tile walls. I was confronted with my reflection. As my eyes looked into those in the mirror, I felt a rumble, a fiery stir tremble in my chest and creep down around my ribs. A feeling of emptiness, then fullness, accompanied by tugs of desire, then waves of hope, like a boat rocking back and forth with the tide. Since there was no way I could take the production I had just witnessed seriously, I wasn't sure where this came from. I studied my face, the stark cheekbones, the wide eyes staring back. What was happening? Was there a message striking to be born, and what was it trying to tell me? Just then Joan entered and pulled at my sleeve, and the moment slipped away as stealthily as it had arrived.

Afterward in the tea lounge, the statuesque yogi who'd presided at the temple service sat in a corner in his white robes, erect and immobile, surveying the room with gentle, unwavering eyes. His face was smooth and ageless, surrounded by layers of pure white hair.

The hostess approached.

"Please take tea. Your first time?" she asked, and when I nodded she smiled. "Wonderful." Was I was familiar with Paramhansa Yogananda and had I read *Autobiography of a Yoga*? I told her I hadn't but promised that I would.

The room hummed with low-key conversations. I noticed a calico cat peering at me from the next room and went over, chirping and holding out my hand. The cat didn't budge, so I sat down on the threshold and ignored her. Finally, convinced my attention was elsewhere, she slunk over and leaned against my foot. In a minute I was stroking her fur.

"But this is remarkable," cried the ladies who began closing in on me and the animal purring at my side. "This cat takes to no one. You must have a psychic rapport with animals." They were convinced I had extraordinary powers. Even Joan was incredulous. I shook my head. Some people will believe anything.

❧ ◆ ❧

I RANG THE FRONT DOORBELL hesitantly. I wasn't sure I wanted to be there. The large two-story Tudor building with steep-pitched roofs and dark-brown beams resembled a dwelling from a nineteenth-century English hamlet. In fact, it contained eight apartments, and the one I stood before was one of four on the lower level. This one was the first in a row of identical Tutor buildings, each surrounded with moist rich lawns, garden beds curving along with walks, and red and white flowered shrubs clustered under the windows. Already I was charmed.

The door opened and before me stood a girl with soft brown wavy hair, a square chin, and stern blue eyes.

"I've come about the room," I said.

"Oh, yes, come in," said the girl, whose name was Mary. Mary led me into the living room where tea and rice cakes were set out on a low modern-style coffee table. A minute later her roommate Eunice came in, seated herself in an armchair by the window, and wrapped her long legs around each other, pretzel style. We set about getting acquainted.

"I'm a senior majoring in comparative literature, minoring in cinema, and—well, I don't want to live alone." I wasn't sure how to explain myself, but when I mentioned I was from Minnesota the girls looked pleased. The word seemed to evoke an image of the clean-cut, stable Midwesterner. I picked up my tea cup.

They were both grad students. "I'm not home much," Eunice explained, taking a long draft of tea. A tall girl with a narrow face and horn-rimmed glasses, she regarded me nonchalantly. "I spend a lot of time at the biochemistry lab at school. When we're here we eat together, but most of the time we're out and about. We take it pretty casually."

As we chatted over tea it became clear that Eunice and Mary had formed a comfortable, functioning relationship. By a stroke of luck, Mary had discovered the apartment—tipped off by one of her professors—and Eunice had moved in six months later. Eunice was good-natured, the type who didn't create waves. Mary proved to be the sensitive one. At first I was put off by Mary's proper demeanor and serene air of assurance, but as I got to know her I discovered she was pleasantly fun-loving, in her own reserved way. Her passion was art and she had been studying for several years with Sister Mary Corita at Immaculate Heart College.

"Meanwhile, I'm pursuing a master's in fine arts at U.S.C.. These are my paintings," Mary she told me with a smile.

I looked around the spacious living room. The effect was cool and modern, with contemporary furniture and high-ceilinged walls. A surround-sound stereo system that Mary had purchased with her great aunt's inheritance dominated one side of the room, with three speakers mounted along the walls. A framed print of Willem de Kooning hung over a hallway table.

But it was Mary's artwork that drew my attention the most—abstract, wildly colorful, and strangely stark at the same time, something between Jean Miró and the cubists. I was mesmerized. As Mary poured tea from a blue-and-white China pot, we conversed about blizzards in Minneapolis, Mary's upcoming art show at St. Scholastica, the French films I was in the process of devouring, and the exigencies and opportunities of graduate school.

Walking up Menlo Avenue I weighed the pros and cons of moving in. On the one hand the well-appointed apartment, complete with two amiable, academically tuned girls, appeared too good to be true. I would have my own room in a quiet corner in the back. The girls' friendly no-nonsense manner was appealing. It would be interesting living with an artist again.

On the other hand a tiny voice warned not to be hasty. I might not get along in a setup where I was obliged to compromise and follow the reigning norms. Was inserting myself with roommates who had no doubt already cemented a bond a good idea? With Mary's affinity for the nuns and her Catholic background she might be conservative and narrow-minded. Would this be more of what I had been fleeing? Would their judgment come down on my offbeat ways? I hadn't had much success with roommates up to now. Could I ever fit in?

It was Mary who persuaded me. Competent and generous, her sweet smile and benevolent air of authority were reassuring. One would be in good hands with her. The house felt spacious and welcoming.

I decided I wanted to be there.

Judy McConnell

Journal Entry

January 10. *Now I am not so lonely. It feels good to hear the commotion of others coming and going. I like Mary. She is devoted to her art and shows me the serigraphs she is working on. Her work has an imaginative simplicity about it. Mary relishes my admiration and spends hours explaining techniques and telling stories of her art teacher, Sister Corita, and the other nuns she studies under.*

January 18. *Mary and Eunice are very religious and make great efforts to be considerate and unselfish. I think we will get along. But to tell the truth I feel out of place. The only common ground we have is consideration and decency. It may not be enough.*

February 1. *I don't think I like Mary and Eunice. They are too nice and considerate. This emphasis on politeness and always thinking of the other person is trying, if not unnatural. I'm afraid to take the last portion of pork chop at dinner—too selfish. The slightest thing requires a "please'" or "thank you so much" or "may I"; phrases that are supposed to indicate appreciation, not replace it. Maybe they are just trying to be careful since I'm new. Eunice raved and raved about the Spanish rice I concocted one night for dinner. It was over-seasoned and the rice was hard, but she couldn't praise it highly enough. This artificiality is demeaning and unnecessary. They go too far.*

February 13. *I am so touchy! And negative! I don't like anyone. Is this lack of ability to give esteem and credit a permanent fixture in my makeup? Does being a loner too long drain one of the more humane aspects of socialized living? I have noticed one thing: the unhappier I am the less warmth I can generate. I expect this is termed taking oneself too seriously.*

March 6. *Several weeks have passed. I begin to think if things go wrong it's not because my roommates haven't tried. For some reason, I trust them and am growing to like them, despite the irritating goodness they display. Yet there is a barrier. Our discussions in the living room or at the kitchen table lack warmth, maybe because I make them uncomfortable by philosophizing over everything, by probing to interminable depths, by holding out the only right opinion. Often I make remarks I later regret, blurting out whatever has come* *into my mind, comments with derogatory or insinuating implications. They make no response, but the silence is heavy.*

My fly-by-night ways don't go over well in this house. Mary and Eunice judge on actions, not words. If I create a racket getting home late at night, no matter how reasonable my apologies, the predominant fact remains that I woke them. No buttering up, no excuses. Now I move through the house on tiptoe, quiet as a mouse, not because I must try to be quiet but because I must be quiet. Being aware of making a mistake is not enough. I start to show up for house meetings on time.

March 12. Actually, I am beginning to like it here. Living in a household with two intelligent girls creates an environment friends like to visit. With such a home base, I have more clout than I did as a single package.

I especially appreciate the way Mary and Eunice handle people. When someone comes over they do not gush, as if the person is doing them the biggest favor. There are standards everyone must live up to, certain courtesies expected. This is made clear, yet no matter how visitors act they are treated with firm politeness and consideration.

If a boy calls me at 11:00 p.m., expecting me to be available, I no longer jump at the chance to get out, regardless of the inconvenience. It is now easier to stay home. It feels good to show backbone, to have an alternative to agreeing to just anything.

The days hurl out in front of me and I meet them with eagerness.

❧◆❧

"Abdul, look out! You're passing too close!" I straightened up in the seat of the old Ford, darting glances at Abdul who sat next to me stiff and upright, hands gripping the wheel, head frozen straight ahead. "I could have shaken hands with the man in that car. Let's get back in the right lane and stay there until you get the hang of this."

"No worry. You see I did not hit him. Everything is fine. I am practicing all week. This car and me, we are friends."

The University of California enrolled a large number of foreign students, and I sometimes visited the International Center to hear a lecture on international affairs or sample an exotic dinner served during foreign holidays. At a lecture on the cold war being waged by the two superpowers, I first encountered Abdul Alquirashi. We slipped into the last two adjoining seats in the front row at the same instant, causing me to turn and meet his brown eyes. After the presentation by a prominent journalist, we fell into a discussion of the actual causes of the war was in Korea that brought us to the front entrance and continued over dinner at a Lebanese restaurant. After that Abdul came calling, stayed for coffee, invited me for long walks or tacos. Since he didn't own a car we rarely left campus.

This was our first drive together. He had borrowed his friend Abdulla's car so we could spend the evening at a highly touted Spanish restaurant on Santa Monica Boulevard. Now, flying along the freeway in the pale evening dusk, I watched with amusement his nervous concentration as he negotiated the freeway.

"Abdul, I hope you see that mammoth truck," I said.

"What? Of course I see it. I am not so blind!"

The restaurant was dimly lit, and as our eyes adjusted we made out black and red upholstery, small marble tables, and flickering candles in iron sconces lining the walls. From one corner, classical guitar music and the crisp clacking of castanets drifted towards us. As we consumed plates of paella, Abdul listened to my lengthy philosophies about life and the state of the world. Then, in a gentle tone, he addressed what he considered my misconceptions.

"Judy, the religion is called Islam, not Mohammedism. Mohamed was a prophet. And you must learn to call me by full name, Abdulaziz."

The 1956 Israeli invasion of Egypt was hot on his mind. When Abdul's passion was roused his English picked up; he became almost fluent.

"The aim of the takeover of the Suez Canal by Israel, along with Great Britain and France, was not to open up its use, as claimed," he said in his calm manner. "It was about imperialism versus nationalism. The goal of the western powers was to topple Nasser, they considered him the force behind independence in Middle East. Countries like Sudan, Tunisia, Morocco, Algeria, and Jordan were joining together against continual Israeli threats to their territory. The claim that Nasser handled the canal badly or prevented Israeli ships from using the canal was a pretense. Israeli ships had been banned since 1948 and no protest from Great Britain. Outlawing enemy ships was common in a state of war, and war was going on for some time. The United States took the same stand in the Panama Canal when it prevented access to Red Chinese ships.

"Ignoring the United Nations peace negotiations, Great Britain and France invaded the Suez Canal on the pretext of saving it," he went on, resting his dark eyes on me earnestly. "They wanted to get rid of Nasser so they could control resources and keep their influence in the area." All this was said with composure and a humility that belied his keen grasp of foreign affairs and his dark good looks.

We often carried on such discussions. I loved to listen to him. Abdul and his Egyptian friends, Abdulla and Suhail, were enrolled, like him, in the U.S.C. business school. Occasionally the four of us sat in his apartment over mud-strong coffee dissecting our contrasting cultures. I was full of questions, and they claimed I was one American they could speak frankly with about their country. Abdul enjoyed arguing with me and teased that I was an incurable intellectual—a claim that was not backed up by my school grades, although I usually received A's in literature.

My relationship with Abdul remained impersonal. We didn't exchange feelings or confessions of an intimate nature. On the occasion when he tried to fold an arm around me on the couch I slipped out of range. I'm not sure why. Maybe I needed to be bowled over, and fond as I was of him, I was not floating on a silver cloud.

MARY, EUNICE, AND I decided to pool our friends and throw a party. I was especially keen now that I had a spacious place to entertain. We labored for two days, deep-cleaning the apartment, mulling over recipes, traipsing to the grocery store, and chopping and mixing foods.

On Saturday the dining room table was laid with blue-and-white edged dinner plates, bowls of hot cheddar pepper dip, artichoke hearts on crackers, meatballs pierced with colored toothpicks, deviled eggs, and crusty rice cups stuffed with guacamole. Purple hydrangeas flashed in the center, and at one end two crystal punch bowls held raspberry sherbet, ginger ale, and chipped ice—one alcohol free, the other laced with gin. Several wines and bottles of tequila and gin were lined up on the kitchen table.

People took refreshments and grouped in clusters around the room drinks in hand, chatting while the rhythm of Ravel's *Bolero* hummed in the background. Standing by the hall door I surveyed the room. None of the guests wore the Norwegian sweaters, blazers with crescents or plaid pleated skirts typical of the U.S.C. co-ed. Myrna Hartman, a fellow literature major, stood beside a floor lamp wearing a plain navy skirt and white collared blouse, her face hidden behind heavy horn-rimmed glasses and long bangs. Her hands flickered as she expounded on Hemingway's *The Old Man and the Sea*. I noticed several guys from the cinema department. Chester was seated on the couch next to a blonde girl in a rose sweater. Dressed in his usual tweed jacket and tie, pipe in mouth and glass of gin in hand, he looked quite professorial. He was holding forth—he explained later—on his accomplishments as a film writer and novelist, sucking on his pipe between phrases while the girl in the rose sweater regarded him with interest. Chester claimed this approach never failed. Not far from him Joel listened with a close-lipped smile to Joan Aquino's non-stop barrage.

I mingled with a wide assortment of people I'd never met: An older man with a trimmed beard, wearing a neck scarf; a tall pink-cheeked woman in her late twenties, who turned out to be a nun in plain clothes; students in fresh cotton and dirndl, not overly concerned about style; and a man in a felt vest who seemed to know all there was to know about the life-span of the Mexican coati.

Spying Abdul half-hidden among a throng of girls, I moved over to join them. Abdul certainly cut a striking figure. And in his shy way knew how to make himself agreeable.

"I am completing advanced degree in business and marketing," he was saying. "But no, I do not plan to return to Egypt soon—too many credits to finish. Here I work most of the time. If I return home I have to work all of the time."

The girls around him were regarding him with interest. One petite blonde with a square blue scarf looped around her neck looked at him pointedly. "I'm considering a business major myself."

"Very good choice," he replied politely.

I thought that for someone who claimed to be bashful around women Abdul was showing remarkable poise. At this point he turned his head towards me. "This is my friend Judy."

I moved closer.

"So you are good friends?" the blonde girl asked suggestively.

"I would say so," I responded glancing at Abdul, who nodded. This was not a subject I wanted to clarify just then. I quickly went on, "Abdul is a fool for poker. He and his friends play constantly. If you're ever looking for a game, here is the maestro." I liked to tease Abdul about his constant poker playing, and now he laughed.

"I admit it is weakness for me," he said. "Whoever wants to be weak with me is very welcome. I promise not to take too much your money."

"Do you play poker in Egypt?" asked the blonde.

"Oh, no, that is not allowed," he replied smiling. "But I am here to find out about American culture. So I am learning."

"So how do you entertain yourself in your country?" pursued the girl.

"We go to the movies—American movies," Abdul laughed, looking at me and taking a swallow of his non-alcoholic punch.

As the night wore on I drifted out back and sat on the top step, coddling a gin and tonic in my lap. Most of the neighborhood lights had been extinguished, and in the sheen of the quarter moon the outlines of a dogwood tree and bougainvillea vines crawling along the edge of the house were etched in the shadows. It felt good to relax into a weary warmth. The sounds of the party faded as the last stragglers left and I fell into a comfortable reverie.

After a while Mary appeared and settled herself on the stoop beside me. We didn't say much as we gazed into the purple shadows. This was my first time acting as host to a group of intriguing people, and I was relishing a pleasurable sense of responsibility. As I relaxed, chin cupped in my hands, the silence radiated the heat of a thousand summers. It occurred to me I liked it here tremendously. It was good to be back in the land of the living.

As for my roommates, they seemed to appreciate the cooperative spirit that had developed between us, but they remained leery. My reserve created a distance and they still weren't used to my tendency to do my own thing at all costs.

≈◆≪

THE PARTY WAS DEEMED a great success. Mary and Eunice were pleased. After that they warmed up considerably, maybe because the drinks had loosened my reserve and they'd seen me outgoing and smiling for once. As for me, I was still trying to figure them out. Eunice, the science major, was down to earth, focused, and smart. Mary, on the other hand, was artistic. I admired her drive and talent and unending consideration for my point of view. She worked tirelessly on her graduate thesis, an analysis of Gertrude Stein's cubistic writing and how the techniques Stein used to break down language mirrored the techniques of cubistic painting.

Mary espoused the daring innovations of Robert Motherwell and Jean Cocteau, yet upheld her conservative standards with firm religious conviction. Did she believe in the self-denial and restraint demanded by the church, or did she follow the wild and daring as expressed in her paintings? She admired Alan Ginsberg's *Howl*, but did not approve of his free-for-all lifestyle. How did this mesh? How could one be creative without a good dose of spontaneity and anarchy? At first I was unable to reconcile this seeming duality. I had to get used to appreciating an intelligent, creative person housed in a strict conservative mold. Maybe she had to get used to me and my tendency to drift along with the prevailing wind.

After several months I found myself adjusting to the house meal schedule, bringing home special foods for dinner, and following through on household commitments. I experienced a new sense of stability. Peering out my bedroom window at the gleam of blue silk sky above the rooftops, it seemed that that life was good.

ॐ ♦ ॐ

UNPRECEDENTED UPHEAVALS shook through the United States in 1955-1956. The fervor for political change was igniting. Graduate students at the university met in campus cafes or gathered in the student union lounge to deplore the Korean War and champion the Montgomery bus boycott against segregation. We watched scenes of Korean villages being burned to the ground and civilians massacred, and a fourteen-year-old Negro boy hung from a tree for speaking to a white woman in a grocery store in Mississippi. Sitting in deep chairs amid clouds of cigarette smoke, we discussed the latest government cover-up and denounced the lies from Washington and raged against the racial bigotry everywhere.

A song by the Weavers buzzed in the air, "I'll stand it no more, come what may . . ."

Journal Entry

Easter vacation drags. After turning down the family trip to a Texas dude ranch in order to complete a term paper on Thomas Mann's The Magic Mountain, *I'm having a hard time sticking to my schedule. Here I am alone in L.A. while Mary and Eunice and everyone else are off vacationing. The personal writing I'd intended to work on is dead in the stall. My short story is standing still. I haven't written a line for two days. I keep thinking, what is all this worth? So what? I'd give anything to be able to plunge into a work that would be the primary drive and focus of my life. But can I?*

Maybe I am too attached to life. So many authors are unstable types, forced to create a world to live in because they don't fit in the actual one. They press to exorcize their demons and try to form harmony out of the chaos of their world. Maybe it's preferable to delve into life itself, to use one's artistry to bring symmetry into one's surroundings, to arrive at happiness directly. Do I really want the career of the tortured artist, constantly struggling? Wouldn't it be better to fix up my life?

Why is it so hard to knuckle down? I dream of sprawling in an open car in the warm evening air.

Later. *Today is the last day of Easter vacation. I am walking through the deserted campus, headed nowhere. I feel inexplicably depressed. The city is full of sunshine and the streets I walk along burst with light; the house gardens are overrun with flowers. All the allure passes over me, useless, a mocking contrast to the shadowland where I reside.*

MARY AND I STRODE down the path eagerly. The crowd was swarming around the stage, faces flushed and expectant in the open air. Most were on the young side, students or graduates or drifters dressed in sport shirts, halters, or checked blouses, some in striped serapes and sandals, some with long hair drooped around their faces. They scrunched on blankets shoulder to shoulder and sat in rows of metal chairs lined up in front of the platform. On a nearby hill a handful of children scurried among the rocks. The grass sparkled in the spring air and the odor of fresh grain and moss drifted from under the trees. Behind the distant rooftops, ribbons of vermillion and orange trailed a sinking ball of sun.

The excitement in the air was palpable. A hum escaped from the crowd as a fifth-wheeler pulled up, growing louder as several men jumped from the back. A crew flew about adjusting lights and monitors, positioning backdrop screens, checking mics and stage lines. The audience straightened, every eye turned to catch a glimpse of the performer, in a pitch of feverish enthusiasm.

Finally the stage cleared, and with an agile leap a figure gained the stage and strode up to the microphone. He was dressed simply in casual slacks, with rolled up shirt sleeves and a banjo slung over one shoulder, looking like an Eagle Scout. Cheers and wild applause rang out over the field. After warming up with "Good Night Irene," "Kisses Sweeter than

Wine," and other of his popular folk songs, Seeger sang out "If I had a Hammer," and "This Land Is Your Land." The crowd was eager for a message and his lyrics resonating through the evening air said everything they were waiting to hear. They clamored for more, hollering, clapping, until Pete raised an arm, poised his banjo, and in the quick silence launched into his latest hit, "Where Have All the Flowers Gone? / Long Time Passing / Where Have all the Young Men Gone? / Long Time Ago . . ." His face reflected every word that left his mouth, and his voiced, full-throated and sincere, carried over the fields and into our hearts. I felt my throat tighten. I wanted to do something, to rise up, to yell, to protest. I glanced at Mary. She had the same fervent look on her face. Our eyes met and in that instant I knew that somewhere in the fabric of our beings a thread of humanity bound us, forging a bond as tight as the strings on Pete Seeger's quivering banjo.

On the bus home we discussed the burgeoning number of youth groups who defied authority and questioned American leadership. There was growing alarm about the war in Korea that was destroying a country and killing its citizens for a questionable American cause. Mary and I were in total accord. We were convinced the aim of the military was not to protect our land but to protect our foreign interests, largely economic. I was overjoyed to hear Mary speak so heatedly, breaking out of her usual orthodox reserve.

"Judy," she turned her serious face from the window, "Pete Seeger is the voice of justice, seeking to make the world a better place. He didn't crumble under the assault on him at the House Un-American Activities Committee hearings." We recalled his words at the time: "I resent very much and very deeply the implication of being called before this committee that in some way because my opinions may be different from yours, or yours, Mr. Willis, or yours, Mr. Scherer, that I am any less of an American than anybody else.'"

She quoted Elliot's *The Waste Land*, "*Here is no water but only rock . . . dry sterile thunder without rain.*"

As the bus nosed towards the streets of south Los Angles, the discussion turned to the Lost Generation writers. We admired the

American expatriates who settled in Paris after World War I to break from the materialism and conformity they could no longer tolerate in the United States.

"The Parisian writers, Gertrude Stein, Hemingway, and Dos Passos, and the like showed resistance by questioning the rigidity of American society. They were the first." Slipping a mint drop into her mouth, Mary curled her hands in her royal blue skirt.

"Then twenty years later Jack Kerouac and William Burroughs come along and turn American culture upside down with their Beat anything-goes preaching and lifestyle," I said. "They remained in America and lived the destruction they preached."

"Yes," exclaimed Mary, "I remember the words of Kerouac: '*The only ones for me are the mad ones . . . mad to life, mad total.*'" Her admiration for these cultural rebels appeared to have no bounds. Abruptly she turned to look at me. "What do you think of their heavy use of psychedelic drugs and attempts to legalize LSD?"

"It's crazy. Their whole lifestyle is adolescent," I replied, "But at least they challenge the status quo. They've torn into the old complacency and paved the way for change."

Mary nodded with a look of satisfaction.

By the time we reached our stop, the closeness between us had tightened. We might have emerged from different religious zones, Mary and I, but we were in agreement, coursing down the same path. Would wonders ever cease? Would life ever bloom so splendidly?

A LETTER FROM MOTHER asking me to pick an upscale restaurant for my graduation ceremony and to bring any friends I wanted. Why don't you stay with Dad and me at the hotel? Oh, dear—how could I explain that I wanted no part of the graduation claptrap? That I considered such ceremonies officious and irrelevant, promoted to uphold the platitudes of authority and outdated traditions. Plus, I had no fancy friends to invite to dinner at an upscale restaurant. Luckily, my lack of academic planning with an advisor saved me. I hurriedly sent off a reply:

> *Dear Mother, I have been informed by the standards office that I am missing credits for the completion of my degree. No one noticed this before. My graduation is off. It looks like I will have to remain for the first summer session to catch additional science classes. I will receive my diploma by mail in August. I'm afraid you will have to forgo your trip.*

IT WAS A HOT SUMMER evening the day before my departure. A single strand of cloud inched across the sky, tracing a shadow path across the sun-tamed lawns. I sat on the front stoop listening to the Spanish melodies that drifted over from the Tudor building across the street— love songs from former days and sweet memories that spoke of devotion, passion, and oneness. Carlos, smiling widely and full of good humor, and his fiancée Manuela, dazzling in her flowing Mexican skirt and rose- colored blouse, stood on the stoop across from me and sang duets, their voices blending in easy harmony. They moved with abandon, looking into each other's eyes or slipping their arms around each other's waists.

Often I'd gone over and chatted with them, trying out my weak Spanish phrases that made them laugh. Sometimes they brought out bottles of chilled Jarritos and told me of their life together while Carlos strummed softly on his guitar.

Now they were smiling at me and singing my favorite song. The childish tune sent shimmers through me, peals of longing and hope. The words stirred a flash of sadness in the hidden corners of my mind.

> *A penny a kiss, a penny a hug*
> *We're going to put our pennies in a big brown jug.*
> *A penny a kiss, a penny a hug, oh how rich we're going to be.*
>
> *I'm going to save a penny every time I hold you tight,*
> *And we're going to watch the pennies grow.*

I'm going to save a penny every time we kiss goodnight,
And darling when we're married we can build a bungalow.

A penny a kiss, a penny a hug
We're going to put our pennies in a big brown jug.
A penny a kiss, a penny a hug, oh how rich we're going to be.

As they sang one song after another, I listened to the play of harmonies skimming the air like flower petals. The sky shown iris blue and the warm stoop felt golden under me. Tomorrow I would be leaving U.S.C. for good. Classes were finished, the streets deserted. I would miss my cinema brothers, Mary, Abdul. But campus life had reached a dead end.

I was about to enter a new stage—a flight into a loftier realm, fortified with a BA degree and an encouraging letter from my creative writing instructor Ariel Arnold. Life was in my own hands—just as I wanted. I must plunge ahead and just see. That's what I must do.

From an open window a clock chimed out the hour, each stroke ringing out a promise. Emblazoned by sun tips, a million bright stars shone ahead, each within my reach. I felt alive, every fiber inflamed by the eternal sunshine.

I was ready to travel into the rest of my life.